Winning
with the
News Media

by

CLARENCE JONES

A Self-Defense Manual
When You're the Story

2001 Edition

070.1

J 7C

Published and distributed by:

>   Video Consultants, Inc.
>   5220 S. Russell Street # 40
>   Tampa, Florida 33611
>
>   Voice : 813.832.4137
>   FAX: 813.832.9039
>   e-mail: cjones@winning-newsmedia.com
>   Internet website: http://www.winning-newsmedia.com

ISBN 0-9619603-5-3

To order additional copies, see last page or website

Printing history:

Winning with the News Media - 2001 Edition - is the latest revision of:

Winning with the News Media - 1999 Edition
Winning with the News Media - 1996 Edition
How to Speak TV, Print & Radio - Fourth Edition - published 1993
How to Speak TV, Print & Radio - Third Edition - published 1991
How to Speak TV - Second Edition - published 1988
How to Speak TV - First Edition - published 1983

Printed in the United States of America

Preface

Mega-Media Owners
Make Winning Tougher

The rush by international mega-corporations to gobble up America's news media has accelerated. The massive shift in ownership is changing the way the media operate in ways the Founding Fathers could not have imagined.

Internally, they are in great turmoil. From the outside, it is very difficult just to keep track of which corporation owns which outlet. They constantly merge and morph.

We outsiders often wonder — which rules are they playing by today? Newspapers, radio and television — delivered by broadcast, cable, satellite and the Internet — are dramatically different now than they were even 10 years ago.

Monks in the Monastery

The American heritage of press freedom was based on local, Mom-and-Pop newspapers. The "press" was the only for-profit business given Constitutional protection.

In my seminars and speeches around the country, I talk about my changing perspectives of the news media. Particularly newspapers. That was where I grew up. I was one of them.

Now, I view too many newspaper people as isolated monks in their monasteries. Printosaurus Rex. An endangered species unable to grasp what is going on in the reality of the outside world.

At the same time, I recognize that the long tradition of isolated individualism was a marvelous counterbalance. The men who gave birth to this democracy (women were not allowed in Freedom Hall) had incredible insight into the evils that can corrupt a democracy.

They understood the capitalist system too often is driven by greed.

The writers and editors of their time were cantankerous zealots who stood apart so they could freely criticize government and society, and to hell with the consequences. Whether or not you agreed with them, you knew they followed their calling because they had convictions.

They believed their roles were essential in a free society. If their newspapers made a little money, OK. But that was not the Holy Grail.

Times Have Changed

My, how times have changed.

Most news media outlets today are small divisions of huge corporations which view the media as simply a distribution system for other products. Like movies and TV shows, or stock market data. News is a sideline commodity. Almost an afterthought.

The people who work in the news division within the big corporation are not as wealthy or as powerful as the lawyers and executives whose primary instinct and function is to make money.

These are the times that try men's souls, George Washington wrote during the dark hours of the American Revolution.

I believe the dark hours are here again. In the form of tough ethical decisions, when the new media corporations decide whether to tell us the truth, or hide it. Perhaps tell us some of it. But not the whole truth, nothing but the truth, if it will hurt the corporation. That has not been a part of their history or game plan.

The new material in this edition explores that idea in depth.

New in This Edition

In this edition (the seventh) I've expanded the chapters on Crisis Management, Ethics, Libel, Privacy, and Networks. Some of that was prompted by traffic on my website, which I monitor daily. These are the areas that attract the most visitors.

The book itself is eight pages thicker.

Every chapter has been updated. Some have been squeezed a little smaller to make way for the expanded material. The Technology Chapter is gone. I've always tried to keep this book as current as possible. New products, services and ideas are conceived so rapidly now, that chapter could be obsolete before the ink was dry.

The Internet as a resource for research continues to astound me. In gathering new data and statistics for the book, I no longer have to prowl the stacks of remote libraries or make dozens of long distance calls to update the information. It's all there, on the Web, at the other end of my DSL connection. In some cases, the keepers of the information gave me special access to their databases to assemble and update the names and numbers. Wow!

Thank you.

Afraid of the Media

I left the news business and became a news media consultant in 1984, after the first edition of this book took off. My experience with my clients since then has taught me a great deal.

They are almost universally afraid of the media. Afraid of being misquoted. Or taken out of context. Afraid of looking stupid or guilty, when they are neither. Afraid to admit they — or someone within the organization — screwed up.

Afraid of their own lack of skill, experience and understanding. Afraid of media bias — real or imagined. Afraid to face professional journalists whose job it is to cross-examine them.

Reporters often seem like litigators, searching for the vulnerable underbelly that will destroy the witness and win the case.

Allies, Not Adversaries

This book is designed to help you understand the process. In the huge majority of interviews, the reporter is not trying to destroy you. The reporter is simply trying to gather enough for a story. The reporter needs your input.

In too many cases, the fear — the stage fright — make you adversaries when you should be allies.

That's part of what this book is about.

The Most Powerful Force

The news media have become the most powerful force in this society. I can think of no other institution, no other group, with the power of the media. The media have the power to create — the power to destroy. And — unlike those other forces in our culture — they can do it almost overnight.

They are the instruments of change. They set the agenda for us as a people. We do not get around to discussing or solving a problem until the media put it on our priority list.

Executives in government and corporations spend a great deal of time and money learning how to be better managers. All that effort can quickly go down the drain — along with your career, I tell them — if you do not develop your media skills and reflexes.

Attorneys Need This

My experience has also led me to believe that attorneys in both government and corporate life are often responsible for the media decisions that lead to disaster.

In a crisis, they are often put in charge. They act in good faith, and in good conscience. They are doing what their training and experience taught them to do. But they do not understand that the media play a completely different game. With very different rules.

I tell lawyers I believe they are now guilty of malpractice — by not representing their clients' best interest — when they block, or fail to help them balance the legal and media considerations.

No Guarantees

I make no guarantees with this book that you will always win. In fact, if you play the game you will take some hard knocks. Professional athletes are in the game to win. Sometimes they lose. The good ones come back the next week to play again as well as they possibly can.

I know you can win the media game *most* of the time if you develop your skills. If you scout the media team and learn their plays. Their hot buttons. Their value system. How they think. How they decide whether you're a good guy or a bad guy.

You may need to learn the hard lessons of how to be brutally honest in mid-disaster. To show your humanity in public. To apologize when you stumble, and not get arrogant when you win.

It works. It really does. I have had remarkable success with clients who were under attack by the media. And I have taken great pride in watching those I coached develop their sense of self confidence in speaking for themselves and the people around them.

That, too, is what this book is about.

Good luck.

Clarence Jones

Table of Contents

Section One - STRATEGY

Winning with the News Media

Section Two - SKILLS

Section Three - INSIDE THE MEDIA

How to Use This Book

You Can Quickly Find
What You're Looking For

We designed this book so you can quickly find what you're looking for. It's divided into three sections —

- **STRATEGY**
- **SKILLS**
- **INSIDE THE MEDIA**

The section and chapter titles are at the top of each page. Within each section, the chapters are in alphabetic order.

Throughout, there are frequent subheads to help you find what you need by flipping through.

To keep the size of the book manageable, there is no index.

Section One - STRATEGY

This section will help you understand how reporters and editors think. Expanded chapters in this edition on **Crisis Management**, **Ethics** and **Selling Your Story**.

Section Two - SKILLS

Personal skills you need in dealing with the news media. Read the chapters on **Interviews**, **Good Guys/Bad Guys**, **News Conferences**, **Off the Record**, and **Talk Shows** before:

- You talk for quotes — in person or on the phone
- You leak information to the news media
- You participate in a television or radio talk show
- You hold a news conference

Section Three - *INSIDE THE MEDIA*

The chapters in this section take you behind the scenes to give you more insight into how the media do their thing, how they make money, and their future as economic models and owners change. Current data on newspaper circulation, TV ratings, advertising spending and media ownership. Expanded chapters in this edition on **Libel**, **Privacy** and **The Internet**.

How to Order This Book

The last page is a handy form to help you easily order more copies of this book, including discount rates for carton-lot orders and rates for expedited shipping. The cover price includes basic shipping and handling.

Court Decisions on the Web

Many of the chapters in this book cite court decisions that established current law and practice.

The absolutely best place to find just about anything about the U.S. Constitution, the law or the courts is on the Internet at findlaw.com. This is a free, public resource with the complete text of every U.S. Supreme Court decision back to 1893, and many before that. The text of U.S. Circuit Court decisions are also there, and easy to find.

Findlaw.com claims to be the most frequently visited site on the Internet for legal information and research. The home page is:

- **http://www.findlaw.com**

Supreme Court decisions can be searched by any name in the case title, by date, or citation, and the search engine is extremely easy to use. It's at:

- **http://www.findlaw.com/casecode/supreme.html**

From findlaw.com, you can link to state court websites to find decisions in your state in the same area of the law. After you find the Supreme Court decision you're looking for, findlaw.com even provides links to other court rulings citing that case.

In the 1999 Edition of this book, I listed several legal resources on the Internet. Findlaw.com has improved so much since then, it's the only place you need.

Section One

STRATEGY

Accuracy
Crisis Management
Ethics
Fighting Back
Lawyers & Lawsuits
Media Policy
PIOs
Selling Your Story
Ten Commandments
of Media Relations

STRATEGY

Accuracy

If That's the Story, I Must Have Been Somewhere Else

It is my impression that the media are much less accurate these days. Why has accuracy deteriorated?

I believe the major cause is the intense pressure to increase corporate profits. Most daily news outlets in America are now owned by large, distant corporations. (See **INSIDE THE MEDIA/Networks** and **Newspapers**) The final decision-makers are corporate executives a thousand miles away. They closely watch ratings and circulation figures. Higher ratings and circulation mean you can charge more for advertising. The company's profits and stock price will increase.

The Business/Newsroom Wall

In the middle part of the 20th Century, news reporters and editorial writers were completely divorced from the business side of journalism at newspapers and broadcast stations run by ethical owners. Accuracy was the highest single goal for conscientious reporters and editors.

As a young newspaper reporter, I thought it unethical to even think about circulation, or advertising, or company profit.

When I moved to TV, I was bothered at first by the newsroom's awareness and concern with ratings. Then I realized we had tough competition, and ratings were the scoreboard. My newspaper had not had a serious competitor. My second TV station had a rule — no advertising people in the newsroom. The manager did not want anybody to even suspect that profit could influence news.

Profit Oozes Into the Newsroom

As the ownership of the American media changed, the drive to be profitable oozed into virtually every newsroom. Today, there is enormous pressure on reporters and editors to get the sensational story. Too often, in my opinion, they publish or broadcast first, then check the facts later. (See **STRATEGY/Ethics**)

Unfortunately, this same competitive force makes the media echo each other's stories. They do not want to be left out of the major, breaking story which draws readers/viewers/listeners. It is pack journalism at its worst.

And so the story generated by an unconfirmed rumor, a shaky or fictitious source, is quickly relayed from one news outlet to another. Whether true or not.

The Internet Adds to the Problem

The Internet, with its immediacy, its capacity to circle the globe within seconds, and its attraction for wackos who are wannabe publishers, has added a new dimension to the problem. (See **INSIDE THE MEDIA/The Internet**)

The news business has always been competitive. But there was a different motive in previous generations. Journalists took enormous pride in beating their competition because it proved they were better at their craft. They wanted the scoop, but not at the risk of spreading a false or flawed story that would disgrace them.

Recent Examples

There are a handful of recent, high-profile stories that were published or broadcast too quickly; repeated by virtually every other media outlet; then found to be untrue or substantially different than first reported.

- Richard Jewell was fingered by the *Atlanta Constitution* in August, 1996, as the Atlanta Olympics bomber. The story was quickly echoed by virtually all media. After the stories forever altered his life, he was found to be completely innocent.

- The *Dallas Morning News* reported in March, 1997, that Timothy McVeigh had admitted to his lawyers that he was the Oklahoma City Federal Building bomber. This was before his trial. The story was relayed by other media, then retracted.

■ In January, 1998, it was widely reported that an unnamed, former Secret Service agent had seen President Clinton and Monica Lewinsky together, in an intimate encounter at the White House. But when the agent was tracked down and identified several days later, his story was very different.

■ In early June, 1998, the *New Republic* admitted that more than two dozen stories it published — all written by 25-year old Associate Editor Stephen Glass — were at least partially fabricated. Six of his *NR* articles were pure fiction. Glass had also written stories for several other national magazines.

■ In late June, 1998, *Boston Globe* columnist Patricia Smith resigned after confessing she had invented both people and quotes to enhance her columns. Earlier in 1998, she was a Pulitzer Prize nominee and had won the American Society of Newspaper Editors Distinguished Writing Award.

■ In July, 1998, CNN and *Time* retracted their June stories about "Operation Tailwind," a U. S. military foray into Laos during the Vietnam War. They had reported the raiding force used nerve gas to kill American defectors there. When the stories were attacked, CNN hired famous media attorney Floyd Abrams to investigate. Abrams studied videotaped out-takes from interviews, and talked to CNN's anonymous sources. In his report, Abrams said two primary witnesses the story relied on were shaky. In some instances they were quoted out of context, or had denied in out-takes the story's basic premise.

Good Reporters Sweat

Believe it or not, an inaccurate story is extremely painful for good reporters. They take immense professional pride in their ability to get it right. Better to miss the scoop than be wrong.

Sometimes, after a story is on the air or in the newspaper, ethical reporters suddenly realize there's one angle they didn't check. They sweat. There's a knot in the bottom of their bellies until they check that neglected angle to make sure it doesn't change anything. Good reporters also have the grace to admit it when they're wrong, and correct their mistakes.

I am concerned that the journalistic mantra "Get it first, but get it right" has been overpowered by corporate executives who are not journalists, and whose primary job responsibility is to increase profits. As part of their cost-cutting, many publications have decreased the number of fact-checkers. (See **STRATEGY/Ethics**)

The old ethic to check and double-check will fade as more young journalists learn their craft in this atmosphere, then become editors and news directors. There are other factors, too, that lead journalists to be less than totally accurate.

What Do You Fear?

I often begin a media relations workshop by asking the group to write on a sheet of paper the three things they most fear when they deal with the media. What do you dread? I ask. When you know a reporter is coming to interview you, what concerns you most?

The results are remarkably the same. No matter where the seminar is held — no matter what they do for a living. Bank presidents, police chiefs, corporate CEOs, social workers, doctors, lawyers and accountants all have the same response.

Fear of Being Misquoted

So much so that I forecast what they will say, before I know what they have written. Two thirds of you, I tell them — maybe three-fourths — will have on your list the fear of being misquoted.

There are sly smiles, as if I had some psychic power. Or a mirror in the ceiling. Then I ask for a show of hands. How many of you have on your list the fear of being misquoted? Sometimes, the count is unanimous. Everyone will have written some version of being misquoted or taken out of context.

Incompetence or Bad Motives?

Are inaccurate stories the result of reporter incompetence, insensitivity, or bad motives?

Sometimes one, sometimes the other. Sometimes all three.

Some reporters get tunnel vision pursuing their story. They don't let the facts derail them. If you sense that is the case, you will need to invest a lot of energy to swing the story toward the truth. (See chapters on **Interviews** in the **SKILLS** Section)

You may need to have a meeting with the reporter's editor, or send a detailed letter to the news outlet clearly stating the facts, in contrast to what the reporter seems to believe. (See **STRATEGY/ Fighting Back**)

Preconceived Assignments

Another major factor in media inaccuracy is the preconceived story. Many story ideas are thought up by the editor, not the reporter. Remember, all of us view the world from our own, isolated cubicles. Editors are no different.

To get ahead in the news business, you do your best to please the boss. I once worked for a newspaper editor who was terrible about assigning preconceived stories. I'll disguise his identity and call him Dave.

Dave would stop at the City Desk when he arrived in the morning, sneezing and blowing his nose. His voice would be hoarse.

"We need a story on the flu epidemic," Dave would tell the city editor.

"Is there an epidemic?" the city editor would ask. He knew the boss' story ideas did not always pan out.

The Flu Epidemic Story

"I've got the flu," Dave would say. "My wife and kids have the flu. Everybody at the club has the flu. Can't remember when so many people were sick at one time."

And so a young reporter would be assigned the flu epidemic.

His first stop would be the county health department. Lowest reports of flu in 20 years, they'd say. When the reporter's findings were put on Dave's desk, he'd shake his head. "Can't rely on those damned bureaucrats over at the health department," he'd grumble. "They could be covering it up. Put a more experienced reporter on the story."

Suggest a Replacement

Remember, the editor has invested time, and the time of a reporter and photographer in this preconceived story. Most newsrooms are understaffed. They can't afford to waste resources.

One technique to deal with the false preconception is to suggest another, legitimate story to replace it. That way, the reporter doesn't go back empty-handed. It will be a lot easier to tell the boss the original assignment didn't pan out.

If you're the health department worker who's asked about a nonexistent flu epidemic, you could say (if it's true), "We've never had so little flu at this time of the year, but boy, the black plague is spreading like wildfire."

Now *that's* a story. Forget about the flu.

Size Up the Reporter

When a reporter approaches you on a story, your first task is to size up the reporter AND the story assignment. I call it the Pre-Interview Interview. You need to get a handle on the reporter's story assignment, intelligence, experience, knowledge of the subject, attitude toward you and your organization. (See more on the Pre-Interview Interview in **SKILLS/Interviews-General**)

If you discover the reporter is working on a preconception that is all wrong, you need to set the facts straight IMMEDIATELY. How strongly you object to the false preconception will often determine whether the reporter changes course on the story idea.

Your first approach should be friendly and informative. "A lot of people assume that's the reason for our action, but they're wrong. Let me tell you what really happened."

Become More Aggressive

The reporter may persist with the original concept. You should become more aggressive. Lay out your case in great detail. Suggest others who can substantiate what you're saying. Produce records that refute the preconception. Provide copies to help the reporter convince the editor the story concept is wrong.

If the reporter is not convinced, be sure your quotes make it clear you disagree, and effectively argue your point of view.

You may discover, in that Pre-Interview Interview, that the reporter knows almost nothing about the subject matter. You will be terribly tempted to educate the reporter — to confer a Ph.D by the time the interview is over.

DON'T DO THAT.

Don't Tell Everything

Don't try to teach even half of what you know about the subject. You'll just confuse the reporter. You'll increase the chance that the story will be inaccurate, the quotes distorted. The reporter is not expert enough, after a brief visit with you, to sort through a mountain of information and choose the most important points.

In a seminar for university administrators, one of my students was public relations director for a very prestigious medical school in the Northeast.

Reporters Who Know Nothing

"I've given up on TV reporters," he told the group. "They send reporters who know nothing about medicine.

"At our school, we're on the cutting edge of research. We're using extremely sophisticated, complex techniques. We work with radiation and lasers and genetic engineering. It takes us a whole day just to give the reporter a basic education in the field. And what do we get for our trouble? Maybe 90 seconds, often inaccurate. Not worth the effort."

You're telling reporters too much, I suggested. They only need to know what time it is. You've been insisting they understand atomic clocks. The reporter's only knowledge of the subject may be a newspaper or magazine clipping the editor handed out with the assignment.

Once you realize the scope of the reporter's ignorance, PROVIDE ONLY WHAT IT TAKES TO WRITE THE STORY YOU WANT. Draw the final conclusions. Get to the bottom line. Sum it all up in one or two sentences.

It gives you an opportunity to control — to a large extent — what will appear in print, or on the air. (See **SKILLS/Defending Yourself** and chapters on **Interviews** in the **SKILLS** Section)

Misquotes — Your Fault

Reporters have been conditioned to look for quotes that fit a certain formula. If you haven't learned to speak Media Language, you may discover that the reporter stitches together a phrase you spoke here, another there, as if they were spoken at one time, in one sentence. (See **INSIDE THE MEDIA/Editing**)

You need to learn how to say what you want quoted in one, quick sentence. Otherwise, you might as well be speaking German or Chinese. Don't make the reporter act as interpreter. Many quotes get lost or distorted if they have to be translated into

MediaSpeak. (See **SKILLS/Interviews** for crafting quotes that will be used and quoted accurately)

If your experience with a specific reporter leads you to believe this reporter has an accuracy problem, a suggestion:

Record the Interview

Record the interview. To make sure the recording is legal, tell the reporter. You say, as you turn on the recorder in plain view, "You don't mind if I record this, do you?"

You can do the same thing in a telephone interview. (See more about the legality of recording conversations in **INSIDE THE MEDIA/Privacy**)

This tells the reporter you have a complete transcript of what you said. There will be no your-word-against-my-word dispute. (See **SKILLS/Defending Yourself** and **INSIDE THE MEDIA/Libel** for elements of truth, news media risks & defenses)

It may be that you do everything right, and you're still misquoted. Or the story is so distorted, you wonder if you and the reporter attended the same event.

You Need to Complain

You need to complain. Set the record straight.

Not a nasty, angry complaint. A careful, straightforward telephone call or letter to the reporter and the editor, showing what was reported and what you really said. Or what really happened.

In most cases, you won't ask for a retraction or correction. But if you don't file your complaint, the flawed story goes into the newsroom library. In the future, every reporter who writes about you or the same subject matter will pull that inaccurate story from the library and repeat the error.

Once it's on the air or in the newspaper three times, it becomes fact. (See **STRATEGY/Fighting Back** for details on how to file your complaint, when, and with whom; the pros and cons of corrections and retractions)

STRATEGY

Crisis Management

Survival Often Hinges on What
You Do and Say in the 1st Hours

In most crisis management scenarios, the outcome depends heavily on what you do and say in the first few hours. What the news media report in their first stories — and how they view your coping skills — will often set the tone for the entire crisis. Chances are, the media's first impression will persist until you have overcome the problem and emerged victorious ... or you've been humiliated, fired, put out of business, arrested, sued, divorced ... the list goes on and on.

What is a Crisis?

A crisis is the imminent risk of death or serious damage. It can threaten you, people you care about, your organization, your property, your reputation and/or your future.

If and when the media discover the crisis, your skill in influencing how they report it — or decide not to report it — are key factors that determine the outcome.

The tone of the early stories usually hinges on how well reporters and editors know you, your understanding of media strategy, your experience and reflexes in dealing with journalists.

One of the most difficult steps in crisis management is making the decision that there *is* a crisis. Wait too late, and you may not be able to save the sinking ship.

Send everybody to battle stations when hindsight shows there was no Armageddon looming, and you'll look like Chicken Little. A poor, paranoid manager who's out of touch with reality.

Worst-Case Scenarios

One way to determine whether you have the potential for a serious crisis is to call a meeting of top people and draw up a list of worst-case scenarios. Then ask:

- If any of these worst-case scenarios should occur, what would it do to our company/agency/career/future/project/plans?

- How likely is it that our worst fears will come to pass?

- How and when will the media learn about it?

Call in Outside Help

If you or the organization could be destroyed or critically damaged, you've got a major crisis, and should probably call in outside public relations counsel to help you deal with it.

Inside PR staff caught up in the emotion and fear tend to not think as clearly as an outside professional. Even if they think about some of the tactics available as options, staff may not be willing to express them. They know how volatile and dangerous those options will seem to other, powerful insiders.

Just because the options are scary doesn't mean they're not viable choices for solving the problem and ending the crisis.

In far too many crises — personal, corporate and governmental — the lawyers are brought in immediately. Virtually all decision-making is turned over to them. SERIOUS MISTAKE. The attorneys need to be *a part of the crisis team* — not run it. Why? Because their instincts for dealing with the news media will almost always be wrong. (See **STRATEGY/Lawyers and Lawsuits**)

Choosing Outside PR Counsel

The outside PR counsel you choose is very important. If the outside PR practitioner needs your business very badly, he/she may be no better than an insider who is afraid to speak the painful truth.

Outside PR professionals brought into the crisis MUST have extensive experience in the field.

They MUST be people of absolute integrity who will give you their best, unvarnished opinions and suggestions. They must be willing to call it as they see it, at the risk of being ridiculed and/or losing you as a client.

Creativity Can Seem Crazy

Sometimes their ideas will seem harsh or off-the-wall. Creativity often seems crazy. At first blush. That's one definition of creativity. Out-of-the-blue ideas nobody else has thought of.

After the boss has heard everybody's assessment of the problem and possible solutions, it's the boss's job to make the tough decisions. That's what bosses are paid to do.

Here are some basic rules for the management of news media crises:

Never Under-Estimate the Crisis

Never under-estimate the crisis.

- If you under-estimate, once they learn the real extent of the problem, reporters will feel like you tried to deceive them

- If you under-estimate, you can be blamed for your lack of knowledge and skill, once we know how bad it really is

- If solving the problem becomes a long, difficult task, the news media expected it to be, and you won't be faulted

- If you over-estimate the crisis and then solve it quickly, it appears you have immense power and skill

The Media Need a "Bad Guy"

The news media need a good guy and a bad guy in every crisis. (See **STRATEGY/Good Guys/BadGuys**)

- A crisis means the gods must be angry; we still practice the ancient ritual of human sacrifice in this society

- To appease the gods, the high priests of politics and the press must find someone to sacrifice

- If you don't understand the ritual, you can easily become the bad guy who is vilified and then sacrificed

- If you did something that caused all or part of the current crisis, take responsibility, and lay out your plan to avoid repeating the error (See **STRATEGY/Ten Commandments**)

- In all your interviews, news conferences and news releases, make clear who the bad guy is

When the radiation first leaked at Three Mile Island in March, 1979, power plant officials brushed it off as inconsequential. When reporters found the leak was more serious than first announced, the story mushroomed into an international, five-alarm event.

Exxon's Oil Spill at Valdez

After the oil spill at Valdez, Alaska, in March, 1989, one of Exxon's biggest mistakes was to diminish the severity of the spill and the damage to the environment.

A company vice president was quoted putting down the media for sensationalizing the situation. No big deal, he said — after all, oil bubbles up from the bottom of the sea as a natural process.

Didn't he understand that in the next moment, TV viewers would see vivid pictures of dying seals and eagles; fishermen and their families unable to work and make a living?

Reporters are human. They do not like being deceived. They have a large arsenal of weapons to get even. It is easy to make you look ludicrous. The bad guy who lies. Remember, they always have the last word.

It took a long time for the president of Exxon to decide the situation was bad enough for him to take a personal look. The media message was:

This is not important to the people who run Exxon. They don't care about the damage to the environment or the fishing villages facing financial disaster. As a global powerhouse, they only care about making money.

You Need to Go There

Russian President Vladimir Putin had his worst public relations crisis after the nuclear submarine Kursk sank in August, 2000. Putin was on vacation at the time. He did not rush back to Moscow to supervise the doomed rescue attempt.

He probably could not have done anything more in the capital. But the impression was that he did not care enough to interrupt his play.

American politicians have learned to speedily go to disaster sites, fly over them in helicopters, then tell the press how much they feel the pain of those involved. It is a political ritual, enacted for the media. But an important ritual. Ignore it at your peril.

Navy's Tailhook Scandal

The Tailhook Association is an old group of Navy pilots who flew planes launched and recovered by aircraft carriers at sea. It gets its name from the cable stretched across the carrier deck, and the hook in the tail of the planes. The hook is designed to grab the cable and stop the hurtling planes as they land.

During their convention in Las Vegas in 1991, a large group of intoxicated Tailhook members gathered in a Hilton Hotel hallway. As women tried to walk down the hall, they were groped, harassed and in some cases, had their clothes ripped off.

Navy Careers Scuttled

Although they were not involved in the melee, Secretary of the Navy H. Lawrence Garrett III and Chief of Naval Operations Admiral Frank Kelso had both attended the 1991 Tailhook convention.

In the aftermath of the scandal, Garrett ultimately resigned. Kelso took early retirement two years later. The news media portrayed them as bad guys who were, in the final analysis, just as guilty as the drunk pilots because they had been slow to investigate the allegations.

Eventually, the careers of 14 admirals and nearly 300 Navy pilots were damaged in some way by the Tailhook scandal.

Slowness to act will often be interpreted by the media as an attempt to cover up the crime — one of this culture's very worst sins. (See **STRATEGY/Ten Commandments** and **SKILLS/ Good Guys/Bad Guys**)

Crash of Valujet 592

Valujet Flight 592 caught fire shortly after takeoff from Miami on May 11, 1996, and crashed into the Everglades, killing all 110 people aboard. The next day, Transportation Secretary Federico Pena held a news conference.

U.S. airlines are safe, Pena said. He was so sure the Federal Aviation Administration (FAA) was doing a good job regulating the airlines, Pena said he would not be afraid to put his own family aboard another Valujet plane. FAA Administrator David Hinson's media interviews echoed the same confidence.

Within a month, the media had learned about 34 safety violations in Valujet's recent history. Media stories said both Pena and Hinson knew about the violations at the time they were bragging about the FAA and airline safety.

They were accused of hypocrisy and deception. The FAA was cast as one of the bad guys.

FAA Conflict

Both men were caught in a conflict of interest within the Congressional mandate that created the FAA. The agency was supposed to regulate airlines and insure their safety, but it was also supposed to promote air travel.

In their management of the crisis, both Pena and Hinson had under-estimated the problem, and failed to assume responsibility for things that might have gone wrong.

Quite suddenly, Pena almost disappeared from news stories. In March, 1997, he was shifted to the Department of Energy, and in June, 1998, he resigned that post. Hinson retired at the end of 1996, seven months after the crash.

The careers of both men and the reputation of the FAA were badly damaged by their missteps in the early hours of the crisis.

The TWA 800 Crash

There was a sharp contrast in the way National Transportation Safety Board (NTSB) vice chairman Robert Francis handled the media in both the Valujet crash and the TWA Flight 800 crash two months later. When the TWA 747 enroute to Paris exploded off Long Island the night of July 17, 1996, all 230 people aboard died.

Francis by that time had logged a great deal of experience in crisis management. The TWA crisis was especially difficult because there were recurring rumors the plane had been destroyed by a bomb or a missile. At every news conference, Francis was exceptionally skillful at reminding the media:

▪ How difficult it would be to prove what caused the crash

▪ That the NTSB would leave no stone unturned

▪ That it would take a very long time

▪ That nobody should jump to conclusions before all the evidence was in

Be Patient With Reporters

Despite extreme fatigue, sunburn and a very tough job in the international spotlight, Francis was unusually patient with reporters who asked stupid, repetitive or antagonistic questions.

It is extremely difficult to maintain your equilibrium when the crisis exerts that kind of pressure. It is also hard to resist the seductive things that happen to your ego if you're on TV and the front page day after day as the crisis unfolds.

Keep Reminding Yourself:

You need to keep reminding yourself:

- I have a job to do; reporters have a job to do
- If they didn't understand what I said, I'll say it over and over, without getting testy, until they do understand
- If I behave badly, the world will see reruns a thousand times
- If reporters behave badly, it will probably not be reported
- I will be a more effective spokesperson if I can remain human, humble, sensitive
- It is OK to admit that I don't know, but I'm working very hard to:
  - ✓ Find the answer
  - ✓ Solve the problem
  - ✓ Prevent it from happening again
- When I know the answer, I'll tell the whole world

Bring the Media Inside Your Crisis

Bring the news media inside your crisis. Brief them frequently. Let them watch at close range how you handle the crisis. At first glance, this seems absolutely absurd. But it works.

Here's why:

- Reporters are, by nature, gossips
- Being inside gives them special knowledge, power and prestige
- By watching your decision-making process, reporters can better understand the options

- They are more likely to report you were the good guy who did the right thing, and made the best of a bad situation
- The Stockholm Syndrome takes over

The Stockholm Syndrome

In August, 1973, a group of robbers armed with sub-machine guns tried to rob the Sveriges Kreditbank in Stockholm, Sweden. The robbery went bad when police surrounded the bank. The robbers holed up inside the bank vault with four hostages. The hostage crisis lasted five and one-half days.

Psychologists and police officers who later interviewed the hostages were amazed that they were sympathetic to the bank robbers, not the police officers who rescued them. The phrase "Stockholm Syndrome" was born. A number of hostage situation studies since then confirm the same bonding phenomenon.

Ruthless Attitude Softens

Lengthy, close contact in a hostage crisis also leads the captors to identify with their prisoners. Their original, ruthless attitude is softened as they learn more about their prisoners as human beings.

Both hostages and hostage-takers are unified by the knowledge that the police outside may harm or kill them all.

Bringing the media into your crisis bunker has similar psychological effects. Those outside, surrounding and threatening you, after several days will be perceived as the bad guys. Those inside the bunker become the good guys.

The Tylenol Disaster

Johnson and Johnson CEO James Burke saved the company during the famous Tylenol poisoning of five people in Chicago in September, 1982. Within an hour after news broke that someone had planted cyanide in Tylenol capsules, Burke was enroute to Chicago to supervise the company response.

He also let the media see the innermost decision-making process. Mike Wallace and a *60 Minutes* camera crew were allowed to film an executive committee meeting at the height of the crisis, with no holds barred. Reporters were briefed regularly. Extensive facilities and staff were provided to help them cover the story.

Helping reporters cover your crisis creates another psychological advantage. You have done them a favor. They sort of owe you one. This will never be spoken or acknowledged. But reporters are human, too. While they claim to be hard-nosed professionals who do what they have to do, they are subtly influenced to write a more sympathetic story when you use this tactic.

Confine the Story

The real damage occurs when a story breaks out of the local media and goes national. The media today have a habit of piling on, once you've been hit by the first, local story. They can smell a scandal half a continent away. Nobody wants to be left out.

My advice is to drop everything and concentrate all your resources and skill on the local reporter who gets wind of a story with disaster potential. If you're not guilty, and you succeed with the local reporter, the story will be aborted.

If your organization slipped up and made a terrible mistake, tell the local reporter that. Admit your crime, correct the problem, do what you can to prevent its ever happening again. The result will often be a small story that stays local.

The Targeting Phenomenon

Once a story begins to spread nationally, a strange phenomenon occurs. For a while, anything that is even remotely associated with an element in the story gets a huge amount of media attention.

If a Boeing 737 crashes, for months afterward, any slight problem that occurs with *any* 737 will get major coverage. The little problems would not normally be news. But for a time, anything to do with 737s will be targeted by the media.

Think Outside the Box

One reason some situations deteriorate into full-fledged crises is the fear of staff to make quick, creative decisions on their own. To do things differently usually requires high-level approval. Perhaps by the CEO or chairman of the board. That takes time.

The Allies' Normandy invasion might have been repelled if the German officers in command had ordered a shift in German forces to the invasion site. Instead, they waited for permission from Berlin. By the time it came, it was too late.

In a media-driven world where crisis news now circles the globe in a matter of minutes, the old, bureaucratic checklists which require high-level approval for dealing with problems no longer work. Everything is on a much faster track.

Crisis at Coca Cola

The scare about contaminated Coca Cola in Europe in June, 1999, is a good example. It took nine days for the Coca Cola board chairman to fly to Europe to show top-level concern about reports that Coke had caused illness in hundreds of people.

Coca Cola staffers in Europe believed from the beginning that their drinks were not the cause of the illness. Government investigations determined much later that they were right.

Being Right Can Be Expensive

Their conviction that they were not at fault kept the company from responding quickly and innovatively when the crisis surfaced.

Media stories (and government reaction to the coverage) cost the company an estimated $100 million in recalled products that summer, and reduced sales for months. The company's stock price, its reputation, and a number of careers were also hammered.

It is not enough to proclaim your innocence, if you are the accused. If it appears that you *might* be at fault, you must quickly take bold, visual, expensive, public, media-savvy steps to make sure things are safe and under control.

The Firestone/Ford Crisis

Firestone and Ford were badly hurt in the 2000 crisis over tires on Ford Explorers throwing their treads and causing scores of deaths. The most damaging accusation was that the companies had indications of problems years ago and covered up, or did nothing.

It is possible that other brands of tires have the same propensity to disintegrate at high speeds if the owner does not keep them properly inflated. But that is an aside, and might distract viewers/readers from the primary media message.

Make no mistake about it. Ford and Firestone are the story.

This kind of coverage can destroy the largest corporation. Even if you're innocent.

Crisis management is crucial.

STRATEGY

Ethics

Do They Make Up the Rules As They Go Along?

When I mentioned journalistic ethics in a seminar, a middle-aged police chief interrupted. "Reporters have no ethics," he grumbled. "They'll do whatever it takes to get a story. They have no conscience. They make up the rules as they go along."

Sometimes, I conceded, that's true. Since the beginning of this nation, the media's ethics have been in constant flux. Some of the ethic is written, some spoken. Some simply understood among editors and reporters. That's what makes it seem so amorphous and strange to outsiders.

Who Regulates the Media?

The ethics for many professions are enforced through state or federal law, usually through regulatory bodies created by statute. Many people who deal with the news media believe there should be similar supervision of the news media.

But the First Amendment keeps popping up:

Congress shall make no law ... abridging the freedom of speech or of the press ...

There was a period in the 1970s and 1980s when the media did a lot to clean up their act. Part of it was the aftermath of Watergate. The media had turned the spotlight on public officials in a new, no-holds-barred way. Before Watergate, the media had often participated in a conspiracy of silence about certain kinds of things that went on behind the scenes in government; certain kinds of behavior among power people, politicians, and media people themselves. (See **INSIDE THE MEDIA/Privacy**)

If we're going to hold politicians and public officials to a certain standard, the media reasoned, we'll have to live by those same standards. People who live in glass houses, the old saying goes, shouldn't throw stones. Journalists have traditionally been the stone-throwers in this society.

And for the first time, the media were willing to report on each other without pulling their punches. Another contributing factor for that was new, increased competition. Newspapers were especially eager to trash their new television competitors, whom they feared and despised. (See **STRATEGY/Selling Your Story**)

Ethics Erosion in the 90s

Unfortunately (in my opinion) a much sharper increase in competition in the 1990s has led to a massive erosion of media ethics and responsibility.

I blame that deterioration primarily on a shift in American media ownership. Television networks, many local TV stations, and about 80 percent of all daily American newspapers are now owned by large, distant corporations. (See **INSIDE THE MEDIA** chapters on **Networks** and **Newspapers** for ownership details)

This is a major cultural shift for the United States. Until the 1970s, most American newspapers were locally owned, usually by a local family, and very provincial.

Unlike other industrial countries, the U.S. has very few national dailies sold all over the country. *The New York Times, The Wall Street Journal* and *USA Today* are about the only ones. With circulation of 1.77 million, *USA Today* is America's largest daily. Japan's largest daily, *Yomiuri Shimbun*, sells 14.5 million.

The Bottom-Line Mentality

The people with final power in the corporations that own today's media rarely have experience as reporters or editors. They have no experience with journalistic ethics. They have a bottom-line mentality. Their primary allegiance is to their stockholders. They crave Wall Street's blessing. If there is a conflict between responsible journalism and profit, profit usually wins.

The ethical slide is also accelerated by the decline of the newspaper as the dominant source of news and information.

"The Cereal Killer"

The most publicized episode in this ethics battle began when Mark Willes was named CEO of the Times Mirror Corp. in 1995. The *Los Angeles Times* was the company's flagship newspaper. Willes came to Times Mirror from his job as vice-chairman of General Mills, the cereal company.

He quickly alienated reporters and editors by going through the entire corporation, slashing jobs and killing highly-regarded publications that were not profitable enough. Journalists within the company gave him the nickname "The Cereal Killer."

Willes' next move was an attempt to move the advertising department into the newsroom. Editors were teamed with advertising "partners" so they could work together to merge the goals of both news and advertising. In June, 1999, Willes appointed as publisher Kathrn M. Downing. She had no newspaper background.

The Willes strategy was financially successful. He made a compelling argument that journalists will have nowhere to publish what they write if their publication does not make a profit.

Guerilla Warfare Behind the Lines

Throughout Willes' reign, there was constant guerilla warfare in the newsroom. Stories about what was happening at the *Los Angeles Times* became staples in the *Columbia Journalism Review* and *American Journalism Review* — the self-appointed monitors of ethics in U.S. journalism. Many of the details were leaked by disgruntled staffers on the *Times* editorial staff.

In late 1997, Shelby Coffee III, 50, the highly-regarded *Times* editor who had led it to four Pulitzer prizes, resigned. He claimed it had nothing to do with Willes. But few believed him.

The Final Battle

The final battle was a 162-page Sunday supplement published October 10, 1999, about the Staples Center — a proposed $400 million sports and entertainment arena in downtown Los Angeles. The supplement was stuffed with $2 million in advertising. *New Times* — a local weekly then disclosed a secret deal to give the proposed center half the $2 million generated by the Sunday supplement.

Otis Chandler, the retired former chairman of Times Mirror, had been largely silent about the business for 13 years. With news of the Staples supplement deal, he could stay quiet no longer. In a four-page letter of protest, he savaged Willes' regime as "the single most devastating period in the history of this great newspaper."

One of the sacred tenets of American journalism ethics has barred reporters and editors from having an undisclosed financial interest in anything they cover.

Downing — the *Times* publisher — admitted that she had kept the Staples Center financial arrangement secret from the editorial staff. In the uproar, she published an apology for the entire incident.

In mid-2000, Times Mirror was merged with the Tribune Co. — parent company of the *Chicago Tribune*. Both Willes and Downing were dumped in the merger.

Newspapers' Terminal Illness

The newspaper as we have known it cannot survive much longer. People will still want printed news, but they will have to print it themselves. Because they had been dominant so long, it took a long time for newspaper people to realize the new technology was taking over. (See **INSIDE THE MEDIA/Newspapers**)

When they finally grasped what was happening in the mid-1990s, they went into survival panic mode. In the evolution of organisms and organizations, the will to survive is often much more powerful than the will to be responsible and ethical.

As the *LA Times* episode illustrated, corporate executives with no background in journalism often have a tin ear for ethical tunes. They simply do not understand what all the fuss is about.

Some cynics question whether the new ownership calls for another look at the First Amendment. The "press" is the only for-profit business granted unlimited Constitutional protection. The Founding Fathers could not have foreseen the media's evolving financial structure. (See **INSIDE THE MEDIA/Networks** and **Newspapers**)

When journalists break their own rules, there are things you can do about it, if you understand the traditional ethic, and the levers of power. I'll try to explain some of those rules, and how you can wield power as a reader/viewer/listener/consumer.

The Out-Take Ethic

For outsiders, there is no ethic more baffling than editors and reporters who refuse to give up out-takes. Out-takes are pictures, audio tape or videotape that were never published or broadcast. In the editing process, they were taken out.

The out-take issue took on national significance in the summer of 1968, after the street demonstrations during the Democratic National Convention in Chicago. Prosecutors decided it was time to treat protesters more harshly.

Chicago - the 1968 Riots

They went to newspapers and television stations with subpoenas, demanding all film (videotape was not yet used by TV news) and still pictures taken during the demonstrations. From those pictures, they planned to prosecute anyone they could identify.

Many editors and news directors had never dealt with the issue before. Some quickly handed over their out-takes, without a fight. Others refused, saying they would destroy the pictures, if necessary, and risk contempt of court.

People outside the media could not understand why reporters, photographers and editors thought themselves immune to subpoenas and court orders. The police were using pictures already printed and broadcast to round up protesters. What was the difference between those and out-takes?

First Amendment Theory

The argument against giving up out-takes uses a First Amendment theory. The news media argument goes like this:

> *If we give you these pictures, and you use them to prosecute people, then our photographers become police agents. At the next demonstration, the mob will attack our photographers to prevent their gathering evidence for the police. We will not be able to do our job. Therefore, the government subpoena violates our First Amendment rights. It abridges the freedom of the press to cover future events.*

After the 1968 hassle, many news organizations adopted a broad policy that says:

We will never give up out-takes to any governmental agency. We will destroy the pictures or hide them and risk contempt of court rather than handicap ourselves in future news gathering.

The hard-liners counter that if you do it once, you set up a precedent that will make it harder to refuse out-takes next time.

Case-by-Case Approach

Other news organizations take a case-by-case approach. In some instances, they believe they can give up out-takes without jeopardizing future freedom to gather news.

It is a tough question.

Suppose, for instance, that a television reporter is shooting a standup in a downtown park. The reporter flubs several times. The sun goes in and out behind the clouds. The photographer is unhappy with the light, so they do it once more. An airplane passes over and the sound is ruined, so they do it again.

They use one of the standups in a story for the six o'clock news. The flawed standups become out-takes.

The next morning, a homicide detective shows up at the newsroom. "I understand you were shooting videotape in Downtown Park yesterday," the officer says. "I'd like to look at that tape. There was an armed robbery in a jewelry store across the street from the park at 2:05. A clerk in the store was killed. Your photographer may have unknowingly captured the killer entering or leaving the store. Right now, we have no other leads."

A Murderer on Tape

Is there now a reasonable argument to deny the police access to the out-takes? Some organizations will give them up in a narrow circumstance like this.

There is a loophole for the station with the "no out-takes" policy. They could look at the videotape, and if it does show someone going in or out of the jewelry store, they could run it on the news. "Do you recognize this man?" Great follow-up to the murder story. Once on the air, it would no longer be an out-take, and the station could honor a subpoena without violating its policy.

Too Cozy With the Police

Forty years ago, there was little concern about reporters becoming police agents. Law enforcement and reporters often collaborated. The police gave reporters story leads, and the reporters passed information to the police. A two-way street.

Some people in the news business now question that kind of coziness. It is not the media's job to make criminal cases, they say. That is a function of the criminal justice system. To become a police informant, they say, compromises a reporter's independence.

In some news operations, one reporter is assigned the police beat. That reporter, for all intents and purposes, becomes a closet cop. The longer on the beat, the more the reporter is trusted.

If there is a critical story about the department, another reporter does it. Reporters who investigate police misconduct are careful not to give or accept any favors from the police.

Reporters As Witnesses

Some news organizations have severe misgivings about their employees testifying in a criminal trial, or before a grand jury.

In the early 1970s, three reporters in separate incidents refused to even go inside grand jury rooms. They had been subpoenaed to testify about illegal activities they had witnessed and written about.

They said they arranged to watch those activities by promising they would never disclose the names of the people involved. If they went into a secret grand jury session, they argued, and their sources were later arrested, the sources would believe the reporters had betrayed them inside the grand jury room.

The Supreme Court's View

The U.S. Supreme Court combined the three incidents because they were so similar. In *Branzburg v. Hayes* (408 U.S. 665 - 1972) the Court ruled reporters have no First Amendment immunity from grand jury subpoenas.

The justices said a reporter might refuse to testify about certain things once in the witness chair, and that refusal might have to be argued in court; but there are many other subjects reporters — as citizens — are obligated to talk about. Some journalists strongly disagree, and would be willing to risk jail if they were subpoenaed.

Deception Through Staging

Television coverage of civil rights and war protest demonstrations made "staging" a major issue in the 1960s. TV was new. It was still exploring the power of the picture.

If the TV crew got there after the rocks were thrown, photographers would sometimes ask demonstrators to throw more rocks, with the camera rolling.

The FCC established severe penalties for stations who broadcast scenes that appeared to be spontaneous and unrehearsed when — in fact — the event had been staged for television. At some stations, rules were written that instructed staff:

If you get to the scene of a demonstration, and nothing is happening, it may become clear they were waiting for you to arrive. Leave without filming anything if you determine the demonstration was staged purely for TV.

Photo Opportunities

This is a slippery concept.

In the 1950s, politicians and celebrities quickly learned to create "photo opportunities" for both TV and print.

A publicist announces a politician will go to the scene of a chemical spill for a personal inspection. Is that staging?

Yes. It is an event created primarily for media exposure. The argument that he needs to visit personally, as part of his campaign or government duty, is very transparent.

Enhanced Media Events

An event can be greatly enhanced for the cameras through staging. During presidential campaigns, if the candidate is in a motorcade, it is not unusual for campaign workers to recruit people to enlarge the crowd.

Large crowds are arranged in the vicinity of the TV cameras. There may be blocks without a single person to wave at the candidate. But the crowds near the cameras give the perception that multitudes were hysterically enthusiastic along the motorcade route.

It is staged. It is deceptive.

Sometimes the media tell us about the staging. Sometimes, they don't.

Dramatizations

In 1989, the use of dramatizations became popular in TV news. Actors re-enact an event for the camera. On television, the agreed-upon ethic decrees that if dramatizations are used, the audience must be told very clearly this is not the real event.

One of the landmarks in this issue was an ABC News television story about an alleged espionage case. ABC videotaped a reenactment of a State Department employee handing national security secrets to a Russian agent.

The Phony Spy Tape

In broadcasting the story, it was not made clear this was a reenactment. The videotape had been shot amateurishly, as though it were authentic counterspy surveillance. The story caused such an uproar, many TV news organizations for a time outlawed all reenactments and dramatizations by their news departments.

But the re-enactment technique gradually crept back into respectability. Shows like *America's Most Wanted* use re-enacted crimes as a weekly staple.

Exploding Truck Scandal

An even larger ethical debacle took place in November, 1992, when *Dateline NBC* ran a safety story about General Motors pickup trucks.

The videotape showed a broadside crash which seemed to cause the truck's gas tank to explode. The fuel tanks were mounted on the underside of the chassis.

General Motors began an intense investigation to defend its design and disclosed in early 1993 that the *Dateline* crash had been rigged. A contractor-technician for NBC had attached incendiary devices to the truck to make sure it would explode.

The disclosure led to a major investigation within NBC; the resignation of three *Dateline NBC* producers who had worked the story; and the reassignment of the correspondent to a network-owned station.

Most ethical issues swing like a pendulum. After you get a speeding ticket, you drive more carefully.

For a while.

Print Holier-Than-Thou

Newspapers are particularly holier-than-thou in their coverage of any television news controversy.

But virtually every newspaper in the nation publishes staged pictures every day. If you've been at the award ceremony, you know the still photographers line people up, position them, tell them to hold still, and then hold still for "one more."

Are the standard "grip and grin" pictures in virtually every newspaper staged? Yes. But because the action is so innocuous, we don't seem to mind.

Spot News Photos Rare

Television news from the beginning invested heavily in helicopters and other equipment to reach news events and broadcast them live. That was an important element in their becoming the dominant source of news for most Americans.

Because television can beat them so badly, many newspapers no longer even try to photograph most breaking news stories. Virtually every picture in the newspaper is posed.

Television has conditioned Americans to expect video of major events, as they happen. If we see it, it must be so. Not necessarily, as the spy handoff and the pickup truck videotape showed.

Doctored Photographs

The ethics of doctoring photographs has now become a major concern for both print and broadcast media. Newspapers with the latest technology no longer need to make prints of photographs that will appear in tomorrow's editions.

Film negatives are fed into a scanner which displays the photograph on a computer monitor. Or the picture is taken with a digital camera. There is no film. The image is stored electronically.

With complex software, a photo editor can manipulate the image. The picture can be cropped, enlarged, shrunk. Colors can be changed or enhanced.

Items or people can be inserted, or wiped out. The manipulation cannot be detected when the picture is published. The same thing can be done with videotape. Television is going digital. More and more television news video is edited on a computer.

This was the technique used in the movie *Forrest Gump*, where one of the actors appears to be missing his legs, and where Gump seems to be talking to the President in the White House.

The CBS Billboard Coverup

To mark the turn of the century on New Year's Eve, 1999, Dan Rather anchored the *CBS Evening News* from Times Square in New York. Over his shoulder, you could see a large billboard advertising CBS.

The billboard was not really there. It had been inserted electronically to cover the *real* billboard, which advertised NBC.

When other news media ran stories about the billboard coverup, Rather said he did not know about it until after the newscast. But he said nothing publicly until news stories about the billboard broke almost two weeks later.

Rather said then, "At the very least, we should have pointed it out to viewers ... By not doing that, we run the risk of undercutting our credibility." CBS President Leslie Moonves called the storm of criticism "Ridiculous ... It's much ado about nothing."

Jennings' Precaution

ABC Anchor Peter Jennings was wary that he might be accused of similar visual sleight-of-hand at the political conventions in 2000. In each newscast, Jennings told his audience the convention floor that appeared to be behind him was not really there.

Jennings would then let the audience see a shot from the side. He was in the convention hall, but he was sitting in front of a blank wall. The live shot of the convention auditorium that viewers saw behind him was inserted electronically. (Read how weather maps are created the same way in **INSIDE THE MEDIA/Newscast**)

In the past, newspaper artists routinely used air brushes to remove distracting objects from pictures. They sometimes pasted people into photographs. But that was much easier to detect.

Junkets and Freebies

A hundred years ago, P. T. Barnum learned how to get free advertising when the circus came to town. First, you hired schoolboys to paste circus posters on the side of every barn within 20 miles. They'd do it for nothing if you gave them free circus tickets.

Newspaper reporters could also be recruited. For a handful of tickets, a reporter would write a glowing story about that wondrous extravaganza of excitement, that colossal collection of color and courage, that stunning display of spine-tingling skill waiting for you under the Big Top. It still works.

Until the early 1970s, it was not unusual for reporters to accept all sorts of freebies. Travel writers took elaborate trips, with an airline or a resort picking up the tab. Political writers traveled with a candidate in planes the candidate paid for.

Press rooms were provided in public buildings for free. Critics received free tickets to the events they reviewed, and sportswriters almost universally accepted batches of season tickets for every conceivable event that was related in any way to sports.

The Free Ticket Furor

In the late 1970s, an investigative story in a magazine caused a major furor. It told how sportswriters at major newspapers routinely accepted large numbers of valuable season tickets, which they could sell or pass out to ingratiate themselves with other people. Embarrassed newspapers began announcing they would no longer accept free tickets to sports or cultural events.

Many news organizations drew up — some for the first time — codes of ethics for their staffs. Most now forbid accepting anything of value from anyone a reporter might expect to cover.

Some are so strict, they won't even let their employees accept a cup of coffee. Or lunch. They pay their pro-rata share of transportation costs when they travel with candidates, and they pay rent for the use of press rooms in public buildings.

Massive Freebies Still

But there are still freebies on a massive scale. Tourist attractions fly reporters, photographers and their families in for a VIP weekend when they open a new section or celebrate an anniversary. Many accept. Media people know a phone call is all it takes to get free tickets at some attractions.

Airlines invite the media along for first-class service when they open a new route. The TV networks have huge, week-long, expense-paid parties to unveil the new season's shows. Some TV critics accept the freebie, others pay their own way.

Those policies are still evolving. Those who refuse freebies argue that if they constantly search for conflicts of interest among public officials and corporate executives, they have to keep their own skirts clean.

Others don't seem to care. Some alibi that travel, sports and entertainment coverage is not real news, and has a different ethic.

Congressional Conflicts

In the 1990s the U.S. House and Senate passed new ethics rules preventing members from accepting large fees for speeches and limiting their ability to be paid advances by book publishers.

The rule changes originated with the media's reporting on book sales by then-House Speaker Jim Wright (D-Tex). Wright would speak for free, but the group he was speaking to would buy hundreds — sometimes thousands — of copies of his book, *Reflections of a Public Man*.

The Speaker's Demise

The media were very harsh on Wright, and the issue eventually ended his term as Speaker. He left the House in 1989. His most energetic tormentor was a young Republican Congressman from Georgia, Newt Gingrich.

The issue erupted again in 1994, when Gingrich became Speaker. Gingrich accepted a $4.5 million advance from Harper-Collins, which contracted with him to write two books.

As it turned out, media magnate Rupert Murdoch controlled the publishing house. Murdoch needed Congress and the FCC to waive the rules for his growing ownership of media properties in the United States. The media had a field day, castigating Gingrich for the conflict of interest. He was forced to return the advance.

As this book goes to press, a similar issue — what to do about "soft money" for political campaigns is once again on the national agenda.

Media Moonlighting

Some media celebrities who are writing scathing reports on Congressional conflicts of interest don't tell their readers/viewers about their own moonlighting. Well-known journalists accept lush payments to speak to special interest groups.

These are groups whose issues the presenters will likely cover as reporters. Some well-known network correspondents and newspaper columnists charge $35,000 to $50,000 to speak.

They rarely tell their readers/viewers they've accepted money, travel and other gifts from those they're writing about.

Accepting anything of value from a group you're covering is a clear violation of the Code of Ethics endorsed by both the Society of Professional Journalists (SPJ) and the Radio-Television News Directors Assn. (RTNDA). The full text of both codes is reproduced at the end of this chapter.

In many cases, journalists who violate the Code of Ethics are so valuable to their employers, nothing is done about it. Sort of like star athletes who misbehave, but aren't disciplined because the team needs them. Another example of the profit motive overwhelming journalism standards in large media corporations.

A Duty to Be Fair

Reporters have an obligation to be fair. To get both sides of the story. To interview you, and give you a chance to answer the allegations against you. The story should be balanced and objective, unless it is clearly labeled as an editorial, a column for the journalist's personal opinion, or commentary.

Truth and Accuracy

Media stories should be accurate and true. Reporters have an obligation to go beyond the obvious in search of the truth — particularly if the story will damage someone. Reporters who accept information with strings attached are morally obligated to honor that contract, which is often a verbal agreement that is virtually impossible to enforce. (See **SKILLS/Off-the-Record**)

Breaking the Law

The U.S. Supreme Court has ruled that reporters and editors must live by the same laws that other citizens do. The Constitution does not give them special dispensation to trespass, to break and enter, to harass you, or wiretap your telephone.

In the real world, reporters break minor laws in order to expose a problem. As an investigative reporter, I bought illegal numbers tickets and bet on horses in illegal bookie joints. My editors and I played God. We decided the public service that would be performed by those stories outweighed the misdemeanor.

In mid-1998, the *Cincinnati Enquirer* renounced a series it had published on Chiquita Brands International, fired the reporter who'd written it, and reportedly paid Chiquita $10 million. The paper said it learned after publication the information for the story had apparently been obtained by tapping into Chiquita's electronic voice-mail system. The reporter was arrested and pleaded guilty.

Undercover Reporting

Undercover work to obtain a story is hotly debated within the news media. Some say reporters should never pose as anything but reporters. They should interview people to obtain inside information, rather than infiltrate their target, posing as someone else.

As an investigative reporter, I took the opposite position. If truth and fairness were my goals, I wanted to see, hear, record and photograph for my audience exactly what was going on.

If you're doing a story on a home improvement scam, do you go to the contractor's office, introduce yourself, and say, "Hi, I'm Clark Kent of the *Daily Planet* and I want to know whether you've been bilking little old ladies."

Not if you want the truth.

The Food Lion Case

This was exactly the issue in the Food Lion v. Capital Cities/ ABC case. In 1992, ABC's *Prime Time Live* sent two producers to the Food Lion supermarket chain to apply for jobs in the meat department. After they obtained the jobs, they worked for several weeks wearing hidden cameras and microphones.

On November 5, 1992, *Prime Time Live* broadcast a riveting segment in which Food Lion supervisors — captured by the hidden cameras and microphones — showed the undercover producers how to dip tainted meat in bleach to kill the smell, then re-package it for sale.

Food Lion sued ABC. But not for libel (defaming its reputation). The truth of the story was not challenged at the trial.

Instead, the grocery chain based its case on the producers' deception in applying for their jobs, their trespassing in the stores where they worked, and for secretly recording and betraying the Food Lion employees who had befriended them. (See **INSIDE THE MEDIA/Privacy** and **Libel**)

Jury Awards $5.5 Million

The jury was not even allowed to see the ABC story about Food Lion. The issue was not the story — it was how the reporting was done. In December, 1996, the jury returned a verdict against ABC with a judgment for $5.5 million in punitive damages. The damage award was later overturned by an appellate court.

After the verdict, newspaper columnists clucked their tongues and shook their fingers at ABC for doing something naughty that newspapers would *never* have done. (See more about the nasty feud between newspapers and TV in **STRATEGY/Fighting Back**)

The print writers seemed to overlook *The Wall Street Journal's* 1995 Pulitzer Prize for Tony Horwitz' undercover series on dead-end jobs that included his working inside a chicken packaging plant. Or Jane Lil's undercover job in a garment factory in 1996 for *The New York Times* to document sweat shop conditions.

The Entrapment Issue

Some journalists argue that inviting the aluminum siding sales-person into your home for the sales pitch is entrapment. Entrapment is a part of criminal law that protects innocent people from being framed by police and prosecutors. The law says defendants cannot be persuaded to break the law, and then be prosecuted.

To be scrupulously ethical, reporters working undercover must be very careful in what they do and say, so the targets of their investigations act on their own, without being coerced or encouraged to do something improper. Where a hidden camera is used, the audience can judge for itself whether the target was improperly influenced. In some states, however, hidden microphones cannot legally be used by reporters. (See **INSIDE THE MEDIA/Privacy**)

"Sneaky" Reporters

"Sneaky" is the word often used to criticize stories and pictures obtained by reporters posing as potential victims or fellow thieves. Yeah, as an investigative reporter I learned to be sneaky.

I maintain that some stories and some criminal cases can never be accomplished any other way. How many of the congressmen in the Abscam investigation would have been successfully prosecuted if they had not been secretly videotaped negotiating bribes and stuffing payoff cash in their pockets?

Newspapers invented undercover reporting and the use of hidden cameras. Now that miniature cameras and microphones enable television to videotape with incredible clarity, some newspapers have taken a sour grapes attitude.

Public Service Responsibility

Journalists often polish their public service halos. Is the public interest served when the news media disclose an undercover police investigation before the case is finished? Or the government's secretly buying land for a new road, to keep the price down?

Journalists say they must defend the "public's right to know." The counter argument asks — if the story had been held a little longer, would not the public good have been better served?

The same debate rages over how much the public should know about a criminal case before it goes to trial. Does the public's right to know outweigh the defendant's right to a fair trial? Those issues will be debated as long as democracy exists.

Anonymous Sources

Anonymous sources are another continuing ethical debate. Watergate would have never happened without "Deep Throat." (See **SKILLS/Off-the-Record**)

But if the reporter is dishonest, the "reliable source" may be fictitious. How will we know? There is a current effort at some media outlets to decrease the use of anonymous sources.

Confidential sources are especially prevalent in stories about government and politics, where the media have virtual immunity from lawsuits. (See **INSIDE THE MEDIA/Libel** and **Privacy**)

Checkbook Journalism

Checkbook journalism became a nasty phrase in the middle 1970s after CBS paid H. R. Haldeman $25,000 for a lengthy interview. Haldeman had been Richard Nixon's White House chief of staff. Throughout Watergate, Haldeman had said nothing to the news media. The CBS interview was a coup that backfired.

The rapid proliferation of tabloid-style TV shows in the 1990s rekindled the issue as paying interview subjects became more and more common.

In 1993, *A Current Affair* reportedly paid $100,000 for exclusive interview rights to three of the four Los Angeles police officers charged in the Rodney King beating.

In stories hotly pursued by the tabloid media like the murder of O. J. Simpson's ex-wife, the William Kennedy Smith rape trial, the death of Princess Diana in 1997, and the 1998 White House sex scandals, witnesses and jurors quickly realized they could get rich.

It became the custom to hire an agent to solicit bids for interviews. News media payments to witnesses in the O. J. Simpson case became an issue at the trial.

A Credibility Issue

When the media pay someone for an interview, it raises the same questions that come up when a paid informer testifies at a criminal trial.

Can you believe people who've been paid to talk? Was there an agreement to avoid certain subjects? Have they enhanced their stories to make them more valuable? Would they have told more if the price had been high higher? Is this really a form of bribery?

It is extremely rare for major "respectable" news organizations to pay cash for an interview. But there are loopholes.

Other Forms of Payment

In my seminars on media ethics, newspaper editors often say, self-righteously, that they would *never* pay someone for an interview. That would be unethical.

But as I move the hypothetical along, they say they *would* charter a jet to help a crime victim confront the defendant; pay for the transportation to reunite a family; fly a critically ill child to a well-known medical center.

The transportation arrangements would be made with a promise of exclusive coverage for the news outlet that paid the bill.

They have a very hard time explaining why providing transportation or hotel rooms is different from cash. I suspect the code of ethics in some editors' minds is there because it has been the custom — not because it has been carefully thought out. Television producers, on the other hand, often see nothing wrong with providing something of value to those who make the story better.

Before the Haldeman flap, "respectable" publications paid people for their first-person accounts after major news events.

Life Magazine signed a lucrative contract with the original group of astronauts for their exclusive, personal stories. That was checkbook journalism, but there were few protests.

Tabloid Journalism

Tabloids like the *National Enquirer,* the *Star* and the *Globe* rarely let the issue of checkbook journalism get in the way of a juicy story.

TV shows like *Hard Copy, Inside Edition* and *A Current Affair* are called "Tabloid TV" or "Trash TV" because their choice of stories — and the way they obtain them — are very similar to the print tabloids.

Sex, crime, aliens from outer space, celebrities, money, family violence, scandal and schmaltz are their standard ingredients.

William Kennedy Smith Case

In 1991, when Sen. Ted Kennedy's nephew was charged with rape in Palm Beach, the case filled every tabloid reporter's wildest fantasies. There, wrapped in one story, were all the elements that drive their coverage.

There was a bidding frenzy for exclusive interviews with witnesses and friends. In the heat of combat for new tidbits of information, a tabloid disclosed the name of the alleged rape victim.

Both NBC News and *The New York Times* quickly followed suit. That had always been considered unethical. There was a great deal of pontificating to justify their breaking the old code.

I suspect the real motives were profit and competition.

Tabloid journalism's influence on news worldwide continues to grow. The "dumbing down" of America's taste in news began with the Smith trial and rapidly grew.

It is often difficult now to tell the difference between network magazine shows and syndicated tabloid shows like *Hard Copy* and *Inside Edition.*

The Slide Into Sleaze

A timetable of stories that gradually led "respectable" media, both print and broadcast, into tabloid territory:

- Beginning in 1992, ongoing stories about marital infidelity by members of the British royal family.

- The Amy Fisher story. In early 1993, all three networks produced documentaries or docu-dramas after the New York teenager was convicted of shooting the wife of her lover.

- The arrest of Lorena Bobbitt in June, 1993, made common in mainstream media the previously-censored word "penis."

- In late 1993, the attack on Olympic skater Nancy Kerrigan by the ex-husband/manager of competitor Tonya Harding.

- The 1994 trial of Hollywood madam Heidi Fleiss, which included testimony about movie stars listed in her "black book."

- The arrest of football star O. J. Simpson for the murder of his ex-wife in 1994, and Simpson's 1995 trial.

- The 1995 expulsion of U.S. Senator Robert Packwood for sexually harassing female staff members. Stories included the titillating details from Packwood's diary.

- The death of Princess Diana in August, 1997.

- Detailed news stories of sexual allegations against Bill Clinton, so prevalent in 1998 that some columnists suggested warnings: "The following contains content not suitable for children."

Rush to Judgment

The speed at which sensational coverage can destroy the target of a media feeding frenzy is accelerating geometrically.

In 1997, after an outbreak of food poisoning that received massive media coverage, the company that had supplied hamburger to Burger King was out of business in two weeks.

It took about 18 months for the Watergate investigation to reach the point where the news media were suggesting the impeachment of Richard Nixon.

Within 48 hours after the Monica Lewinsky story broke in 1998, two major networks ran special reports strongly suggesting this story would result in Clinton's impeachment or resignation.

The concepts of what ethical journalists should publish or broadcast, and how personally intrusive they should be, is constantly changing.

In addition to competition and profit, many of those changes are driven by the media's relative immunity from lawsuits when they write about public figures.

Previewing Stories

Interviewees often ask if they can see a story before it's published or broadcast. That's considered a no-no. If you saw it, and didn't like what the reporter wrote, or the way it was presented, you'd say so.

The reporter might be influenced, and lose independence. In effect, you would become an editor for a story about yourself. You're not very objective about something you're personally involved in.

Some reporters — particularly those at weekly newspapers in rural communities — will let you do it. Most big-city newspapers won't. It doesn't hurt to ask. If the reporter has no objections, it's to your advantage to preview the story.

Everything I Say, or Nothing

If you're doing battle with a news organization, you may not trust their editing of what you say. Many people in this situation say they'll submit to an interview only if the reporter agrees to print or broadcast what they say, unedited.

This kind of offer is almost always refused. Editors don't like to be told what they can print or broadcast. As a part of their FCC licensing, broadcasters accept responsibility for everything they put on the air.

In effect, they would be handing that responsibility to someone else. They can be sued if you use their station to libel someone. You might be irresponsible in other ways, like using four-letter words the FCC frowns on.

There's a way around the problem. Draw up a letter of agreement in which they agree to print or broadcast everything you say — or nothing at all. That leaves them complete editorial control.

But if you expect them to use what you say under that agreement, remember — it has to be brief, and to the point.

Questions in Advance

Interview subjects often ask if they can have the questions in advance. Normally, that is considered unethical. The interview — particularly on television — is supposed to be a spontaneous, unrehearsed conversation between you and the reporter.

If you know in advance what the questions are going to be, you can go to the experts and memorize their information, then make it look like it's yours.

It's similar to letting the lawyer for a witness at a trial stand behind the witness and whisper the answer to every question.

Most reporters consider it ethical to give you a broad idea of what the interview will cover, but not specific questions.

Questions in Writing

In some cases, however, you can insist, and win. This sometimes happens with highly-placed officials, celebrities, or people facing major criminal charges.

Look, they say, I'll answer your questions, but only if you submit them to me in writing. Take it or leave it. Play it my way, or not at all.

In that situation, the media will sometimes play by your rules, but tell their readers, viewers or listeners the terms of the interview so they will not be misled. (See prepared statements in **SKILLS/ Interviews-Print**)

Journalists in Politics

Most journalists consider it unethical for reporters and editors to participate in any kind of political activity. That includes contributions of work or money; bumper stickers on their cars; signs in their yards, attending a political meeting where they are not working as reporters or editors.

Some will even register as "Independent" to avoid any suggestion of bias toward a political party. The extremists do not register at all and do not vote.

Purists in the media also refuse to do work for a charitable organization or serve on any board — private or public. Every journalist draws a different line. It is common in many communities for newspaper editors and broadcast executives with news responsibility to work in local United Way fund-raising campaigns. Some reporters in those newsrooms chafe when their bosses accept those positions.

Hard-liners suspect the people who run United Way chose the boss because they believe they can get better news coverage that way. They probably can.

National Codes of Ethics

There are two nationally endorsed codes of ethics for American journalists. One by the Society of Professional Journalists (SPJ) — also known as Sigma Delta Chi — which is dominated by newspaper people; and another by the Radio-Television News Directors Assn. (RTNDA).

The codes are only models. Nothing in them binds reporters. There is no legal or professional commitment for journalists to live up to them. Many news organizations have much more stringent and specific guidelines for their employees.

But the codes of ethics reproduced in full below will give you an idea of some broad, general areas that most conscientious people in the news media would agree on.

Use It When You Complain

When you complain to the media about their coverage, citing either code is a powerful tool if you believe the media have acted improperly. (See **STRATEGY/Fighting Back**)

The original SPJ code was adopted in 1973. After a great deal of debate, it was completely rewritten. The current version was adopted at the SPJ's September, 1996, convention.

SPJ Code of Ethics

Here's the complete text. Subheads are part of the code.

Preamble

Members of the Society of Professional journalists believe that public enlightenment is the forerunner of justice and the foundation of democracy. The duty of the journalist is to further those ends by seeking truth and providing a fair and comprehensive account of events and issues. Conscientious journalists from all media and specialties strive to serve the public with thoroughness and honesty.

Professional integrity is the cornerstone of a journalist's credibility. Members of the Society share a dedication to ethical behavior and standards of practice.

Seek Truth and Report It

Journalists should be honest, fair and courageous in gathering, reporting and interpreting information. **Journalists should:**

- *Test the accuracy of information from all sources and exercise care to avoid inadvertent error. Deliberate distortion is never permissible.*

- *Diligently seek out subjects of news stories to give them the opportunity to respond to allegations of wrongdoing.*

- *Identify sources whenever feasible. The public is entitled to as much information as possible on sources' reliability.*

- *Always question sources' motives before promising anonymity. Clarify conditions attached to any promise made in exchange for information. Keep promises.*

- *Make certain that headlines, news teases and promotional material, photos, video, audio, graphics, sound bites and quotations do not misrepresent. They should not oversimplify or highlight incidents out of context.*

- *Never distort the content of news photos or video. Image enhancement for technical clarity is always permissible. Label montages and photo illustrations.*

- *Avoid misleading reenactments or staged news events. If reenactment is necessary to tell a story, label it.*

- *Avoid undercover or other surreptitious methods of gathering information except when traditional open methods will not yield information vital to the public. Use of such methods should be explained as part of the story.*

- *Never plagiarize.*

- *Tell the story of the diversity and magnitude of the human experience boldly even when it is unpopular to do so.*

- *Examine their own cultural values and avoid imposing those values on others.*

- *Avoid stereotyping by race, gender, age, religion, ethnicity, geography, sexual orientation, disability, physical appearance or social status.*

- *Support the open exchange of views, even views they find repugnant.*

- *Give voice to the voiceless; official and unofficial sources of information can be equally valid.*

- *Distinguish between advocacy and news reporting. Analysis and commentary should be labeled and not misrepresent fact or context.*

- *Distinguish news from advertising and shun hybrids that blur the lines between the two.*

- *Recognize a special obligation to ensure that the public's business is conducted in the open and that government records are open to inspection.*

Minimize Harm

Ethical journalists treat sources, subjects and colleagues as human beings deserving of respect. **Journalists should:**

- *Show compassion for those who may be affected adversely by news coverage. Use special sensitivity when dealing with children and inexperienced sources or subjects.*

- *Be sensitive when seeking or using interviews or photographs of those affected by tragedy or grief.*

- *Recognize that gathering and reporting information may cause harm or discomfort. Pursuit of the news is not a license for arrogance.*

- *Recognize that private people have a greater right to control information about themselves than do public officials and others who seek power, influence or attention. Only an overriding public need can justify intrusion into anyone's privacy.*

- *Show good taste. Avoid pandering to lurid curiosity.*

- *Be cautious about identifying juvenile suspects or victims of sex crimes.*

- *Be judicious about naming criminal suspects before the formal filing of charges.*

■ *Balance a criminal suspect's fair trial rights with the public's right to be informed.*

Act Independently

Journalists should be free of obligation to any interest other than the public's right to know. **Journalists should:**

■ *Avoid conflicts of interest, real or perceived.*

■ *Remain free of associations and activities that may compromise integrity or damage credibility.*

■ *Refuse gifts, favors, fees, free travel and special treatment, and shun secondary employment, political involvement, public office and service in community organizations if they compromise journalistic integrity.*

■ *Disclose unavoidable conflicts.*

■ *Be vigilant and courageous about holding those with power accountable.*

■ *Deny favored treatment to advertisers and special interests and resist their pressure to influence news coverage.*

■ *Be wary of sources offering information for favors or money; avoid bidding for news.*

Be Accountable

Journalists are accountable to their readers, listeners, viewers and each other. **Journalists should:**

■ *Clarify and explain news coverage and invite dialogue with the public over journalistic conduct.*

■ *Encourage the public to voice grievances against the news media.*

■ *Admit mistakes and correct them promptly.*

■ *Expose unethical practices of journalists and the news media.*

■ *Abide by the same high standards to which they hold others.*

RTNDA Code of Ethics

The Radio-Television News Directors Assn. adopted the following code at its convention in September, 2000. It is a major expansion of the brief Code of Ethics that had previously been in effect. Subheads are part of the code. Here's the full text:

RTNDA CODE OF ETHICS

The Radio-Television News Directors Association, wishing to foster the highest professional standards of electronic journalism, promote public understanding of and confidence in journalism, and strengthen principles of journalistic freedom to gather and disseminate information, establishes this Code of Ethics and Professional Conduct.

Preamble

Professional electronic journalists should operate as trustees of the public, seek the truth, report it fairly and with integrity and independence, and stand accountable for their actions.

Public Trust

Professional electronic journalists should recognize that their first obligation is to the public.

Professional electronic journalists should:

- *Understand that any commitment other than service to the public undermines trust and credibility.*

- *Recognize that service in the public interest creates an obligation to reflect the diversity of the community and guard against oversimplification of issues or events.*

- *Provide a full range of information to enable the public to make enlightened decisions.*

- *Fight to ensure that the public's business is conducted in public.*

Truth

Professional electronic journalists should pursue truth aggressively and present the news accurately, in context, and as completely as possible.

Professional electronic journalists should:

- *Continuously seek the truth.*

- *Resist distortions that obscure the importance of events.*

- *Clearly disclose the origin of information and label all material provided by outsiders.*

Professional electronic journalists should not:

- *Report anything known to be false.*

- *Manipulate images or sounds in any way that is misleading.*

- *Plagiarize.*

- *Present images or sounds that are reenacted without informing the public.*

Fairness

Professional electronic journalists should present the news fairly and impartially, placing primary value on significance and relevance.

Professional electronic journalists should:

- *Treat all subjects of news coverage with respect and dignity, showing particular compassion to victims of crime or tragedy.*

- *Exercise special care when children are involved in a story and give children greater privacy protection than adults.*

- *Seek to understand the diversity of their community and inform the public without bias or stereotype.*

- *Present a diversity of expressions, opinions, and ideas in context.*

- *Present analytical reporting based on professional perspective, not personal bias.*

- *Respect the right to a fair trial.*

Integrity

Professional electronic journalists should present the news with integrity and decency, avoiding real or perceived conflicts of interest, and should respect the dignity and intelligence of the audience as well as the subjects of news.

Professional electronic journalists should:

- *Identify sources whenever possible. Confidential sources should be used only when it is clearly in the public interest to gather or convey important information or when a person providing information might be harmed. Journalists should keep all commitments to protect a confidential source.*

- *Clearly label opinion and commentary.*

- *Guard against extended coverage of events or individuals that fails to significantly advance a story, place the event in context, or add to the public knowledge.*

- *Refrain from contacting participants in violent situations while the situation is in progress.*

- *Use technological tools with skill and thoughtfulness, avoiding techniques that skew facts, distort reality, or sensationalize events.*

- *Use surreptitious newsgathering techniques, including hidden cameras or microphones, only if there is no other way to obtain stories of significant public importance and only if the technique is explained to the audience.*

- *Use the private transmissions of others only with permission.*

Professional electronic journalists should not:

- *Pay news sources who have a vested interest in a story.*

- *Accept gifts, favors, or compensation from those who might seek to influence coverage.*

- *Engage in activities that may compromise their integrity or independence.*

Independence

Professional electronic journalists should defend the independence of all journalists from those seeking influence or control over news content.

Professional electronic journalists should:

- *Gather and report news without fear or favor, and vigorously resist undue influence from any outside forces, including advertisers, sources, story subjects, powerful individuals, and special interest groups.*

- *Resist those who would seek to buy or politically influence news content or who would seek to intimidate those who gather and disseminate the news.*

- *Determine news content solely through editorial judgment and not as the result of outside influence.*

- *Resist any self-interest or peer pressure that might erode journalistic duty and service to the public.*

- *Recognize that sponsorship of the news will not be used in any way to determine, restrict, or manipulate content.*

- *Refuse to allow the interests of ownership or management to influence news judgment and content inappropriately.*

- *Defend the rights of the free press for all journalists, recognizing that any professional government licensing of journalists is a violation of that freedom.*

Accountability

Professional electronic journalists should recognize that they are accountable for their actions to the public, the profession and themselves.

Professional electronic journalists should:

- *Actively encourage adherence to these standards by all journalists and their employers.*

- *Respond to public concerns. Investigate complaints and correct errors promptly and with as much prominence as the original report.*

- *Explain journalistic processes to the public, especially when practices spark questions or controversy.*

- *Recognize that professional electronic journalists are duty-bound to conduct themselves ethically.*

- *Refrain from ordering or encouraging courses of action which would force employees to commit an unethical act.*

- *Carefully listen to employees who raise ethical objections and create environments in which such objections and discussions are encouraged.*

- *Seek support for and provide opportunities to train employees in ethical decision-making.*

In meeting its responsibility to the profession of electronic journalism, RTNDA has created this code to identify important issues, to serve as a guide for its members, to facilitate self-scrutiny, and to shape future debate.

STRATEGY

Fighting Back

I'm Mad as Hell & I'm Not Gonna Take It Any More

When a news story is inaccurate, libelous, unfair, slanted, absurd — or just outrageously stupid, what can you do about it? In the old days, you challenged the editor or reporter to a duel. Or thrashed him (female editors were extremely rare back then) with your cane. Those techniques have gone out of style, unless you want to be the lead story in tomorrow's paper and perhaps make the wire services and network news. Great idea, if that's the kind of coverage you're looking for.

Most people react angrily, in ways that often create more bad stories, and worse public images for themselves. It may make you feel better — just as it would to punch the reporter — but in the end, you'll lose the fight. Here are the most common reactions:

Throw Them Out

Vow never to talk to a reporter — any reporter — again. Hire a bouncer. Issue orders to your staff that any reporter or photographer who sets foot on the premises is to be violently ejected.

This will endear you to all newspaper editors and broadcast news directors. On slow news days, it means they can count on you to liven their news. "Hey, Gorilla," they'll yell across the newsroom, "Go over to Neanderthal's place and try to get in. Keep the camera rolling. We need something to fill the second block."

Great stuff. Will probably earn you a special award at the next Emmy or Pulitzer ceremony. Most Valuable Resource to Increase Ratings and Readership. Marvelous for your public image.

Shut Them Out

Punish the offending station, network, magazine or newspaper by shutting them out. Feed lots of stories to their competition. Hold news conferences and invite everyone else, but conveniently forget to include the offenders.

This is the most common reaction in government agencies — particularly police departments — when they're unhappy with a story. It rarely works.

Public Records Are Public

Most of the records reporters need for daily coverage of a public agency are — by law — public. If you shut them out, they'll go to court, and win easily. The stories about the court process will get lots of coverage. In all of them, you'll be the bad guy.

The news of your fight with the reporter will prompt disgruntled people within your office to make anonymous calls, leaking more dirt and ammunition to the reporter.

You'll wind up with a big LOSER tag around your neck. It'll look like you're trying to hide something. The story of your shutting them out will be a better story than those you're feeding the competition.

Look at the Compelling C's in **STRATEGY/Selling Your Story**. One of the most powerful elements is CONFLICT. Another NO-WIN RESPONSE.

Stop the Advertising

Cancel your advertising at the offending station or publication. Call your friends who advertise there and urge them to pull their commercials or ads.

In a small town this may have some effect. Otherwise, you're a real candidate for Kamikaze School.

Unless you can find another, equally effective medium, your business probably needs to advertise a lot worse than the news outlet needs your money.

At a station or newspaper with ethical management, the advertising staff is completely divorced from the news operation. To prove that advertisers have no voice in news judgment, the news department may come after you with even more vigor than before.

If it is a station with low ratings, or a declining newspaper, dropping your ads may hurt them. But losing the advertising exposure may hurt you more. And it'll hurt a lot more, months from now, when you come back with your hat in your hand, asking if you can place some new advertising with them.

Not a great solution. But in narrow circumstances, better than the first two.

Complaining is Important

It is absolutely vital that you complain when you feel strongly that a newspaper, magazine, TV or radio outlet has published or broadcast an incompetent, unfair, or dishonest story.

You probably don't want a retraction or correction. That often makes matters worse. In the correction, the reporter writes, "What I said yesterday was not exactly right. It's actually much worse."

But if you don't complain, the error will be repeated in every future story. Once it is printed three times, the error becomes accepted fact. Almost impossible to correct.

The complaint should not be made in anger. Wait until you've cooled off to decide how you'll complain.

If this is the first time an editor or news director has received a complaint about a reporter's story, you may get no discernible reaction.

But if yours is the second or third complaint about the same person, the editor or news director will begin to wonder whether there is a problem on the staff who could get the newspaper or the station into much more serious trouble. An expensive lawsuit.

Truth, the Perfect Defense

Remember that in a libel suit, truth is the perfect defense. Editors these days are very concerned about libel suits. Jurors who feel the media abuse their power have a way to even the score.

We're not talking about small amounts here. Libel and privacy suits usually ask damages in tens of millions of dollars. So a reporter who can't report accurately is a multi-million-dollar libel suit, just waiting for the right assignment.

Editors and news directors need to know when they have a reporter who can't write truthfully. For whatever reason. It can be incompetence. It may be the inability to leave personal prejudices out of the copy. The reporter's supervisors are vitally concerned. (See **INSIDE THE MEDIA/Libel**)

In the same way, privacy suits are often lost because of the way the reporter or photographer acted at the scene of the story. Editors and news directors need to know if they have a staffer who likes to bully people. Someone willing to break the norms of human behavior — perhaps the law — if that's what it takes to get the story. (See **STRATEGY/Ethics** and **INSIDE THE MEDIA/Privacy**) Editors and news directors have no way to know about their employees' inaccuracy, incompetence, or nasty behavior if you don't tell them.

How to Complain

Let's go through some of the ways in which you can complain with maximum results.

Suppose the story is inaccurate. Names misspelled, titles wrong, errors in numbers that are not really damaging to you or your organization. A letter is probably the best way to complain. I'd suggest writing the reporter, with a copy to the immediate boss. It should read something like this:

Dear Reporter: The story you wrote in yesterday's newspaper/newscast contained several inaccuracies. I thought you should know, so future stories will not repeat those inaccuracies.

In the first paragraph, you called my organization the Amalgamated Association of Aardvarks. The proper name is The National Association of Aardvark Advocates.

In the second paragraph, you said we spent $3 million lobbying the state legislature last year. The correct figure is $300,000.

Correction? Be Careful

You may ask for a correction or retraction. But remember that reporters and editors have big egos. To distract from the mistake, in the same story that corrects the error, they may unload new information that is even more damaging.

As an investigative reporter, I learned to hold back a trump card. If my target complained, I turned over my ace in the hole.

If You're Going to Sue

If you have any idea of filing a suit because the story damaged you in some way, consult an attorney before you complain. In some states, the form and timing of the complaint can have a major effect on your rights in that future suit. (See **INSIDE THE MEDIA/Libel** and **Privacy** chapters)

If an inaccurate or unfair story has caused real problems for you or your organization, a face-to-face meeting may be the best way to make your case. Here again, I'd suggest that you call the reporter and/or the editor to set up the meeting.

You will need documentation to show how the story distorted the truth, or how outrageously the staffer acted.

The Radio & TV Station Hierarchy

It is critical that you reach the right person with your complaint. The organizational structure at most radio and television stations goes something like this:

The station's **General Manager** hires and fires the **News Director,** who is responsible for everything in the news department. The news director may have an assistant.

The **Assignment Editor** decides how the station's news staff will be used every day. How their time will be invested. Who will cover what. The assignment editor is expected to know what's happening in your area, and cover it, if it's important.

At most stations, the assignment editor is not responsible for the quality or accuracy of the stories, and will not have much input into how those stories appear in the newscast. Unless you're unhappy with the station's persistent refusal to cover stories you suggested, the assignment editor is probably not the person to see.

Each newscast has a **Producer,** who's roughly the equivalent of a page editor at a newspaper. The producer decides which stories go into the newscast — how long they'll be, in which order, and in what form.

At larger stations, there will be an **Executive Producer**, who supervises the producers of each newscast, and whose duties may include review of scripts for accuracy and fairness.

The executive producer is sometimes a sort of assistant news director, with a variety of responsibilities.

Power to Hire & Fire

The news director does all the hiring and firing within the broadcast station's news department. Reporters and photographers work under the direction of producers and the assignment editor, but their competence and any disciplinary action will eventually be decided by the news director.

Most station managers will meet with or talk to their news directors several times a day. Newscasts are the major local revenue and image producers for many TV stations.

Remember, if the station is a network affiliate, the station has no control or responsibility for the network programming it broadcasts.

News directors and station managers are human, too. When you complain, their natural reaction will be to defend their employees, and their stories.

Make Your Own Tape

Documenting a broadcast error can be difficult. In the past, the FCC required broadcasters to keep a copy of their scripts or a tape of their broadcasts. Not any more. They are not required to provide you with a copy of what they said.

If you have any advance warning that a story may be slanted or antagonistic, you should at least make an audio recording of the broadcast. A videotape recording of a television story is much better, because part of the inaccuracy or slant may be created visually.

The audio or video tape will be the only way you can prove you were misquoted, or how the story was inaccurate.

The Newspaper Hierarchy

At newspapers, the top editor in charge of everything to do with news is the **Managing Editor** or **Executive Editor**, who may or may not have jurisdiction over the editorial page. Many newspapers have an autonomous **Editorial Page Editor**.

The person with overall supervision is the **General Manager** or **Publisher.** But in most cases, the general manager or publisher is more concerned with the paper's mechanical and financial operations. They leave journalism to the top editor.

At most newspapers there will be a **City Editor** or **Metro Editor** who supervises all stories in the local area. A **State Editor** will be in charge of stories and reporters outside the local area but inside the state. There may be a **National Editor**, a **Political Editor**, an **Investigative Projects Editor**. (See **STRATEGY/Selling Your Story**)

Here are the steps to take if you have a complaint about a story:

Complaining, Step One

Call the reporter. Discuss the story. Find out who the immediate supervisor is, or the editor who was in charge of the story you're unhappy with. If it's a simple complaint to correct numbers or names for future stories, tell the reporter you'll send a letter confirming the call, as I suggested earlier. If you're unhappy with the reporter's response, take the next step.

Complaining, Step Two

Write the reporter's editor or news director a detailed letter describing your complaint with the story or a staff member's behavior. Quote from the offensive story and write, in detail, your version of what happened; or how the story was inaccurate or unfair.

Repeat. *Don't file your complaint in anger.* Suppose you've headed a study commission that produced a final report. The story about your study is grossly inaccurate. If you're writing a newspaper editor, you may want to include a copy of the study, a copy of the story, and something like:

> *Dear Editor: I thought you would want to know that a story you printed Monday was very inaccurate. If you'll compare the enclosed study with what your reporter wrote about it, I think you'll come to the same conclusion.*

If you are badly misquoted, your letter to the news director should say something like:

> *Dear News Director: I thought you'd want to know that I was quoted entirely out of context in the story you broadcast Monday night. I recorded the entire interview with your reporter. I'm enclosing a transcript. The way in*

which my interview was edited created a false and very damaging impression. Once you compare the story with the transcript, I think you'll come to the same conclusion. If you'd like to see the videotape (hear the audio tape), I'd be glad to meet with you.

If you're still unhappy with the results, go to Step Three.

Step Three for Radio & TV

Write the station manager the same kind of detailed letter. This time make it clear you're angry. Send a copy to the president of the company that owns the station. You can usually get the name and address by calling the station manager's secretary.

If not, go to the station and ask to see the **Public File**. This is a file required by the FCC which will include fairly complete details of station ownership and corporate officers; and what the station committed to do when it applied for its license with the FCC. If your complaint involves fairness or deception (which might lead to a lawsuit or formal FCC complaint) send a copy of this letter to the corporate vice-president for legal affairs.

Step Three for Newspapers

Write the managing editor or executive editor the same kind of detailed letter, but this time make it clear you're angry. Send a copy to the CEO of the corporation which owns the newspaper. Ownership will usually be included in the masthead on the editorial page. If not, call the general manager's secretary and ask for the name and address of the corporate CEO.

Complaining, Step Four

Now it's time to write the president or CEO of the corporation directly, if you're still unhappy.

Local radio and TV stations are usually much more responsive to complaints than newspapers. They're always concerned about their public image. Anything that turns off viewers lowers ratings.

What they charge for advertising time is directly related to how many people watch. It's a lot easier to change channels than to change newspapers. In most cities, you *can't* switch to another daily newspaper. There's only one.

Many station managers require their telephone switchboard operators to keep a daily log of calls — both complaints and praise. It gives them a daily survey of audience reaction to their programming.

Until the mid-1980s, the FCC required stations to compile voluminous "ascertainment interviews." These were personal interviews with people from all segments of the community, asking them to list and rate the community's major problems and issues.

At license renewal time, the station was supposed to show how its programming had served the community's needs, as outlined in those interviews.

As part of the gradual deregulation of broadcasting that began in the 1980s, ascertainment interviews are no longer required. But veterans in the business still reflexively respond when you complain that the station is violating its public trust and responsibility.

If you're contemplating a lawsuit against the station, you should consider having your lawyer look at each of your letters before you send them. The attorney might want to send along a cover letter.

Tell the Competition

Competing local media may be interested in reporting the competition's goof or breach of journalistic ethics.

Regional magazines often cover local media better than newspapers or broadcasters.

This idea of the media tattling on each other is fairly new. In some cities, they still refuse to report each other's indiscretions. After all, editors think, the next embarrassing story could be about me, if this thing gets out of hand. But that's changing.

If your complaint involves a broadcaster, write a letter to the editor of the local newspaper.

Media Critics

If the newspaper has a TV critic, there might be a story there. Newspaper people hate TV and the people who work in it. (See **STRATEGY/Selling Your Story**) They're always ready to jab TV, for the slightest slip or indiscretion. Newspaper Sunday supplements and regional magazines are often interested in stories that expose shoddy television reporting or policy.

A few television stations have media critics. They're rare, but they're always looking for material. They'd love to hear from you if there's a story of sloppy, inaccurate reporting or slanted, unfair treatment. In some cities, public television stations have regular reviews of local reporting.

Westmoreland vs. CBS

In 1983, *TV Guide* wrote a scorching story criticizing a CBS documentary that had suggested General William Westmoreland conspired to hide or distort reports on enemy strength and casualties in Vietnam.

Hodding Carter, former press secretary for the State Department, also did an investigative special for Public Broadcasting on the same CBS documentary.

Eventually, Westmoreland sued CBS for libel. After weeks of testimony and high-intensity media coverage, Westmoreland dropped the suit, claiming a moral victory. (See **INSIDE THE MEDIA/Libel**)

At the time, one medium criticizing another so harshly was highly unusual. But things have changed. Like tobacco companies, the media have been a favorite target lately and are much more vulnerable to critical coverage by other media.

The Time-Warner Flap

In 1995, a major public debate erupted over the content of Time-Warner's "gangsta rap" music on CDs and video. The lyrics were sexually explicit, depicting women as sex objects who should be abused. Some encouraged the assassination of police officers.

Former U.S. Education Secretary William Bennett, as co-chair of the advocacy group Empower America, attacked Time-Warner as a corrupting influence on American life.

Because Bennett was very media-savvy, his efforts were covered extensively by virtually all news outlets.

Politicians began introducing legislation to censor obscene and violent media. Although it claimed the decision had nothing to do with the controversy, Time-Warner quickly sold the division that had been producing gangsta rap.

There are several national publications that might be interested in your complaint about how the media have covered you.

Brill's Content

In June, 1998, a new, monthly magazine to cover the media was born. The goal of *Brill's Content* is to critically review the performance of the American news media. The chairman and CEO is attorney Steven Brill, who had earlier founded (and then sold) *Court TV* and *The American Lawyer* magazine.

Brill is a cantankerous journalist from the old school who believes his publication should be filled with tough, take-no-prisoners reporting, with no sacred cows allowed.

His magazine, Brill says, will cover the media with these guidelines in mind:

- Writing that purports to be non-fiction should be true

- Non-fiction reporting should include truth-in-labeling and sourcing, so that consumers have some idea where the information came from, and how reliable it is

- There should be no hidden motives, especially concerning advertisers or friends of the journalists or publisher

- Reporters and editors should be fully accountable for their work, and their mistakes

To help carry out that last guideline, Brill hired Bill Kovach, curator of the prestigious Nieman Foundation for Journalism at Harvard University, as the magazine's first ombudsman. In September, 2000, Kovach was succeeded by Michael Gartner, a distinguished newspaper editor and former head of NBC News.

Brill set a goal of 500,000 subscribers within five years. It had reached 325,000 by late 2000.

If you think the magazine might be interested in your perspective on the news media, contact:

    Brill's Content
    1230 Avenue of the Americas
    New York, NY 10020

    Internet — www.brillscontent.com

Columbia Journalism Review

The *Columbia Journalism Review*, founded in 1961, is generally considered the conscience of American journalism. In the first edition, it stated its purpose:

To assess the performance of journalism in all its forms, to call attention to its shortcomings and strengths, and to help define — or redefine — standards of honest, responsible service ... to help stimulate continuing improvement in the profession and to speak out for what is right, fair, and decent.

Bi-Monthly Darts and Laurels

The *Review* is published every other month by the Graduate School of Journalism at Columbia University. In each issue, there is a section called "Darts and Laurels," in which the magazine praises or roasts networks, local stations, and the print media. The section pans or praises specific incidents, journalists, and stories. The editors are always looking for articles about the media, particularly performance or policy that violates journalistic ethics.

CJR's circulation is about 25,000. Most of its readers are journalists, journalism professors, and public relations people. Take your complaint to:

> **The Columbia Journalism Review**
> **Columbia University**
> **2950 Broadway**
> **New York, NY 10027**
>
> **Internet: http://cjr.org**

American Journalism Review

Founded in 1977 as the *Washington Journalism Review*, the name was changed to *American Journalism Review* in early 1993. It is a monthly, with circulation of about 25,000.

The magazine is slickly produced, with sharp, interesting writing, often by journalists rather than academics. Its stories have the flavor of "insider" gossip and intrigue during power struggles at places like *The New York Times*, the TV networks, *The Atlanta Journal-Constitution*, and *The Washington Post*.

It publishes continuing analyses of major media issues. Like news coverage of Independent Prosecutor Kenneth Starr's White House investigation, and the demoralizing effect in newsrooms as corporate profits take precedence over good journalism.

AJR was privately owned until May, 1987, when it was given to the University of Maryland's Journalism School. The Journalism

School has been able to maintain the commercial look and appeal the original publisher gave it. Most of the current issue content is available online. You can contact *AJR* at:

> **American Journalism Review**
> **1117 Journalism Building**
> **College Park, MD 20742-7111**
>
> **Internet: http://ajr.newslink.org**

SPJ and Quill

The Society for Professional Journalists (SPJ) — also known as Sigma Delta Chi — has created the most widely-recognized code of ethics for journalists. You'll find the complete text of that code in **STRATEGY/Ethics**. Most major cities have a local SPJ chapter.

In most of those chapters, newspaper people will be much more active than broadcasters. Call the city desk at the local newspaper to find the name of the SPJ president in your town. The initiative and strength of the local organization vary considerably from city to city. A strong chapter, incensed over a story that was inaccurate, unfair or unethical, might pass a resolution condemning the offender.

Quill is SPJ's national magazine. *Quill* also publishes articles that criticize journalists' performance, but its circulation (about 12,000) and influence are smaller than *CJR* and *AJR*. Contact:

> **The Quill**
> **3909 N. Meridian St.**
> **Indianapolis, IN 46208**
>
> **Internet: http://spj.org/quill**

Local Journalism Reviews

Some cities have local journalism reviews, often written and distributed free among local journalists. They are frequently semi-underground publications, where local reporters write anonymously about scandals inside their own workplace.

Complaining to a Network

Effectively complaining about a network news story is much more difficult than complaining locally. The networks have regional bureaus across the country. Correspondents work out of those bureaus. They spend about four days a week on the road. If you're interviewed by a network correspondent or producer, you'll probably never see either of them again. Their supervisor will be a bureau chief hundreds of miles away. The people with the real power are in New York, Atlanta or Los Angeles.

Know the Producer

If you're contacted for a story by a network, find out which bureau is originating the story and the name of the field producer.

A network crew will usually include the correspondent, field producer, photographer and sound technician. The correspondent is the one you'll see and hear when the story is broadcast. The producer scouts the story, sets up interviews, gathers documents, manages travel arrangements, and often writes the script the correspondent voices.

Work Your Way Up

If you try to call a network bureau to complain to the correspondent or producer, they probably won't be there. They're running to catch a plane halfway around the world. So start working your way up the hierarchy.

1. **Phone the bureau chief.** Give your assessment of the story and its failings. During the conversation, ask who the bureau chief's immediate supervisor is. Each network is organized differently. After the call, if you're not satisfied —

2. **Write the bureau chief's supervisor.** At each stage, send a copy of your letter to the next one up the ladder. Then —

3. **Write the head of network news.** The title of the news division boss varies from time to time. It may be president of XYZ News, which is a division of the XYZ Network. Or the network may have several vice-presidents — one of them in charge of news. Remember to be detailed and specific with your complaint. And if you're still not happy —

4. **Write the president of the network.** If there's any thought of a lawsuit, send a copy to the vice-president for legal affairs. You can get the names and addresses of network executives on the Internet, or by calling ABC, CBS or NBC in New York. CNN is headquartered in Atlanta; Fox in Los Angeles. Call the

local affiliate to get addresses for smaller broadcast networks, the local cable company for cable TV and satellite networks.

Complaining to the FCC

The FCC processes complaints on virtually every kind of problem in broadcast or cable news — from allegations of unfair or distorted coverage to gripes about the quality of the picture or sound. Most of the people who complain receive a form letter asking for more detailed information. Here — more so than with a complaint to a station or network — great detail is extremely important if you expect to have any impact.

You Must Give Details

You have to give them the station or network that broadcast the story, the date, which newscast, the correspondent or anchorperson who read it, quotes from the story (a transcript of exactly what was said will impress them) and why the story was inaccurate, unfair or deceptive.

The FCC website is extensive, and includes the rules that govern broadcasters. You can even file a complaint there.

Send your complaint to:

> **Federal Communications Commission**
> **Enforcement Bureau**
> **445 12th St. S.W.**
> **Washington, D.C. 20554**
> **Internet: http://www.fcc.gov**

The revocation of a broadcast license is extremely rare. Virtually every revocation in the history of the FCC was based on some kind of deception. But the loss of its license is so threatening, any complaint that prompts an FCC inquiry will get their attention.

Nixon-Agnew vs. Media

Government has never used its power to intimidate and harass the news media as energetically as it did during the Nixon Administration. Vice-President Spiro Agnew was Nixon's lead hatchet man for the press. It was Charles Colson's job at the White House to simultaneously watch all three network newscasts each evening.

If he saw something he didn't like, he called and demanded to talk to the anchorperson immediately, while the newscast was in progress. Occasionally, he succeeded, during a commercial break.

National News Council

Agnew kept suggesting that the news media had become too powerful. That some agency ought to be created to control them. How that could be done without repealing the First Amendment was never clear.

In that atmosphere, the National News Council was born, as a privately financed effort to investigate complaints about the news media. It was hoped a private review of complaints would slow the campaign to create some kind of governmental control.

Only the Power to Embarrass

The council had no power — except the power to embarrass within the profession — when news organizations were dishonest, inaccurate or unfair.

The council's major drawback was the limited circulation of its findings. They were published in the *Columbia Journalism Review*. Many newspapers, including *The New York Times*, wouldn't carry the stories. They opposed, on principle, the idea of the National News Council. In 1984, the News Council quietly died.

Minnesota News Council

Current dissatisfaction with the media has revived interest in a new National News Council — as well as news councils in individual states.

One of the most active is in Minnesota, where complaints are given full hearings that include witnesses and evidence. After hearing the evidence, the Minnesota News Council issues its report. You'll find more about the Minnesota Council's activity at:

http://www.mtn.org/newscncl/

Schools of Communications

A school of journalism or communications in your area probably has personal contact with some of the people in local news. The editor or news director may be a graduate. While a journalism school usually has no formal way to investigate or criticize poor journalistic performance, the dean might be able to quietly shake his finger and influence the station or newspaper the next time a similar situation occurs.

Special Interest Groups

A number of national organizations are designed to fight for specific issues — particularly television's coverage of those causes. They lobby for what they believe would be good for society. Things like less violence, better children's programming, less sexuality, no smoking or drinking in dramatic shows, more programs of one kind or another.

Some of these organizations have money and staff to help you carry a complaint to court, to Congress or the FCC. Most of them, however, will be interested in your complaint only if it fits their narrow area of interest.

Accuracy in Media

The most vigorous of the special interest media watchdogs is Accuracy In Media, a politically conservative non-profit group formed in 1969 to combat what it feels is a liberal slant in American journalism.

AIM publishes *The AIM Report* twice a month, detailing media coverage it labels inaccurate or unfair.

The group produces a radio report called *Media Monitor*, broadcast by about 150 stations. About 150 newspapers use a syndicated AIM column by Chairman and CEO Reed Irvine. Reed's column is also available by e-mail.

AIM buys advertising in major newspapers to castigate the media, and also owns a token amount of stock in some major media corporations. An AIM staffer who tries to get on the agenda has become a fixture at annual stockholders' meetings.

The group also sponsors a speakers' bureau and a monthly luncheon in Washington, D. C.

You can reach AIM at:

> **Accuracy in Media**
> **4455 Connecticut Ave., N.W., Suite 330**
> **Washington, DC 20008**
> **Internet: http://aim.org**

FAIR — a Different View

A more liberal perspective on media criticism is available at Fairness and Accuracy in Reporting. With about 40 per cent of its funding from foundations, FAIR calls itself a research and information center. Its primary contention is that large corporate ownership of multiple media outlets is not good. That this kind of ownership inhibits media competition, investigative reporting and the broadest possible coverage of major issues in the society.

FAIR was created in 1986. It publishes a magazine, *EXTRA!*, and a newsletter, *Extra! Update*, which alternate every other month. In late 1992, it began a syndicated radio show called *CounterSpin*, broadcast by more than 110 non-commercial stations in the U.S. and Canada.

The Media Beat is FAIR's syndicated newspaper column on media and politics. It's also available on the FAIR website, with past columns archived there.

Advocacy and Research

FAIR publishes how-to kits for advocates. Everything from letter writing to organizing demonstrations. Its website includes contact lists for national newspapers, magazines, TV networks and PBS radio stations.

FAIR operates specialized research and review desks. The Economic Review gives a weekly analysis of economic reporting in the *The New York Times* and *The Washington Post*. It is broadcast by e-mail, and previous editions are archived on the FAIR website.

The Women's Desk and Racism Watch Desk analyze those topics — in both news coverage and newsrooms. If you think FAIR would be interested in your complaint, contact:

Fairness and Accuracy in Reporting
130 W. 25th Street
New York, NY 10001

Internet: www.fair.org

STRATEGY

Lawyers & Lawsuits

In a Media Crisis, Your Lawyer Will Be Wrong

When you get to work and find the *60 Minutes* crew waiting in your reception area, you know it's going to be a bad day. The first thing many executives do is call their lawyer. Particularly if they know a lawsuit has been filed — or is about to be filed. Some don't even bother to call the attorney. They've been conditioned to believe that lawsuits automatically mean "no comment."

WRONG.

If you take news media problems to an attorney, you'll usually get bad advice. My presentation at a symposium sponsored by the American Bar Association was titled: "In a Media Crisis, Conventional Wisdom, Your Reflexes, and Your Lawyer Will Always Be Wrong."

Lawyers Do Not Understand

You need to call your lawyer for LEGAL advice. But not for advice about dealing with the news media. All over America, executives in both government and industry have abdicated. In any kind of crunch, they hand over their power to their attorneys. They ask them what to do, and then do it religiously. Even when their high-priced media consultants are telling them to do something entirely different.

Most lawyers do not understand the news media game. This is a different arena. A lawyer's training and experience — the instincts developed in the courtroom — will often lead to disaster in the media. By following the attorney's advice, you will probably lose the media battle, and perhaps the war.

And/or the corporation. And/or your job.

You need to hear the attorney's assessment of the legal problems you may create by talking to a reporter. PLUS the opinion of a skilled, experienced media consultant. THEN you carefully weigh all the risks and benefits in both arenas.

In many cases, critical media coverage will do much more damage to your organization than a jury's verdict. Even if that verdict costs you millions of dollars. Bad media stories can destroy employee morale and productivity, turn customers away, depress stock prices, and influence future jurors who will go into court already prejudiced against you.

I maintain that it is your job as an executive to listen to *both* your lawyer and your media consultant, then decide what to do. It is *your* job and *your* responsibility to make the final decision, not your lawyer's.

The Lawyer: 'Say Nothing'

I know exactly what most lawyers will tell you if a lawsuit is looming. "Say nothing. Tell them no comment. Whatever you say to a reporter can come back to haunt us in court."

But "no comment" has taken on many dark shades of meaning in today's media-driven society. (See **STRATEGY/Ten Commandments of Media Relations**) Newspaper readers and television watchers hear something else. When they see you or your attorney running turning away from the cameras, perhaps holding your hand over the lens, they think:

The plaintiff in the lawsuit must be right. The defendants are guilty. Otherwise, they would talk to the reporter. They must have something to hide. Or —

The rich, powerful people who run that organization (or the rich, powerful person who is the defendant) don't even care about this poor plaintiff. They're as insensitive now as they were when the damage was done.

Many people believe — because lawyers have said it so often — that you can't comment on a case that is in litigation.

THAT IS SIMPLY NOT TRUE.

I tell lawyers that they may be guilty of malpractice and unethical conduct if they tell their clients to stonewall the media.

Why are so many good lawyers so dead-set against talking to the media — or having their clients talk to the media?

Why Do Lawyers Avoid the Media?

- **They don't understand the media**, and have no media skills or instincts. They don't want to mess around in an area where they are so incompetent and inexperienced. They don't want to show their lack of expertise.

- **They live and work in an isolated, insulated system.** The legal system has a long history of elitism, dating back to its foundation in England. American lawyers do not wear robes and wigs, as British barristers do. But once they are admitted to the Bar, they are members of a private club where commoners are not allowed. Attorneys get their strokes, recognition and prestige from fellow lawyers who judge them by what happens inside the legal system.

- **In the legal system, there are very rigid rules.** The lawyer who best knows the rules and how to manipulate them often wins. The legal system is based on precedent and history. There are written, predetermined guidelines for almost everything. The media have very few rules, and those that do exist are constantly changing. The precedent that drives today's news decision is whatever the competition did yesterday.

- **Reputable attorneys are ashamed** of some of their colleagues who use the media to advertise their practice. The headline hunters are more interested in getting their names out to the public than in serving the best interest of their clients. Some very good, successful lawyers are so offended by their ambulance-chasing colleagues, they avoid doing anything that would even suggest that they are seeking publicity.

- **Some lawyers truly believe it is unethical** to talk to the news media. They cite sections of the Canons of Ethics that are designed to protect the right to a fair trial. But there is also a Canon that says ethical lawyers must represent the best interest of their clients. To act as if the news media do not exist, I maintain, is often not in the best interest of a client.

Some Cases Will Always Be News

I am not suggesting that an attorney take a case to the media to influence the judge or the jury. Some high-profile cases, because of the status of the litigants — or the human interest in the circumstances — simply cannot be kept out of the spotlight. If the attorney happens to represent that kind of client or case, I maintain the legal ethic now *demands* helping that client deal successfully with the media.

If attorneys for the other side are presenting their evidence in the media, it is suicidal to sit back and say nothing. By the time the case gets to court, the media damage can be so massive, the company or agency may no longer exist. It will be bankrupt. Defunct.

Lawyers like to win. That's why you hire them. But remember that their primary responsibility is winning *in court*. It is your job to find the delicate balance between winning in court and winning in the media. Often, you can win in both places. Just remember that the attorney will always err on the side of caution to protect the legal case. If you do something that — in the attorney's mind — may put the court case at risk, you are jeopardizing the attorney's ego and reputation for winning.

Attorneys Never Admit Fault

Lawyers have been trained and conditioned to never admit their client is guilty or at fault. Yet one of the best media strategies (if your client is guilty, or at fault) is to quickly confess your sins and tell the world what you will do to make it right. (See Commandment Number Eight in **STRATEGY/Ten Commandments of Media Relations**)

If you have made it right, and the plaintiff is now trying to make a lot of money off your mistake, media coverage can tilt or level the playing field in court.

A large, well-known company brought me in as a media consultant when an employee who had been fired threatened to sue. She claimed she was terminated because of her age, gender and national origin. On the surface, she seemed like a tragic victim of this national firm which she claimed was prejudiced and had no sensitivity for little people like her. If the company remained silent, it would become the villain in the media stories.

There's Often More To It

But there was more to it. She was a longtime employee who had started out as a bookkeeper. The company kept growing. By the time it was ready for an initial public offering of stock, her title was comptroller. She simply did not have the experience or expertise to supervise the complicated Wall Street transition.

So someone else (younger, prettier, but also female) was brought in as comptroller. The former bookkeeper was given a series of other assignments, none of which made her happy. She wanted her old title back. When she continued to complain and shirk her duties, she was let go. When she was fired, through stock options and profit-sharing, she became an instant millionaire.

My advice to the company was to take this position: "After all we did for her, it is tragic that a lawyer with dollar signs in his eyes wants to kick us in the shins." Hard to cast a bookkeeper who became a millionaire as a corporate victim. Instead, I suggested, make her greedy lawyer the bad guy in this scenario.

Hypocrites Make Great Targets

A repentant sinner asking for forgiveness is hard to kick. A hypocrite makes a wonderful media target. If you goofed, and the media know that, a quick confession and correction will often end the story. (See **STRATEGY/Ten Commandments**)

The court system is different. There, even the most guilty defendant can sometimes beat the system. But not if the guilty party has confessed. So attorneys will almost always tell you not to admit fault.

The lie or cover-up are much better stories than whatever it is you're trying to hide. That was the major lesson of Watergate. The interminable Whitewater investigation of Bill and Hillary Clinton was not really about money. The media and the independent counsel were trying to prove a cover-up. When it expanded to include Monica Lewinsky's relationship with Clinton, that, too, (legally) was about perjury and obstructing justice, not sex.

After the oil spill at Valdez, Alaska, one of Exxon's biggest mistakes was to diminish the severity of the spill and the damage to the environment. When the radiation first leaked at Three Mile Island, power plant officials said it was inconsequential. When reporters found the leak was more serious than they had been led to believe, the story mushroomed into an international, five-alarm event. (See **STRATEGY/Crisis Management**)

Reporters are human. They do not like being deceived. If they feel you have tried to hide something, they have a large arsenal of weapons to get even. Remember, they always have the last word.

The Media Love Victims

The media love victims. So do juries. Especially little people who have been damaged by big corporations or government bureaucracies. The entire court process is supposedly designed to help little, powerless people get what's coming to them from powerful people and corporations. Often it is not a matter of whether the jury will find the big company at fault. It is just a matter of how much money the company with deep pockets should pay the tragic victim/plaintiff. Reporters and editors also consider it one of their Missions From God to make things right. To bring justice to a world full of injustice.

The complaint in a civil suit often casts the plaintiff as one of those victims. One of those little people, whose property and/or quality of life have been badly damaged — perhaps destroyed — by the incompetent, insensitive, evil defendant. These kinds of cases make a great stage on which reporters can play folk hero, rescuing the "good guy" victim; wreaking vengeance on the "bad guy" defendant. (See **STRATEGY/Good Guys/Bad Guys**)

The Overly Aggressive Lawyer

You often choose a lawyer who is extremely aggressive. A human dynamo with the killer instinct. An oversupply of testosterone. Occasionally, that will help if you are in combat with the news media, and the attorney understands media strategy.

But more often, this kind of lawyer will try to prevent your carrying out the most disarming media strategy — admitting you made a mistake and making every effort to fix things. "I don't want to look like a wimp," this kind of lawyer will tell you, "And I'm sure you don't want to look that way, either. We're not going to give an inch. We're going to ram this thing down their throats."

In the judicial process, this kind of posture often leads the other side to cave in and settle quickly, rather than become involved in a very long, expensive legal battle. But the media can cast that aggressive lawyer as the Goliath out to destroy the small, courageous David. The symbolic David carries with him the virtue and honor of victims everywhere. (See **SKILLS/Good Guys/Bad Guys** for postures that can make you the good guy or the bad guy in media coverage)

It Doesn't Have to be True

In our system, publishing or broadcasting the plaintiff's claim has no legal liability. It doesn't have to be true. The filing of the suit makes it a public record. The allegations can be published or broadcast with impunity, so long as the story simply repeats what is in the court record. (See **INSIDE THE MEDIA/Libel**)

If you are the defendant, and you don't tell the media the other side of the story, readers and viewers will believe everything said by the plaintiff is true.

After all, Joe Sixpack thinks, *they couldn't put that stuff on TV or in the newspaper if it wasn't true.*

WRONG.

Guilty Until Proven Innocent

In America, you are supposed to be innocent until proven guilty. If they were ever taught this in high school civics, most people in American seem to have forgotten. With massive media coverage of allegations against you, the reverse is true.

You will be considered guilty until you prove your innocence.

I believe the ethical lawyer representing you needs to be constantly telling the media there is another side to this story. If the evidence you have can't be disclosed now for tactical reasons, you should at least be reminding the audience that there is more to this than meets the eye.

Or the camera.

Too Many Facts Get in the Way

When you're not guilty, you have been led to believe that you will be exonerated, once the public knows all the facts. All you have to do is give a detailed, well-organized, reasoned explanation to reporters. This cloud of suspicion and malevolence will lift.

WRONG AGAIN.

Many court cases have very powerful, emotional angles that appeal to a mass audience. This increases circulation and ratings.

Corporate lawyers have great success with smart, talented judges by designing well-reasoned arguments. No emotion. Lots of footnotes and legal citations. They often use that same technique when they talk to reporters. It doesn't work.

Reporters don't have time for the lengthy, technical reasoning. Get to the point! How do you feel? In less than 10 seconds, tell us what this case is about.

Emotion Sells Products & Ideas

We sell products and ideas in America through emotion, not reason. Commercials for personal hygiene products are based on the fear of offending, failing, losing someone you love — or would like to love.

Luxury cars are sold in TV commercials by suggesting visually that the people who drive this car are wealthy, powerful, sexy, respected, smart. Candidates are sold by appealing to the most basic human emotions — fear; the desire for safety and security; love of family or country; anger at some real or imagined injustice.

Criminal attorneys with a lot of jury experience understand this. They appeal to jurors with high drama and emotion:

Let me explain to you what was going on in the mind of this defendant. If you had been there, you would have done exactly the same thing. You would have been (fill in the blank) afraid/angry/proud/satisfied this was the right thing to do. My client is only guilty of being human, and should not be punished.

That doesn't mean the client didn't do it. It just means the client was justified in doing it. The client is not *morally* guilty.

Once the litigant on the other side casts you as the villain and invokes one of those emotions, it is extremely difficult to change the public's attitude.

Wait Until We Know More

Lawyers have learned in legal cases not to move too quickly. Never make a motion or take the testimony of a witness until you know everything. Attorneys almost universally wait until the very last minute to file motions or briefs. They use every second available to learn as much as they can before they make their move.

Attorneys who have not dealt with the media do not understand that the news media's deadlines are absolute. They think they can present their case later. The media do not grant continuances. If you are to defend yourself, you must do so in the first news stories about this case. Today, by about 3 p.m., if the story is to include your point of view; if the reporter is to be persuaded that this is not exactly an open-and-shut case.

We Can Always Appeal

Another conditioned reflex serves lawyers badly when they are engaged with the media. In court, if you lose at the trial level, you can always appeal. In the judicial system, it is very important to build a meticulous record. This is your backup.

So the lawyer deals with the media the same way. Long, intricate, footnoted sentences. Most lawyers do not speak in soundbites. They cannot understand why reporters fail to quote them.

In the news media, there is no appeal process, once they decide you're guilty.

Incomplete Court Transcripts

In the legal system, appellate judges never see the witnesses or the evidence. In the cold, distant isolation of their chambers, they read the court record. They examine the procedure. The technicalities. Whether every T was crossed, every I dotted.

Court reporters do not record the tears, the smiles, the quick glances, the smells, the murmur from the spectators.

Timing is everything, they say. Milliseconds make all the difference for standup comedians delivering their punch-lines and for lawyers delivering their final arguments. Trial transcripts do not convey the timing. Whether the lines were delivered with a shout or a whisper. They are simply words on paper. Lawyers become terribly concerned with words. Many of them do not know, instinctively, that style can be much more powerful than substance in media stories.

Newspaper and magazine reporters transmit the courtroom proceedings in words, too. But they work very hard to convey all the human sidelights that accompany the words.

The Lawyer's Leverage

Lawyers have enormous leverage. You have invested a lot of money in their advice. To ignore it seems stupid. They sometimes tell you they will abandon you if you don't do everything they say. Just the thought of starting all over again with another lawyer is terribly frightening.

In-house public relations staffers are often former reporters. They rarely have a higher rank in the organizational pecking order than the vice president for legal affairs. If they suggest taking your case to the media, the CEO may believe they are catering to the media because of some inherent, pro-media prejudice.

The outside PR consultant, brought in for the crisis, is pitted against the in-house lawyer who better understands the corporate culture. (See **STRATEGY/Crisis Management** for suggestions on how to choose a public relations agency)

The CEO's Bias

The CEO carries a bias from personal experience. The CEO socializes with lawyers; plays golf with them; respects their wisdom, skill and loyalty; has invested a lot of money in them. They have walked through a lot of fires together, and emerged victorious. Perhaps built the company together.

Most CEOs have a lot more experience with lawyers than with reporters. When the media fire breaks out, that past experience can lead the CEO to quickly accept the lawyers' advice, and dismiss the counsel of the public relations expert.

That decision may put the organization in great peril. It is a difficult balancing act. It is easy to turn everything over to the lawyers. It is hard to hear both sides, and then make the tough decisions.

But that's what bosses are paid to do.

STRATEGY

Media Policy

You Mean I Can't Tell Them to Buzz Off?

I believe most organizations should have a written media policy. The larger the organization, the more detailed the policy should be. Once the policy is written, the boss should personally tell employees why the policy is there. AND WHAT IT REALLY MEANS. If you don't make your intentions very clear, you'll get a lot of different interpretations. Staffers should be given specific scenarios in which reporters might approach the organization, and how they should handle it.

Too Many Thou Shall Nots

Many media policies are just lists of Thou Shall Nots. Don't talk to reporters. Don't talk about company policy. Don't let reporters or photographers enter without an escort. Don't violate client confidentiality. Don't contradict the governor's political stance.

Don't. Don't. Don't.

With all those don'ts, many employees decide the safest course of action is to avoid reporters at all costs. If a reporter shows up, cover your face and hide under the desk.

Corporations and government agencies send their top executives to my seminars, to learn how to deal effectively with the media.

A real problem is that reporters' first contact is often an entry-level employee who knows nothing about media relations. The reporter scares them. They look very defensive. Guilty.

The First Contact

The reporter may interpret that employee's response as the official company line. A story that was slightly critical may suddenly head toward a full expose of scandal in the executive suite.

That's why the written policy is so critical. I suggest that written policies stress the positive aspects of media relations first. Then get around to specific things you should not talk about, and how to refer the reporter up the ladder of command.

At the end of this chapter, I've reproduced portions of model policies I've written for clients. They can be easily modified to fit your organization.

The Basic Points

I believe every media policy should contain these basics:

1. We need to tell the public who we are and what we do.

2. Public knowledge of our organization is vital to our success.

3. Reporters and photographers need to be treated courteously and diplomatically. Their impression of you becomes their impression of the entire organization, and that is reflected in their stories.

4. Discuss with reporters only those facts you personally know about. Don't speculate.

5. If you don't have personal knowledge, help the reporter reach someone who does.

6. If you would give a customer or a client public information the reporter is asking for, give it without hesitation to the reporter.

7. Let a designated executive (usually the PIO) know as soon as possible after any contact with the media. We need to be aware of stories that involve us, so we can provide additional information.

8. Refer media questions about policy or complicated technical issues to the PIO or other designated executive.

9. Return all reporters' calls within 15 minutes. If a message is left and the person the reporter called can't be reached, someone else should return the call. "Can I help you?" We do

not want to be surprised by tonight's newscast or tomorrow morning's newspaper. A story about this organization should never say we "could not be reached for comment."

10. Every story about this organization should include our perspective or point of view. That can't happen if we don't talk to the reporter.

11. Never say, "No comment." It sounds like you're hiding something.

12. Certain kinds of issues should not be discussed with reporters because of (fill in one or more): (a) the law; (b) our ethics or rules of procedure; (c) client confidentiality; (d) business competition; (e) some major harm that might result. Make sure the reporter understands why you cannot answer the question. Refer the reporter to a designated executive.

13. The news media have a legal right to observe, to photograph and to record any event or any person in a public place.

14. Other elements in **STRATEGY/Ten Commandments of Media Relations**.

Only the Boss Talks

Some organizations have a policy that says only the boss can talk to reporters. That means stories will be written without the organization's point of view when the boss can't be reached.

If only the boss is allowed to speak, reporters get the idea the boss doesn't trust the staff. They're either too dumb to speak for the company or have been muzzled because there's something to hide.

There may be a need to designate specific spokespeople for special kinds of situations. In a police department, for instance, the lead investigator working a homicide may be the only proper source for the media on that case. That investigator is best qualified to know whether the release of certain information might harm the investigation.

A fairly open policy will — in the long run — best serve most organizations. The single most disarming factor for a suspicious reporter is a friendly, wide-open media attitude.

I recommend the Home Depot technique. When a customer asks an employee where something is, the Home Depot employee doesn't just tell the customer where power saws are. The employee *takes* the customer there. The customer feels: *this company wants my business. I like that. This is a good place to shop.*

In the same way, your staffer should personally take the reporter to the PIO, or to someone who is better situated to know what the reporter is asking.

A Policy for Bankers

Private corporations and government agencies need to approach media policy with a slightly different tone. Here are portions of a model policy I suggest for my clients in banking. It can be modified easily to fit other kinds of private business.

A SUGGESTED MEDIA POLICY FOR BANKERS

To better serve our customers and the community, we need to tell them more about who we are and what we do here at the bank.

That message is often conveyed by the news media. And so the entire staff needs to be more aware of how we can cooperate with the news media, in ways that will best accomplish that goal.

A Word About Confidentiality

Never forget that the confidentiality of our customers' financial affairs is a sacred trust. Every employee of the bank can protect that confidentiality, and still be courteous and cooperative with members of the media.

Reporters Are Part of the Public, Too

Reporters have the right to answers for any questions you would answer for any member of the public.

EXAMPLE: "What is the bank's current interest rate on new car loans?" We'd answer that question for any potential customer who's shopping for a car. We'd be unusually helpful. We want their business. You should give reporters that same kind of information and help.

Be sure your answers to reporters' questions are accurate and current. If you don't know the answer, make a special effort to find the person in the bank who CAN get the information.

Reporters Have Deadlines

Remember, reporters are working against a deadline. They usually need their questions answered quickly. A prompt, courteous reply is good public relations for the bank. It's good business.

Banking News Is Important

The public today is more involved in finance than ever before. Reporting on banking and business is at an all-time high. This is a complicated subject. Good reporters need explanations and data we can provide. In doing so, we perform a major public service.

When a reporter asks about a generic financial or banking concept, you should — within reason — use your knowledge and the bank's resources to help that reporter.

> *EXAMPLE: "What is the relationship between banks and the Federal Reserve?" Or, "How does the Federal Deposit Insurance Corporation work? What must a bank do to qualify as a member? What does it cost the bank?"*

The answers to these questions are available elsewhere. They're not specifically tied to our bank. But by helping the reporter, we build a relationship with that reporter that's important to us. That reporter will come back to us in the future, both as a reporter and as a customer.

Notify Our Media Specialist

As a matter of policy, after you've given this kind of generic information to a reporter, notify the bank's media specialist. The media specialist's job is to work closely with reporters.

We'd like to keep track of how reporters use the information we give them. Perhaps we'll call later with follow-up suggestions after the story is printed or broadcast. If the reporter's inquiry would require extensive use of bank employee time or resources, you should also clear that with the bank's media specialist, before you commit to do the research.

Matters of Bank Policy

If the reporter's question involves a policy of the bank, or a specific incident or personnel decision, the reporter should be courteously referred to the bank's media specialist.

These questions are sometimes sensitive, in terms of our competitive position with other banks. How much information we provide the public is often a policy decision that can only be made at the administrative level of the bank.

> *EXAMPLE: "We have a tip that you plan to open a new branch and appoint Mary Moneycounter as president of that branch. Can you confirm that?" Or, "To compete with other financial institutions, some banks are offering*

> *innovative Internet services to checking account customers.*
> *Is your bank considering such a service?"*

We might be, but we might not want to advertise it just yet. The bank's media specialist will confer with top officers of the bank before deciding how we should answer that question.

Remember, on some questions you can give away the answer just in the way you say you can't answer. So refer the reporter to the media specialist without hinting at the answer.

Never Lie or Try to Deceive the Media

It's much better to say, "I'm sorry, I can't answer that question right now," than to give a deceptive answer. Explain why you can't answer. Avoid saying "No comment."

Reporters respect honesty more than any other character trait. So do our customers. In fact, honesty is our stock-in-trade. We must NEVER give even a suggestion that we're evasive or deceptive. If you give that impression to a reporter, it will probably be passed on to the reporter's readers, viewers or listeners.

Our Bank Is the People Who Work Here

Our bank is not a building or a corporation. It is the people who work here. We are constantly judged by the public's perception of our staff. When a customer or a reporter finds an employee helpful and friendly, then our bank builds its reputation as a helpful, friendly place.

When an employee is grumpy and uncooperative, then that customer or reporter gets the idea that everybody in the bank is that way.

What Is News?

News is the unusual. It can be good or bad news.

News is information people need in their daily lives. It can be information that makes their lives more enjoyable and profitable.

It can be information that warns them to take special precautions. Bad news always seems to leak out. Gossips thrive on stories of human frailty or failure. And once they spread their gossip, the media have a responsibility to publish or broadcast it, if they decide it will serve the public interest.

But news is also simple, human stories that remind us of life's joys and special times. Stories that renew our hope in humanity.

"Good news" often goes unreported. Not because the media aren't interested. Because they never heard about it.

One of your responsibilities here is to make sure our media specialist knows about possible human interest stories. The media specialist will know who to call in the local media to see if they're interested. But the call will never be made unless you bring the story to the specialist's attention.

EXAMPLE: After a customer had a heart attack in the bank lobby, a group of tellers decided to take CPR classes on their own time. The next time that happens, they'll be better prepared to help until the paramedics arrive.

EXAMPLE: An elderly customer cashed a check and left $100 in cash on the ledge at the teller's window. The next customer in line — a high school student — found the money and told the teller. When the customer who'd misplaced the money returned in panic an hour later, she and her cash were reunited. Without it, she wouldn't have been able to pay her rent.

EXAMPLE: A group of students who couldn't find summer jobs wanted to start a service to "house-sit" the homes of people on vacation. But they had no money to advertise. The bank's loan department decided they were a good risk, and loaned them the money to get started. They've paid off their loan and built a very successful business.

News Pegs

The news media are constantly looking for local stories that tie to a national story. They call these stories "news pegs." They're local stories pegged to a larger, national or international story.

There are many national financial stories that could generate local news pegs. Here again, the local media may not know of the local angle or connection unless we tell them.

Keep that in mind when you know that we're somehow involved in some banking activity that could be pegged to a national or international incident. Tell the bank's media specialist so the story can be passed along.

Cameras In the Bank

Reporters and photographers have the same right to enter public areas of the bank as any other citizen. They do not have the right — in this privately owned, public place — to interfere with banking business or our customers' expectation of privacy.

When a news photographer enters the bank and begins taking pictures, the media specialist or a bank officer should be notified immediately. The officer should approach the photographer courteously and ask what the pictures are for.

Remember, rudeness — on camera — always gives a bad impression of the bank. If the reporter or photographer is rude, we won't see that in the news. But if YOU are, we'll probably see just HOW rude on tonight's news. And tomorrow's news. And in future stories about this bank.

As a matter of policy, we'll be glad to help the news media photograph banking operations. We'd like to know in advance just what they want and need, so we can arrange the photography with the least interference to our customers, bank security, and our normal business.

If the photographer is belligerent and uncooperative, politely ask him to leave. In this kind of conflict with the media, make sure you're not the one who behaves badly.

A Policy for Human Services

The following is a model policy I suggest to human service agencies. By law in most states, these agencies cannot discuss anything about a client. The law and their professional ethic make it extremely difficult to defend the agency when it is attacked unjustly, by people making false allegations. This policy can be easily modified to fit most government agencies.

A SUGGESTED MEDIA POLICY
FOR HUMAN SERVICE AGENCIES

This department exists to serve the public.

The people in this community are vitally concerned with human services. How we meet the needs of those who cannot provide for themselves determines, to a large extent, the character of our community — its priorities and standards — its conscience and human dignity.

The people of this community provide the financial support and encouragement that make effective human services possible. They have the right to know, through the news media, how we carry out our duties and responsibilities.

We have nothing to hide. We will not have the support that we deserve as dedicated public servants unless the community is fully aware of the problems we face, and how we deal with them from day to day.

The News Media Can Help Us

The news media can often help us do our job. Many of our clients and potential clients cannot be reached in any other way. They will not know of our services if they do not hear about them through the media. News stories can rally the community to provide special needs in times of crisis. The news media are often invaluable in helping locate elderly clients who wander away from home; in identifying abandoned babies, and other similar cases.

It is Our Policy to Help the News Media

It is the policy of this department to make information available to the news media as quickly and completely as possible, except in those instances where the release of that information might violate the client's right to confidentiality or interfere with the fair administration of justice. When we cannot release information for legal or ethical reasons, those reasons should be carefully explained to the reporter. In some cases, it might be helpful to give the reporter copies of the law and the regulations governing what we can and cannot discuss publicly.

Returning Reporters' Calls

Every reporter's phone call should be returned in less than 15 minutes. If you cannot be reached, make sure your staff returns the call, and refers the reporter to someone who can answer the reporter's questions.

We do not want it to be said that we "could not be reached for comment." We do not want to be surprised by tomorrow's headline or tonight's newscast. Stories about us should always include our response or point of view.

Client Confidentiality

We have a legal and ethical responsibility to protect the confidentiality of our clients. In some cases, the legal process removes that cloak of confidentiality. If it has not been removed, we can still talk to the media about the way we help clients without naming a specific client.

We can explain to reporters, just as we would to anyone who asked, the rules and regulations concerning our services; the way those rules are put into effect; the numbers and amounts of money involved that are a part of the public record, or will eventually become part of the public record.

Every Staffer May Speak

Every staff member is free to speak to the media about departmental matters so long as the basic policy set forth here is not violated. The employee at the site of our services is often the best witness and can give the most accurate account of what happened.

Public Information Office

It is the role of the Public Information Office (PIO) to serve as coordinator of information with the media. A sort of tour guide. Reporter's inquiries should be referred to the PIO unless they can quickly be handled by the staffer who is contacted.

Often, the reporter simply needs a number or an explanation of how a program works. You may be better qualified to give that explanation than the PIO. But it is a good idea to let the PIO know about the reporter's inquiry. There may be other activity on the same subject within the department that you are unaware of. If the PIO is fully informed, they may be able to give more assistance to the reporter and improve our rapport with the media.

Have Personal Knowledge

You should speak to the media only about those matters of which you have personal knowledge. Do not speculate. This restriction is intended to prevent the relaying of inaccurate information to the news media.

Human Interest Stories

The news media are always looking for strong human interest stories. We often complain that the media cover us when we have problems and ignore us when we do things right. This is a chance for us to tell the public about our successes. It is the responsibility of the PIO to suggest these stories to reporters and editors. But the PIO cannot know about them unless you alert them. Remember, some of these stories need substantial lead time for the media to cover them effectively. Let the PIO know as soon as possible about clients or staffers who are involved in human interest situations that offer news story possibilities. Because it is the job of the PIO to work closely with the media, they can often arrange ways to cover those stories that do not invade clients' confidentiality.

Legal Rights of Privacy

The news media have a legal right to observe, to photograph and to record any event or any person in a public place. On private property, the owner of the property has the final word on who shall be allowed inside the premises. A court order which gives our staff the right of entry does not automatically give that same right to members of the news media. So long as the media are physically on public property — or on private property with the consent of the owner — they have the right to observe, photograph and record events that may be occurring on private property.

On-Scene Coordination

Many of the conflicts between human services staff and the media occur at the scenes of great human emotion and suffering. Under these difficult and often confusing circumstances, many members of the media will arrive about the same time we do. The ranking staff member on the scene should be responsible for coordinating release of information to the news media until a public information officer arrives.

Who Should Discuss Policy

Staff members should make every effort to be courteous and diplomatic in dealing with the news media. In matters of policy, the reporter should be referred to a staff member responsible for setting or carrying out that policy.

Not to Be Released

Staff members shall not release for publication, or in a manner which is likely to result in publication, information in the following categories:

1. The identity of a client, or confirmation that a person is a client, without the written consent of that client.

2. The names and addresses of victims of sex offenses.

3. The names and addresses of juvenile offenders.

4. Until next-of-kin have been notified, the names and addresses of people who die. The names shall be released after a reasonable time if notification of next-of-kin cannot be accomplished. Reporters may be given the names of dead people so long as they pledge that they will not publish or broadcast them until next-of-kin have been notified, or until the department approves release of the names. This will usually be done as a convenience to the media when notification of next-of-kin is expected before the reporter's deadline.

5. Information which might jeopardize an investigation.

6. Any opinion as to guilt or innocence of a client, or the merits or evidence in a case where a client's identity has become public through an arrest or other action outside this department.

7. The performance of any medical examinations or tests; their results, or the refusal of a client to submit to a medical examination or test.

8. The home address or telephone number of staff members, without the express consent of that staffer. The purpose of this provision is to strengthen the off-duty privacy and safety of the staffer and his/her family, not to make the staffer inaccessible to the media. Media requests for information that may be known only by an off-duty staffer can often be relayed to the staffer by the PIO or the staffer's superior without giving reporters a home phone number.

9. (Insert other localized items)

Records That Are Public

State and local ordinances provide that the following records shall be open to the public: (Insert local application)

Records That Are Not Public

State and local ordinances and departmental policy provide that the following records shall not be open to the public: (Insert local application)

Beyond these explicit guidelines, members of this department are encouraged to be open and cooperative with the news media. Although the department has a public information office, its existence does not imply that staff members should refer all inquiries to that office.

Every member of the department is expected to know the contents of this policy, and to abide by it. The director is willing to trust your judgment about what to say to the news media, and how to say it.

Every member of this department is a public information officer.

STRATEGY

PIOs

What Exactly Do Public Information Officers Do?

Most companies and government agencies of any size now have at least one public information officer (PIO). When they get that assignment, many PIOs have no training or experience with the media. Many of them don't have the foggiest notion of what they're supposed to do. Or how to do it. Nor does the boss.

I guess you write press releases, and answer reporter's questions?

Right.

But there's a lot more to it. The learning process can be very painful for the PIO, the boss, the organization, and reporters who have to deal with a new PIO.

Choosing is Difficult

If you're the boss, choosing a PIO is one of the most difficult personnel decisions you'll ever make. You'll need to consider:

- Should the job be full-time or part-time

- Should it be a veteran employee who knows the company, but may not know much about the media, or

- Should it be a media person who can be persuaded to leave the news business and represent you

More important than any of these, I believe, is the PIO's basic personality, intelligence and motivation. Does this individual personify the organization? How hard is this person willing to work? How well does this person perform under stress?

Winning with the News Media

How Reporters Rank PIOs

As a reporter, these are the things I valued most in PIOs:

- **Good PIOs are bright**, and they learn quickly
- **Good PIOs have great people skills**; they're patient; they know how to communicate, negotiate and mediate
- **Good PIOs have integrity**; they will not lie; they project sincerity and credibility; reporters, photographers, and the people within their own organization trust them

The most common misuse of PIOs occurs when the boss creates the position and announces the PIO will be the primary spokesperson for the organization.

Often in this kind of structure, no matter what happens, only the boss or the PIO will speak to the news media. The boss often wants to use the PIO as a buffer. As a barrier to keep the media at a safe distance. Not good.

Relays Are Too Slow

In this scenario, the PIO becomes an information relay. It takes a lot of time to gather the answers to a reporter's questions and then get back to the reporter, who by then has thought of several other questions.

If you miss the reporter's deadline as a result of a lengthy search, your point of view will not be in the story.

Every time information passes from one hand to another, it becomes more stale and less personal. The chance for error multiplies.

How Did It Feel?

Most important — the PIO wasn't there when it happened. Can't answer the media's most pressing question — How did it feel? (See **SKILLS/Interviews**)

A cop is shot in the chest at close range. His only injury is a bad bruise. His bulletproof vest saved his life. Reporters want to talk to the officer, not the PIO. They want pictures of the bruise.

How did it feel to be shot and live to tell about it? What went through your mind? How much pain is there when a slug slams into a bulletproof vest? Do you wear the vest all the time?

Only the officer can answer those questions.

The PIO's function *should be* to arrange the interview, not speak for the officer.

Tour Guides for the Media

Good PIOs are tour guides for the media. They are walking encyclopedias. They know the organization as well as the boss — perhaps better. They can quickly lead reporters and photographers to the right place, the right people, the right information.

Good PIOs are credible. If they know the answer, but can't tell the reporter, they say so. One deception, and the credibility can never be restored. Reporters have very long memories. They have ways to get even.

Good PIOs are respected and trusted by their colleagues within the company or agency. They can be trusted not to leak. Unless the organization wants something leaked.

Which leads to the chain of command. Who should the PIO answer to?

The Chain of Command

In the best organizational structure, the PIO or public relations director reports directly to the chief executive officer. The PIO has constant access to the decision-makers and is included in all major discussions and decisions.

If the PIO is not included, information can be released to the media that's not true. The PIO *thought* it was true. When reporters learn the truth, the PIO becomes — in their minds — either a liar or a flack who's out of the loop and doesn't know what's happening within the organization.

Public vs. Private

PIO for government agencies and private companies should have different perspectives. Similar, but different.

In the private sector, part of the job involves putting the company's best foot forward. It is part public information, part marketing and promoting the company.

Too many public information officers in government fail to understand the perils if they adopt those same objectives. They think it is their job to make the boss, or the agency, look good. In doing that, they may stall, or try to block a story. They may fail to disclose something. They may lie.

Switching to Attack Mode

The news media seem far less critical of deceptive games when private industry plays them than when the players are government officials or employees.

Nothing switches reporters to attack mode quicker than a lie or the belief that you're hiding something. It whets their appetites. There's got to be a Pulitzer Prize somewhere under that mountain of misinformation, they think. They dig harder. (See **STRATEGY/Ten Commandments of Media Relations** and **SKILLS/Good Guys/Bad Guys**)

Who Are You?

In its simplest definition, good media relations tells the public:

WHO are you?

WHAT do you do?

If your organization has good people who do a good job and turn out a good product or service, that's the message you need to convey.

In a society drowning in information, PIOs have to become more and more creative to get the media's attention, so they can deliver the basic message. (See **STRATEGY/Selling Your Story**)

News Conference Role

At news conferences, the PIO's role is to:

- Choose the best place and time
- Alert the media and invite them to attend
- Act as stage manager, to make sure the physical layout will accommodate both the spokespeople and the news media
- Provide handouts before the news conference begins
- Explain any special ground rules, and introduce the people who will take reporters' questions
- Close the conference when a pre-set time limit is reached, or when questions taper off

- Help set up individual interviews if reporters ask for them after the conference (See **SKILLS/News Conferences**)

PIOs Are Always On Call

PIOs should generally be on call 24 hours a day. News does not operate on a schedule. Your organization needs to have its perspective in every story that mentions it.

In some types of operations — fire, law enforcement, medical and emergency services, utility companies — you may need assistant PIOs on call at night or on weekends. Otherwise, the PIO will never be able to sleep.

Spend Time With Media

PIOs need to spend time with the reporters and editors who will be covering their organization. The PIO for a large bank should have lunch regularly with the business editor of the dominant newspaper in the area. The PIO for a hospital should do the same with medical reporters.

PIOs should ask to spend a day or half-day occasionally watching news people do their job. Ride with a TV camera crew, then watch them edit the story. Try your hand at writing an accurate newspaper headline in the limited space for headlines.

It gives you a much better understanding of the problems media people have getting their stories in the paper or on the air. Accurately and on time.

Enlarge Your List

Watching over their shoulders not only educates you. It sends a strong message that you're interested in what media people do. That you want to do a better job, helping them.

In that visit, you'll enlarge your list of media contacts. Next time you call, trying to sell a story, they're much more likely to listen.

The single most important strategy in dealing with the media is to convince them you're willing and anxious to help them get a better story. That's why my Number One Commandment is: Be Open and Cooperative. (See **STRATEGY/Ten Commandments**)

Becoming a Resource

Reporters need resource people. Major national associations realize that, and run advertisements in magazines that cater to the media. "If you have questions about our industry, we have people with answers," the typical ad says.

One of your goals as a PIO should be to have your name, office number and home number in the phone index of every reporter and editor in your community — and perhaps at the networks, and major publications like *The New York Times, The Wall Street Journal, Time* and *Newsweek.*

News is Free Advertising

Every time you're quoted, with your company affiliation, it's free advertising. It creates prestige and name recognition for the organization. It won't hurt your career, either.

Knowing all that, the full-time vs. part-time question really depends on how many media contacts the PIO must handle. You may want to begin with a part-time assignment, keep track of how the PIO spends the time, then decide whether it should be expanded to full-time.

The Staff Must Understand

Part of managing an organization also involves educating the entire staff to function as a team with the PIO. Public information officers can't be everywhere at once. They need to be tipped by others within the organization when there is a potential favorable news story or media problem.

I believe every organization of any size should have a written media policy, so there will be no doubt about exactly what is expected of employees. Managers need to let staff know exactly what the policy means. Particularly if it has been changed.

I recommend periodic staff meetings to go over hypothetical situations to make sure employees understand the organization's stance when dealing with print and broadcast news outlets. (See **STRATEGY/Media Policy**)

In a crisis, remember — the media's first contact will not be with a highly-trained, media-skilled executive. *Every* staff member should be aware of your organization's media attitude and policy.

STRATEGY

Selling Your Story

Wow! Have I Got A Story For You!

Many people try to get the news media to cover their story, fail repeatedly, and can't understand why.

They don't realize that their approach turns off editors. They don't know what news is. Or how to sell it.

News is the exception. The unusual.

Mayor Sober Today

If the headline says, "Mayor Sober Today," we assume he is drunk most of the time. What would your reaction be if tonight's newscast told you:

- No children were murdered today
- No airliners crashed
- No bridges collapsed
- No banks failed

News Is What's Different

News is what happens that is different.

It is news when a doctor walks into a hospital with a submachine gun and kills half a dozen people before turning the gun on himself.

It is not news that thousands of other physicians spent the day saving lives and relieving the misery of their patients.

Information You Need

News can also be information people need. Information that will in some way affect their lives. In a democratic society, we need to know that the school board is contemplating a tax increase so we can support, or try to stop it. We need to know that a certain brand of sardines is contaminated so we can throw them away and not get food poisoning.

To successfully sell stories on a regular basis, you must know your media market, the specific styles and audiences of each outlet.

Many of the stories that are staples for newspapers are not visually interesting for television, and have no appeal whatever for radio. Videotape of the school board's hearing on property taxes is not nearly as visually appealing as a warehouse fire. Because the number of people watching is so critical to television profits, the decision is easy. Air the fire. Dump the school board hearing.

The Compelling C's

There are eight broad categories for news stories — I call them the Compelling C's:

Catastrophe	**Crisis**
Conflict	**Change**
Crime	**Corruption**
Color (human interest)	**Celebrities**

If you, your department or your company are going to be in the news, the story will usually have an angle that fits at least one of these categories. And it must be unusual.

A caller says, "I don't want to give you my name, but you should look into what's happening at the Zebra Club. The treasurer embezzled $200,000 and ran off with the president's wife. The children's hospital we support is about to run out of money because of the theft. There's a big internal fight now, on whether to prosecute the treasurer, who — by the way — is a priest."

Now, That's News

Now, *that's* news. Crime, corruption, crisis, conflict, color.

Back to the school board budget hearing. Let's see if the story there might be more interesting than usual to the media.

LIGHTS! CAMERA! ACTION!

School board member: "Looks to me like the school superintendent has sold out **(corruption?)** to the realtors who are fighting this tax increase **(conflict)**. If this tax is not approved, we may have to shut down some of our schools **(crisis)**."

Veteran politicians understand the technique and use it all the time to get news coverage. The people they attack understand the game. They get on their soap box and fight back, and their point of view gets time on the air, space in the paper. Nothing personal. A lot like attorneys who seem to have a grudge match going in court, but play golf together every Sunday.

Manufactured Conflict

The 1988 Democratic convention was a great example of manufactured conflict to hold the media's interest. Gov. Michael Dukakis had the nomination locked up long before the convention. We knew the outcome. The primaries had dissolved any chance for suspense. Sort of like reading a murder mystery, when the author tells you in the preface who did it. Why bother?

So the balloon of a possible dogfight between Dukakis and Jesse Jackson was inflated and released. Jackson had been out of sight. Was he pouting, itching for revenge? Did he plan to torpedo Dukakis? Would it get messy and destroy the harmony the Democrats had worked so hard to promote?

The media hit the bait and ran with it. Many reporters at the convention knew they were being used. But there was nothing else to write about. Everything was cut and dried.

The broadcast networks began cutting back on their political convention coverage in 1988. Only C-Span and some other cable networks now provide for gavel-to-gavel coverage.

Conflict is news, and that now takes place in the primaries, not the conventions. Even the vice-presidential choices were made before the 2000 conventions. So they got very little coverage by the broadcast networks. Covering them became a kind of public service chore. There was little news there.

Wake Up the Stockholders

Want extensive coverage of your next stockholders' meeting? If the news media believe a group of stockholders are terribly unhappy and demand the resignation of the CEO, reporters will be there. If your association's conferences are rarely covered by the media, here's how to change that:

Anti-Yawn Conferences

If you're a medical group, invite a speaker who will attack ambulance-chasing lawyers as the cause of the massive medical insurance fraud problem.

If you're a bar association, invite a chief executive from a major insurance company who believes outrageous premium increases for auto liability coverage are the result of marginal doctors who milk every dime they can from accident victims.

Bring opposing points of view to the speaker's platform for a hair-pulling, eye-gouging debate. The Q&A session after the debate will lead to great quotes and pictures. CONFLICT is the key ingredient that makes most novels and movies work. It is a guaranteed way to sell a story to get news media attention.

It Is a Game

It is a game, very much like professional sports. To communicate effectively, you need to learn the game. It must be played very skillfully. If reporters suspect they are being manipulated with a phony issue, the technique can backfire.

One reason professional sports gets so much coverage is that they incorporate these basic elements. **Conflict** is central — one team using all its skill and stamina to beat the other. There is a new **crisis** every week — what happens if they lose? Will there be **changes** in the coaching staff? **Catastrophe** when the star quarterback is injured. And **color** everywhere. Rugged, macho, **celebrity** players. Ecstatic, sexy cheerleaders. Big money. Crowds, music, applause. The glory of victory, the agony of defeat. And all too often lately, stories of **crime** and **corruption** off the playing field.

In news, the game is life and death, success and failure, the come-from-behind underdog vs. the powerful champion.

Too Much Conflict?

In his book, *Breaking the News* (Pantheon Books, 1996) magazine editor James Fallows makes a powerful argument that the media's obsession with conflict is undermining democracy in

America. In a series of real-life anecdotes, Fallows recounts how journalists have avoided society's critical issues in recent years and spent their time and space covering conflict instead. Conflict sells.

Effect of Community Size

"My civic club elected officers last night, and I knew you'd want to do a story," the caller tells the city editor. In large communities, there are hundreds — perhaps thousands — of civic club elections each year. Not news.

In a small, rural community, with two or three civic clubs, the election of a new Rotary president may grab the front page. News often depends on where it happens.

Timing is Everything

Timing can be everything, when it comes to news coverage. On a slow news day, they still have to fill the print pages and the newscast minutes.

If there is still empty space on the page as the deadline approaches, a personality profile of the Water Buffalo Lodge president gets more and more attractive to the editor.

The day Princess Diana dies in a car crash, a five-alarm fire may get only two paragraphs.

Weekend Strategies

Newspaper editors need a lot of copy to fill the big Sunday edition. So Saturday can be a good day to release a story.

Because government and business are closed for the weekend, broadcasters have difficulty finding stories for their Saturday and Sunday newscasts. The same is true for Monday morning's paper. It may be easier to place a story then.

The downside is that both newspapers and broadcast stations work weekends with a skeleton staff. Those who work the weekend shifts may be newer, less talented reporters and editors.

One solution: Release the story on Friday, with an embargo. The media must agree to hold it until Sunday.

Some newspapers traditionally have a large "news hole" on Wednesday or Thursday, because that's the day the grocery stores buy entire sections of display ads.

If you expect to sell stories to your local news media, you need to know local editors. (See **STRATEGY/Ten Commandments)** When you call to offer a story, they'll know your name. They'll know you have a sense of news value. They'll listen more closely.

On many story tips, you should notify the editor in advance, in writing. Then follow up the news release with a phone call the day before the story breaks, or early that morning. Try to time your call for the editor's least busy time of day. (See **SKILLS/News Releases**)

Pitching the Story

For the assignment editor at a radio or TV station, the slack time is mid-to-late-afternoon, the day before the story. The call should sound something like this:

Ed? This is Tom Tipster. I sent you a news release earlier this week about the environmental protest we're planning in front of Koffalot Chemicals. We expect to have about 500 people there, willing to go to jail, if necessary. Just wanted to see if you need any other information.

Be careful not to push too hard. A good story doesn't really need to be sold. Selling too hard makes the editor suspicious that there may not be real news there. If there's an unusual element in your story idea that's not obvious, make that clear.

Timing for City Editors

You'd make a similar call to the editor of an afternoon newspaper about 1 or 2 p.m. the day before the story will break. By that time, the last deadline has passed. Time to work on tomorrow's early morning assignments.

For a morning newspaper, the call should be between noon and about 2:30 p.m. the day before, or in the early evening. Just after lunch, the city editor has issued most of today's assignments.

The afternoon editors' meetings that decide which stories will be in tomorrow morning's paper haven't begun yet. The call may also lead to a story in tomorrow morning's newspapers, giving readers a preview of what's going to happen.

In the evening, you can tip the night city editor, who leaves notes for the early morning staff.

Radio assignment editors need to know the day before, and may appreciate calls through the day to keep them up to date as the story unfolds.

Remember — television needs more advance notice, because they have to collect videotape to cover everything the reporter will write about.

Look for News Pegs

You need to contact the media while the issue is hot. If a national story develops on any subject, local editors and news directors look for a local angle. They call it a local "news peg" or a "news hook." It is a reflexive response. If you're the first to call with a suggestion, you'll usually be the person they interview and include in their story.

When O. J. Simpson was charged with the murder of his ex-wife, the record of his threatening and beating her became public. That triggered thousands of local, "pegged" stories all over the nation. When local police are called to a home, and there is clear evidence that the spouse has been beaten, what happens then? How tough are local judges on husbands who beat their wives? How often do local police go back to the scene of a previous domestic dispute to investigate a murder or murder-suicide?

The Easiest Sell

A news peg is the easiest story you'll ever sell to an editor. The national or international story has already established the story's priority. Editors and news directors put the localizing of stories very high on their agenda. But you have to hurry if you or your organization are to be part of today's locally pegged news. Your competition may beat you in tipping the local media.

If you work in a hospital or medical research facility, there will be many national health stories you can "peg" to. Call the editor and say, "There's a story this morning in *The Wall Street Journal* about fingernail transplants. Did you know we've been doing that here for three years? We invented the technique."

If you're a bank executive, there are daily financial stories for which you can suggest news pegs for the local business section. "I saw the story on *The Today Show* about the rising cost of home mortgages. Did you know our interest rates haven't changed in two years? We're considerably below other banks in the state."

Local telephone and power companies can often peg to national stories about new kinds of technology and services.

Stereotypical Stories

There are certain types of stories that are absolutely predictable. Stories that are repeated year-in, year-out.

The journalists simply insert new names, faces, numbers. When the mapping of the human genome is completed, they will find that editors have an unusual, aberrant gene which compels them to publish and broadcast these kinds of stories. And that all of us have a gene that makes us want to hear, see and read them.

Because these stories are so formularized and repetitive, reporters and editors sometimes squeeze the facts a little to make the current version fit the stereotype. Easy to sell one of these —

The Hypocrites

Something about our species makes us truly salivate over stories that unmask hypocrites. Stories like:

- The sanctimonious preacher whose wife catches him in bed with the choir director
- The IRS accountant charged with failing to file her own return
- The labor union president partying at a Caribbean resort with the CEOs of the companies where his members work
- The narcotics agent caught selling drugs, or the firefighter charged with arson
- The conservative "Family Values" politician who abandons his marriage to move in with his gay staff member
- The liberal politician who champions minority causes who is unmasked as an abusive slumlord in an incredibly bleak ghetto

Where does our attraction for these kinds of stories originate? Why do we love to see saints defrocked, the strong brought down?

Maybe we like them because it proves they're no better than we are. No different, after all, despite their pretensions. The stories of fallen idols seem to level the playing field.

Anniversaries

The anniversary story is a news media staple. Most commonly, the anniversary of a disaster or a major crime that got a lot of coverage when it happened.

The assassination of President John F. Kennedy, the death of Princess Diana, the bombing of the Oklahoma City Federal Building are good examples.

On the anniversary for several years, the stories will be revisited. Anniversary stories usually disclose very little that is new.

The anniversary story recurs at the five-year mark, the 10-year mark, then jumps to 25- and 50-year commemorations.

If an airliner crashes near your city and kills a lot of people, expect anniversary stories. The same will be true for major floods, earthquakes, criminal trials, storms, fires and industrial accidents.

If you have a point of view — an angle you'd like to see published or broadcast — several weeks before the anniversary will be an excellent time to sell that story idea to an editor.

History Lessons

History lessons are really a sub-category of the anniversary genre. As this book goes to press, major events in the Korean War and the Cold War are hitting their 50th anniversaries, with extensive media coverage. Often, newly-discovered angles — like the alleged massacre of Korean civilians by American troops — are timed to coincide with anniversary coverage.

Without these kinds of stories, young people today might have no sense of their heritage. From the pictures and sounds recorded on film and tape, I have learned more history from television documentaries — and I retain much more of it — than all the history courses I ever took in school.

Bureaucratic Bungling

The fall guy in bureaucratic bungling stories is usually some government agency or a big corporation. If the power company sends you a bill for $120,000, that becomes a news story. If reporters discover that NASA paid $1,500 for a tool that was available at Home Depot for $25, the stories get huge play and a lot of head-shaking. They trigger Congressional investigations.

Another version of this story is the bureaucrat or corporate bean counter who follows the rules precisely, instead of using common sense. If a monstrous miscarriage of justice or overspending results, that will get extensive, gleeful coverage in the media. (See **SKILLS/Good Guys/Bad Guys** - Conformists)

The media have a kind of conventional wisdom of their own. One of its tenets is that most people who work in government or large corporations are dumb, lazy and/or incompetent. The bungle story shows that the CV is right.

Dragon-Slayers

Another staple, stereotypical story makes heroes of little people who have the courage and/or temerity to fight a government agency, or a big corporation. Perhaps the social service agency which is trying to take custody of their child. (See **SKILLS/Good Guys/Bad Guys** — David vs. Goliath, Idealists, Risk-Takers)

Because we live in a society short on knights in shining armor, these stories are especially prone to distortion as reporters bend or exaggerate some of the facts so the story will fit the classic mold.

Frequently, those stories do not disclose everything about the crusaders. A whistle-blower's personal bankruptcy, drug addiction, mental instability or criminal record would tarnish the shining armor. So it somehow escapes mention in the story.

Ringing the Fire Alarm

The media leap on any wisp of a story that will alarm their audience. After all, news is the unusual. We subscribe/tune in partly to protect ourselves and our loved ones. So stories like these get big play:

- A professor's thesis on the chances of a meteorite striking the earth and destroying all life

- A remote study that claims apple pie will make you sterile

- A laboratory test that indicates milk might be a carcinogen

- Similarities in a string of murders that suggest a serial killer could be prowling the community

- The sudden death of a celebrity who was taking a popular medicine — and experts who say it should be banned

John Stossel did a piece for an ABC *Prime Time Special* called "Are We Scaring Ourselves to Death?"

In the documentary, he cataloged a number of stories the media had trumpeted that frightened us and made us wonder if our days were numbered.

In his conclusion, he charted the statistical risk for each of the dire threats over which the media had wrung their hands. Most of them were so remote, they were barely visible on the chart.

But if you really want to worry about something, Stossel suggested, look at the hard data on the risks posed by tobacco and automobile accidents.

Now, that's something to be frightened about. But those stories are so old and repetitive, they get very little news space or time.

Egocentricity

Journalists travel through life in their own special group (as most of us do). We not only work with people who have very similar interests, we party with them. Play sports and spend leisure time with them.

This gives all of us a very restricted view of the rest of the world. For journalists, it inevitably affects their news judgment.

If a custodian who worked at the local newspaper for 30 years dies, his death will get a large news story. How many other janitors who die get that kind of sendoff in the paper?

If a television anchor or sportscaster receives a truly inconsequential award from some remote civic group, it will get more coverage on the 11 o'clock news than this year's Nobel Prize winners.

First Amendment issues — "The People's Right to Know" — get a lot of news space and time. That's because those issues are critical to reporters and editors.

So if you want to get coverage for your issue, look for some way to bring a journalist into your circle to make them personally aware of your cause.

If your issue is the search for the cure for a certain kind of disease, you might want to find a journalist who has a close family member with that kind of disease. A story about foster homes will be very appealing to a reporter or editor who grew up in foster care. Research local journalists to find their personal niche.

Lobbying Your Issue

When legislation is pending, or the courts hand down a decision affecting your special interest, you need to let local people know how that law or decision will affect them.

Media coverage at the local level has a powerful grass roots effect. In Washington and the state capitol, officials who will decide the issue are much more influenced by local media stories reaching their constituents than by coverage in the capital city.

But local editors may not be aware there IS a local peg unless you call them. This is one of the most effective ways to campaign for an issue. For most people, a hometown person is more believable, more compelling than a national or state figure. The local authority puts it in perspective for local people.

You'll Become a Regular

Once you develop a reputation as someone who understands difficult issues — who can decipher them, so ordinary people understand them — you'll discover reporters come back to you for future stories. You become an expert they can rely on. If you're skillful, you make their story better. You make them look good.

The payoff for you (in addition to effectively arguing your point of view) is a subtle form of public relations for your organization. It won't hurt your role as community leader, either. Or your standing with your supervisors.

Here's the hierarchy at the local news media, so you'll know who to contact when you have a story to sell:

Managing/Executive Editor

At most newspapers, the top editor overseeing daily news stories is the **MANAGING EDITOR** or **EXECUTIVE EDITOR**. This editor is the final word on almost everything that happens in the newsroom; supervises all other news editors; and may even have authority over the editorial page editor.

At many newspapers, the news and editorial pages are kept separate. This kind of organizational chart is designed to make editorial writers more independent. It is a reminder that editorial writers express their opinions, and news reporters should not.

Newspaper Publisher

The managing editor answers to the **PUBLISHER**. At large newspapers, the publisher has almost nothing to do with daily news coverage. The publisher's function is to represent the owners and give overall supervision to keep the newspaper financially healthy. Some publishers write a weekly column. The publisher is often the newspaper's representative in community affairs and civic clubs.

General Manager

At small newspapers, the publisher may also be the **GENERAL MANAGER** who oversees circulation, advertising, and the mechanical portion of the paper. General managers traditionally have no voice whatever in news content. This avoids the suggestion that advertisers can influence news coverage.

City/Metro Editor

Local news is supervised by a **CITY EDITOR** or **METRO EDITOR**. The city editor is responsible for the local staff, and coverage within the immediate city and nearby suburbs. Many morning papers also have a **NIGHT CITY EDITOR**, to supervise the local staff from the time the city editor goes home in the evening until the last deadline, sometime after midnight.

State News Editor

State news (news within the state, but outside the local community) is the responsibility of the **STATE EDITOR**, who may also double as **POLITICAL EDITOR**, since the reporters at the state capitol bureau are within the state editor's geographic area.

Business News Editor

There's probably a **BUSINESS EDITOR** at your local newspaper who handles most financial stories. Business news coverage has increased dramatically in the last decade. The stock market, interest rates, banking policy, inflation and unemployment statistics have all become much more newsworthy to average readers. Many newspapers have a special business section, published on the same day every week. That section has a voracious appetite for detailed stories on local firms and the people in them. A great opportunity to sell a story about your company.

Editorial Page Editor

Editorials, syndicated columns, letters to the editor, and other material printed on the page opposite the editorial page (they call it the **Op-ed Page**) are under the control of the **EDITOR** or **EDITORIAL PAGE EDITOR**. The editor and editorial writers make up the **EDITORIAL BOARD**. At some newspapers, a representative from the newsroom also sits on the editorial board.

Editorial Board

It is the custom in many communities for political candidates, government officials, and leaders of major causes to visit with the editorial board. It is like an audience with the President or the Pope, in which you respectfully appear, hoping for their blessing. You make the board aware of your cause or point of view and subject yourself to cross examination. The goal is to garner editorial support or endorsement for yourself or your issue. At most newspapers each editorial writer is assigned specific areas, based on experience, interest, and expertise.

Features Editor

The **FEATURES EDITOR** supervises long-term reporting projects that are normally not produced on deadline. Stories like profiles of people in the news; an extensive look at controversial issues; magazine-length pieces where writing style is encouraged and enhanced. The section devoted to feature stories is now given a variety of names, like Style or Lifestyle.

With the advent of gender equality, the old "Women's Section" was abandoned. Many of the stories that would have once been in the Women's Section are now in the features section.

Favorite Topics

Favorite topics are human interest stories, personality profiles, animals, marriage and family issues, diets, medicine, moral conflicts like abortion and assisted suicide. The features editor may be called editor of this section, whatever its name.

Investigations Editor

Some newspapers with long traditions of investigative reporting have an **INVESTIGATIONS EDITOR** who supervises a team of specialists. At most papers, investigative projects will be directed by the editor who would normally supervise other stories in the same area. The overseer of investigations into political corruption will be the political editor. Investigations of local government will be monitored by the metro editor, etc.

Radio and TV News Director

At radio and television stations, the person in charge of all news operations is the **NEWS DIRECTOR**. The news director makes all decisions on hiring and firing — roughly the equivalent of the managing editor or executive editor at a newspaper. The news director answers to, and works closely with, the **GENERAL MANAGER**, who reports to the station owner.

Broadcast Assignment Editor

The **ASSIGNMENT EDITOR** is the person who decides how reporters and photographers will be dispatched to cover stories. If you'd like to have radio or TV coverage of something you're involved in, you need to let the assignment editor know about it.

Assignment editors are the most harried people in television news. The typical assignment editor sits in the center of the newsroom, totally immersed in noise and confusion. On the desk, a bank of telephones are constantly ringing. With one ear, the assignment editor must monitor several squawking police and fire department radio scanners.

Noise and Confusion

On top of that, a dozen camera crews out in their cars need directions to addresses they can't find.

They are reporting by radio every few minutes to say their camera or tape recorder has broken down; they arrived 30 seconds too late to catch the bridge collapse; the convention they're supposed to cover doesn't begin until next week, that the massive protest against police brutality is actually a little old man who hand-delivered a letter to the mayor's secretary.

Assignment editors also must eavesdrop on the two-way radio conversations of the competition and check e-mailed news releases.

No Respect

If the assignment editor happens to get a crew to the right place at the right time, and they come away with a great visual story, the reporter and photographer usually get the credit. If the assignment editor misses a story, the news director has a nasty habit of screaming, banging on the desk and shouting obscenities. Good assignment editors are born. Those that aren't, but try to remake themselves into assignment editors, sometimes have nervous breakdowns.

Show & Story Producers

The **PRODUCER** of the newscast decides the length of stories, their format, and their placement in the newscast. Producers are the equivalent of a page or section editor at a newspaper. The stories gathered at the direction of the assignment editor are turned over to the show producer. Network TV crews have a **FIELD PRODUCER** who travels with the correspondent and photographer, does most of the research, and manages the details.

The field producer may also videotape an interview, but is rarely seen or heard on the air. Local stations will occasionally assign a field producer to a crew for a major series or documentary. Since there are several newscasts each day, the producers of each show may be supervised at larger stations by an **EXECUTIVE PRODUCER,** who also serves as deputy news director.

Public Affairs Director

Virtually every TV station had a **PUBLIC AFFAIRS DIREC-TOR** back when the FCC required licensed radio and television stations to dedicate a certain amount of air time to items that served the "public interest."

The standard format for public affairs programming was a weekly talk show, in which someone discussed a current event or project. Those shows were polite and often boring. A completely different breed, compared to today's talk shows (Transvestite

Mothers Who Seduce Their Children's Pediatricians! Don't miss this afternoon's guests on Wired and Wierd!).

With the deregulation of broadcasting, many stations have phased out their public affairs departments. The surviving local talk shows are often produced by the news department. The old talk show format, however, is still a Sunday morning staple on network television. CNN invented today's redesigned talk show on public issues which speeds the pace, increases conflict, and invites viewers to participate by telephone. (See **SKILLS/Talk Shows**)

Editorials & Commentary

Broadcast editorials and commentary are written, produced and performed by the station's **EDITORIAL WRITER** or **COMMEN-TATOR**. They are usually supervised by the station's general manager or public affairs director. At some stations, the editorials are delivered on the air by the general manager.

Under the old FCC Fairness Doctrine, stations were required to give opposing points of view a chance to air their position. Although the doctrine has been abolished, many stations still abide by it, and that gives you another opportunity to sell your story.

The FCC's rules on Personal Attack and Political Editorials were abolished by a federal judge just before this book went to press. But if you scream about fairness, you might get air time. (See **INSIDE THE MEDIA/Fairness and Equal Time**)

Ride-Alongs

When the fighter pilots who fly in the Navy's Blue Angels acrobatics team come to town for an air show, their first stop is every local newsroom. We can take one person up for a ride, they tell the editor.

The result is almost always a huge story, with dramatic pictures and breathless copy.

Syndicated reality TV shows like *Cops* use this technique. If reporters and photographers ride along, you'll get better stories.

The Ringling Brothers and Barnum and Bailey Circus has historically used a similar technique to get great coverage. The circus animals are paraded from the train yard to the place where they'll perform. Reporters and photographers are invited to ride the elephants — perhaps perform in the show as clowns.

The secret of good coverage is often to bring reporters into your life or work. Let them ride in your cockpit — walk a mile in your shoes. Only then can they see the story from your perspective.

Do It When You're Under Attack

And the very best time to bring them in is when you're under attack. It goes against your reflexes to do it then. The normal reaction is to barricade the building; avoid reporters at all costs.

But there are many, many cases where reporters switched from attack dog to awed reverence, once they experienced, first-hand, the problems insiders were coping with.

National journalism magazines in recent years have run essays warning reporters about riding along with their story subjects. *Be careful*, the stories warn. *If you spend very much time with them, you'll begin to like them. You will no longer be objective.*

Targeting the Audience

When people buy advertising, they shop for the medium that can best reach their target audience. You don't sell cemetery plots on a hard rock station. Or acne remedies in a magazine for retirees.

Advertising agencies know the number of people who read, listen to, and watch local outlets. They have the demographics. In some cases, through market research and focus groups, they practically know what the audience had for breakfast.

Advertising Agency Data

If you need to sell stories on a regular basis, visit a local advertising agency and learn more about the audiences for each local media outlet.

Find out how many subscribers, listeners, viewers each has. How old are they? Male and female breakdown. Income and education levels.

When you have a story to sell, you may want to place it so it will reach the widest possible audience, or you may want to target a small, specific group. Consider all the opportunities. There are many you may not have thought of.

Here's a checklist for placing stories as widely as possible:

Radio Story Opportunities

- News
- Talk shows
- Special reports & documentaries
- Editorials and editorial replies
- Commentary and commentary replies

Television Coverage

- Daily newscasts
- Special issue coverage
- Live interviews inserted in newscasts
- Talk shows
- Series and documentaries
- Editorials and editorial replies
- Commentary and commentary replies

Newspaper Stories

- Local news
- State news
- Special sections
- Editorials and editorial replies
- Letters to the editor
- Columnists and columnist replies
- Special columns written by outsiders

Association Newsletters

Virtually every association publishes some kind of newsletter. You may not realize how many associations there are in America. Professional associations. Business associations. Associations to promote the use of dairy products or nuclear energy. Associations for virtually every major issue. Most states have several hundred associations. Nationwide, there are tens of thousands. They're always looking for stories to fill those newsletters.

To find the association that might be interested in your story, search the two-volume *Encyclopedia of Associations* at most public libraries. The American Society of Association Executives is headquartered in Washington, D.C. The state association of association executives will usually be located in your state capital, and most of them publish an annual directory. Obtain a copy so you'll have a specific name and address to call when you have a story idea that would appeal to their members.

Local Magazines

Don't forget the local and state-oriented magazines that are always looking for fresh ideas involving local people and issues. Many local chambers of commerce now publish magazines that concentrate on business, finance, and community development. Lots of opportunities there.

Think Pictures That Sell

Your success in selling a story idea to a radio or television assignment editor will often hinge on your suggestions for sound and pictures. In many cases, you can supply the sound and pictures. (See applications of this idea in the **SKILLS** Section chapters on **News Conferences, News Releases,** and **Talk Shows**)

Unfortunately, much of government and business is dull, by comparison with other, more visual stories. How do you show a smooth-running water department? How do you photograph a record stock dividend? So much of government that has been traditionally covered by newspapers is almost entirely ignored by television.

Even Watergate — the biggest story of the 1970s — was poorly covered by television. There was little that television could *show* until the impeachment hearings began. Most of the Watergate story had to be *told*.

Photo Opportunities

Public relations agencies and government public information officers have created a new event — the "photo opportunity." This is an event generated specifically for news media pictures. It is neither spontaneous nor unrehearsed. In many respects, it is phony. Everybody knows it's phony. But the appetite and demand for pictures is so great, the media play along. Your success in selling a story may depend on your ingenuity in creating a photo opportunity.

Television and radio miss many stories simply because they don't know about them in time to get a camera or microphone there. A newspaper will usually have about five local reporters for each reporter at a TV station.

Newspapers assign reporters to beats, and those reporters spend their entire day at city hall or the courthouse or the police station. They're expected to know, and report, everything that happens there.

Television and radio depend on newspapers, and on listeners and viewers who call to tip them to stories.

Don't Cry Wolf

Public relations firms have a bad habit of trying to sell stories that really aren't newsworthy. Once an editor gets burned by a story tip that flops, he'll hang up on you when you call to report you just found Jimmy Hoffa hiding in your basement.

Give the editor accurate times so the staff won't waste valuable minutes waiting for people to show up or the event to begin.

Who Gets it First?

If the story is not an event that needs to be photographed, you sometimes have to decide whether to give it first to radio, newspapers or TV. Or to all at the same time. It's very rare to choose radio as the medium that will get it first on an exclusive basis, largely because coverage will be brief. It will not reach nearly as many people.

The Newspaper-TV Feud

There is intense dislike — hatred, really — among newspaper people for television news. This can affect how your story will be covered. In many cities, newspapers try to ignore television. If television beats them to a story, they won't touch it. It is an ego thing. Newspaper people look down their noses at both the TV medium and the people who work in it.

Television, in their minds, is fleeting, shallow, delivered by people who are hired for their looks, not their ability or intelligence. It is showbiz, not journalism.

If television got it first, it's hard for newspaper editors and reporters to admit they were beaten by the medium they spend so much time criticizing. So they decide it's not much of a story. Several weeks later, they may revive the story with a new twist, trying to make it look like they found the story and broke it first.

It's Not Old for TV

Television is not so concerned about competing with newspapers. News directors will kill to beat a competing TV station to a story, but they assume most of their viewers don't read newspapers. Just because it's in the newspaper this morning doesn't make it old news for the TV audience.

The rivalry between TV and newspapers over being first with a story varies from place to place. You have to test it in your market area.

To get the broadest possible coverage, give your story to the newspaper first. Because they got it first, they'll play it bigger. Radio will read it straight out of the newspaper. Television assignment editors read the newspaper every morning, looking for story ideas. Newspaper coverage can make TV more interested in a story that may be visually dull. It is another variation of the news peg idea.

Post-Times Certification

The same phenomenon takes place with national stories. TV network bureaus send story proposals to New York. New York says it's not interested, and the story idea is trashed. Two months later, the story appears in *The New York Times* or *The Washington Post*.

The network news desk in New York jerks the bureau chief in Los Angeles out of bed at 5 a.m. Rent a jet. We want this story for tonight's newscast.

"Hey, I told you about that story two months ago, and you didn't want it," the grumpy bureau chief complains.

"It wasn't news then," New York says. "This morning, it's in *The New York Times*."

STRATEGY

Ten Commandments

Basic Techniques for Better Media Relations

Unless you've been caught in the crossfire of a pitched media battle, you will have a hard time understanding what it's like. It may be the most difficult experience of your life. Remember the scene in *Apocalypse Now* when the helicopters are staging an early morning attack on the Vietnamese village? The air is thick with choppers. They swarm like dragonflies. Napalm is exploding. There is gunfire from all directions.

Everything moves so swiftly it is hard to keep your sense of balance and direction. It is confusing. You feel naked, out in the open, not knowing when the incoming fire will suddenly target you. You feel death and disfigurement whistling by, very close. People around you, people you know well, are dropping.

An All-Out Media Attack

That's what it feels like when you become the center of a national or international story. Reporters and photographers arrive by the hundreds, from all over the world, in helicopters and Learjets, armed with tons of exotic, space-age equipment. They surround your office, your home, your church. They camp there, round-the-clock, crushing the tulips. Throwing their Big Mac wrappers and coffee cups on the lawn.

You and your family cannot move without running the gauntlet of microphones and cameras. You may be followed everywhere you go for weeks at a time. You will feel invaded. Under siege. A captive. Your life, your career, the stability of your home and family will suddenly seem to be at great risk.

Fight or Flee Syndrome

That's the worst-case scenario. But the Fight or Flee Syndrome will also seize you when a reporter shows up, unannounced, and begins to ask questions. If it is a television crew, stage fright will be added to the stress.

To help you cope, I developed the Ten Commandments of Media Relations. Some of them are just basic common sense. But your fear of the media often leads you to do strange things. The commandments should also help you develop some regular routines and policy for coping with reporters, editors and photographers on an everyday basis.

The Ten Commandments

1. **Be Open and Cooperative — Never Lie.**
2. **Personalize the Organization**
3. **Develop Media Contacts**
4. **Take Good Stories to The Media**
5. **Respond Quickly**
6. **Never Say, "No Comment"**
7. **It's OK to Say, "I Don't Know" (But I'll Find Out)**
8. **If You Screw Up, Confess and Repent**
9. **Use the Big Dump**
10. **Prepare, Prepare, Prepare**

1 - Be Open and Cooperative

Let's go over them, one at a time.

When you close the door in the face of a reporter, or refuse to provide a document, you may not realize the visceral reaction you trigger. Particularly if the reporter has a legal right to enter that door, or see that document.

As a young reporter, I quickly realized I was too sensitive covering stories that involved death and human tragedy. The emotions got in the way of my objectivity. They prevented my seeing and hearing everything.

So I set out to desensitize myself. I attended executions. As a college student, I covered a shooting one afternoon. The sheriff's deputy asked me if I'd like to attend the autopsy that night. I ate a big dinner and then watched the coroner open the skull and chest cavity of the shooting victim. I knew my exercises were succeeding as I watched, fascinated, with no sense of nausea.

Those exercises were extremely valuable to me later in my reporting career. I was caught in the middle of several riots. In separate incidents, I just happened to be very close when two major industrial accidents occurred, each killing half a dozen people and injuring many others. I was able to walk through the carnage, cool and deliberate, taking notes, shooting pictures. Surgically recording what was happening, so I could give my readers or viewers an objective, clear account.

You Challenge the Reporter

And yet, after 30 years of conditioning to be unemotional on a story, I sometimes felt an adrenaline rush that made my pulse jump and the hair stand up on the back of my neck. It happened whenever someone told me I could not enter. Or I couldn't look at a public record. They challenged my skill as a reporter. They sharpened every combative instinct I possessed. They were hiding something. It was my job to find what they were hiding and tell the entire world.

I was no longer Clark Kent. I stepped into the phone booth and came out — SUPERMAN! Fighting for truth, justice, and the American Way. I usually found what they were hiding and wrote a much larger story about it. I was able to obtain a copy of the document they hid, and put it, full-screen, on the next newscast.

Nixon's Private Meeting

Richard Nixon thought I bugged him during the 1968 Republican Convention. I didn't. But he pulled the trigger that challenged my reporting skill. He announced he would hold a private meeting with all the Southern delegates to discuss his position on school busing. School busing to end racial segregation was a big issue that year. The night before the private meeting, my managing editor called me over to his desk. "Jones," he said, "You're a good reporter. I want you to find out what Nixon says tomorrow morning about school busing."

My first attempt to infiltrate the meeting didn't work. The guards on the door were too good. So I stood out of earshot, looking for delegates I knew. I was carrying a large audio tape recorder. Two delegates refused to help me. The third grinned and said, "Sure." He slung the tape recorder over his shoulder, in plain sight, flashed his credentials at the guards, and waltzed in. He sat under a loudspeaker.

When Nixon began speaking, my secret agent turned on the recorder. He brought me back a studio-quality tape. The next morning, across the front page of *The Miami Herald*, we stripped the story, then jumped inside for the complete transcript. Nixon had violated the First Commandment.

 # 1A - Never Lie

There is a sub-commandment here. Never lie. The lie, in the Good Guy/Bad Guy scale, is usually worse than the sin you lie about. As an investigative reporter in TV, I did whatever I could to get you to talk to me on camera. If you were the villain I thought you were, you would lie. And I could use the lie to destroy you.

In the past, people who lied to reporters could later claim they were misquoted. No longer. With audio and videotape, you do not lie once. You lie at 6 o'clock; at 11 o'clock; on the morning show; again at noon. We may hear the lie played over and over as long as you live. Even after you die. Break some of the other commandments, but don't lie.

 # 2 - Personalize

Americans do not like big government or corporations. They have a negative mindset for almost anything that smacks of bigness and bureaucracy. They carp about the phone company, the military, lawyers, doctors, public schools — you name it.

But their attitude about any large group changes when they get to know someone inside. The medical profession is just a big bunch of quacks, my next-door neighbor says. Go in for an operation, they cut off the wrong leg. The dandruff prescription gives you cancer. Except for my cardiologist. A saint. Saved my life.

Who Are You?

To be successful with the media, you have to become very creative at showing us real people in your organization. All public relations boils down to one simple concept. You need to communicate effectively:

Who are you? What do you do?

The media have created myths about virtually every profession and job. The stereotype in Joe Sixpack's mind may be very distorted. That will change only when reporters watch people in your group, close-up, being who they really are — doing what they really do.

People Stories

Virtually all news stories today are people stories. When hurricanes strike, earthquakes rumble, major rivers flood, we are told the story, one person — one family — one business at a time.

Over the shoulder of the TV correspondent, we can see the townspeople filling sandbags, trying to protect the country store in Missouri. They've been at it for two days now. One of the people interviewed drove 75 miles to help. Doesn't know the store owner. Just wanted to do something to help.

But the water creeps higher. Then, the sandbag levee breaks. The water rushes in. People run up the hill as the floodwaters surge into the store. The store owner and his neighbors weep.

That's just one business, the correspondent tells us somberly. There are a thousands of others whose homes or businesses have been destroyed. As viewers, we understand the story's impact.

 # 3 - Develop Media Contacts

Let's be frank. You develop personal relationships with reporters and editors so you will get better coverage. As you cultivate the contact, you know that. They know that. But you never say that. It is a strange game in which you collect poker chips which you will someday cash in. But it is done without a word.

As a young reporter, I covered federal court arraignments every morning. I wrote small stories about the procession of car thieves, pimps, moonshiners, draft dodgers and occasional bank robbers who appeared to enter a plea and have their bail set.

My Doctor, the Defendant

I walked into court one morning, glanced over at the group of defendants, and my jaw dropped. In the group was a prominent local surgeon whom I knew very well. He had corrected my hernia a few months earlier. Before I could check the docket to see what he was arrested for, his attorney scurried over to me. I knew the attorney, too. He was a state senator I had covered on a daily basis during legislative sessions at the state capitol. "I'm here representing your doctor," the senator said earnestly. "Please, please don't write a story. It will destroy him."

My curiosity was really aroused. What did they get him for?

"Please, Clarence, no story."

Why is he here, senator?

"The game warden caught him. He shot too many ducks."

A Strange Ethic

Normally, I would not have written a game warden arrest story. But that day, I was compelled to. Why? To prove my relationship with the defendant and his attorney could not influence my unbiased, objective coverage. In retrospect, it is a strange ethic.

How do you develop contacts? Invite them to lunch. They'll probably insist on paying their own check. (See **STRATEGY/ Ethics**) At lunch, make it clear that you are available when they need a resource. Emphasize Commandment #1. Just want you to know that we have an open door to reporters and photographers at our place. Call. I'll do my best to help you.

Good Reporters Need You

Good reporters have many contacts. They depend on them. Contacts call with story tips. Volunteer inside information they know will help on today's major story. And when it's time for a story about your profession or organization, you'll be the one who's quoted. It enhances the positive image of your group. And it won't hurt your career, either.

Remember, all stories are not black and white. Reporters have tremendous power in deciding which stories will be written — which will be thrown away. Stories take a slant or tone by the choice of a word or a phrase. When you're having problems, the reporter who knows you personally — respects your competence and integrity — will write a very different story than the reporter who is a stranger.

After you develop contacts, they call you when they get tips suggesting something's wrong at your place. Rumors — and the stories they generate — die when you assure your reporter contact the rumors are false. When the rumors are true, you must NEVER, NEVER suggest that the reporter owes you a break. If you do that, the game is over. You lose all your chips, and a good media contact. Go directly to the front page. Do not pass go.

4 - Take Good Stories

The side dish with most American dinners now is a generous helping of blood and guts. Night after night, we watch bodies dragged across the screen. Our TV sets are smeared with blood.

If not a double murder, then a plane crash. Or a tenement house fire, with mothers dropping their babies to the pavement. From every corner of the world, we see tears, pain and human suffering. National Public Radio wakes us each morning with news of the latest terrorist bombing somewhere in the world.

Why Always Bad News?

Why·do they always bring bad news? Because people *want* to hear and see it. Because they *need* to know.

It is not just morbid curiosity. It is part of our instinct for self-preservation. We *need* to know there is a killer stalking children so we can protect our children. We *want* to know about the design defect in a new airplane so we can take a different flight.

We have always pictured ourselves as caring people who value human life. But because most of us never venture into the ghetto, we do not think about inadequate or unenforced building codes until we see children die there. We have become so isolated from each other, so insulated from our own neighborhoods, we do not notice problems unless there is a disaster to grab our attention.

The Media Set the Agenda

Once the news media bring those issues to our attention, we put them on our agenda. The reform of drunk driving laws in the United States swept across the nation in the 1980s as local and national media focused on the terrible toll of death and permanent disability caused by drunk drivers.

The same thing happened with the destruction of the environment. In modern-day America, we do not believe a problem exists unless we *see* that problem spotlighted in the news media. And if you are a problem-solver, we will not believe you are doing anything until we *see* you working to solve that problem. (See **STRATEGY/Selling Your Story**)

We Are Insulated from Life

There is another theory, too, about the crowds that gather to stare at people dead, or dying, in the street. In this sterile, high-tech society, most of us have never seen the struggle and wonder of birth, the anguish of a nervous breakdown, the pain and loneliness of old age. Most of us have never seen someone die.

We hide life's basics in hospitals and nursing homes, or in a code of behavior that says we must never, never let anyone know what we are feeling, or who we really are.

We are terribly alone, and often bored, in our sanitized lives. We need to touch reality. And so we are drawn to — fascinated by — death and violence, human triumph and tragedy.

That is one reason cops, reporters, doctors and lawyers are the central figures in so much of contemporary television drama. Their jobs put them in touch with humanity. We want to look over their shoulders. We envy their opportunity to experience life with the wraps off.

How Much Gore?

In newsrooms everywhere, there is constant debate over just how much to show. How much blood should they let seep into your living room? How close should the camera zoom in on the face of the dead child?

There are excesses, and after a long string of bodies every night, editors and news directors write memos ordering less blood and gore. The media are always trying to sense just the right balance. Enough to satisfy the viewers' cravings — not so much to disgust them and make them stop watching, listening, or reading. Enough to inform and motivate without turning them off. (See **INSIDE THE MEDIA/Privacy**)

We Forget Good News

There is another phenomenon here. We remember the BAD NEWS stories and forget the rest. In every newscast, newspaper or magazine, there are lots of GOOD NEWS stories. Many local stations now have their equivalent of *Charles Kuralt On The Road*. Newspapers were doing it long before Kuralt. Folksy visits with little old ladies who still chop wood for their kitchen stoves. Trained pigs that bring in the newspaper. Kids who have defeated birth defects through sheer courage and determination.

We forget the story about the cop who saved a life, and remember the one who sold his badge to the dope peddler.

Looking For a 'Kicker'

In more than a thousand TV newsrooms across America, they are searching right now for tonight's "kicker." By decree in the television news industry, every newscast must have a kicker.

The kicker is the last story in the newscast. It is a warm, fuzzy, feel-good, overcome handicaps, success story. It is a story that picks us up and makes us feel that people are basically good, despite what we've been told in the previous 28 minutes. It reinforces the maxims our mothers taught us as children.

The kicker concept was devised years ago by TV news consultants who interviewed focus groups on their reaction to TV news.

Maybe We Shouldn't Watch

"You know," people in the focus groups would say, "We watch the news every night while we eat dinner. And after all that blood and pain and tears, we get indigestion. We've talked about watching re-runs of *Gilligan's Island* instead of news."

The consultants came up with an easy cure — run a kicker as the last story, and the audience will forget the blood and pain and tears. They'll feel good, and come back tomorrow night. And so virtually every newscast in America ends with a kicker.

Bad News Leaks

The bad news almost always leaks out. You assume that good news leaks, too. It doesn't. Gossips inside your organization take bad news to the media. It is a phenomenon of natural law.

To get positive coverage, you must create a system where everyone in the organization is sensitive to good stories. There must be a way for those ideas to reach the person who is responsible for public relations. It is that person's job to try to sell the good story. Thousands of good stories die every day simply because the media never hear about them.

5 - *Respond Quickly*

If you are under attack, **YOU MUST RESPOND BY 3 P.M. TODAY**.

Your lawyer can be a real problem here. Lawyers have learned in the judicial arena that delaying as long as possible will usually help them win. Good legal advice can be horrible media advice. (See **STRATEGY/Lawyers & Lawsuits**)

Tylenol's PR Victory

When someone planted cyanide in Tylenol capsules, the attorneys at Johnson and Johnson counseled CEO James Burke to say absolutely nothing. The giant corporation would surely be sued for billions of dollars. Whatever was said could come back to haunt them in court. Tylenol was responsible for a third of the corporation's revenue.

Burke thanked his lawyers for their opinion, and then did exactly the opposite. The doors of the corporation were flung open to any reporter who called. Burke went on *The Phil Donahue Show* and took questions from the audience and anonymous callers. Mike Wallace and a *60 Minutes* camera crew were allowed to cover a top-level executive meeting at the height of the crisis, with no holds barred.

Most people in the public relations business consider Burke's gutsy decision the most successful PR coup of the 20th Century. If Burke had followed the legal advice, the company might have gone belly-up. (See **STRATEGY/Crisis Management**)

Scheduling Media Trials

The media do not grant continuances, as the judicial system does. Once the allegation surfaces, the trial will be scheduled for tonight's newscast. The longer version will be in tomorrow morning's newspaper.

Let's look at what happens when you stonewall. The nightly newscast opens with the anchor saying, "Well, there's more trouble at Widgetworks tonight. Frank Ferrett, our investigative reporter, has been following that story and tonight he has the latest development. Frank —"

It is 20 seconds after six o'clock. Ferrett now assumes the role of prosecutor, or plaintiff's attorney. His opening statement to the jury lays out the charges and allegations. He calls several witnesses to the stand. In those interviews, they are not cross-examined. Ferrett puts several documents into evidence. We see them on the screen, with key portions circled or enlarged for emphasis. They are not challenged or questioned.

The Prosecution Rests

Then Ferrett rests.

If you have attended courtroom trials, you know that the prosecution presents its case to the jury first. Then the defense has its turn to dispute the allegations.

In this media trial, the defense rests its case without presenting any witnesses, or introducing a single piece of evidence. "Officials at Widgetworks refused to talk to us," the script says, as we see them going into their offices, closing the door, covering their faces.

Ferrett now makes his closing argument. He sums up all the evidence, which has not been challenged. The defense chooses not to make a closing argument. Their attorney says curtly, "We will have nothing to say at this time." The case goes to the jury. This is a speedy trial process. It is now one minute and 40 seconds after six. At 6:01:45, the jury returns with a verdict.

Guilty On All Counts

I know, before the clerk reads it, what the verdict is. GUILTY ON ALL COUNTS.

Several days or weeks later, the attorneys go to the Widgetworks CEO. Let's ask for a rehearing in the media. A new trial. We now have the evidence to prove we are absolutely innocent.

The media court has different rules of procedure. New trials are extremely rare. Re-hearings, if they take place at all, are often two paragraphs back by the hemorrhoid ads.

Once you are cast as the villain in a story, it is difficult — often impossible — to change that image, no matter what you do.

The media policies I write for clients require someone on staff to return all reporters' phone calls within 15 minutes. This prevents you from being surprised on tomorrow's front page. You need to know what the reporter is working on. Every story about you should include your viewpoint.

Sometimes, the reporter simply needs information. You become a resource. You're an expert. Your image is enhanced by the story. (See **STRATEGY/Media Policy**)

6 - *Never Say No Comment*

Never say, "No Comment."

Why? It violates Commandment Number One. We hear something else. We assume you are hiding something. Evading. If you haven't done anything wrong, why not talk to us?

In reality, there are times when you shouldn't talk to the media. If the detectives tell us too much about the kidnapping, the child may be killed. If the CEO discusses the proposed merger, the negotiations can fall apart.

The grand jury witness who tells reporters what happened in the jury room will be held in contempt and jailed. So what do you say when reporters ask questions you shouldn't answer?

The Oliver North Posture

During his first appearance before the Iran-Contra Congressional committee, Marine Col. Oliver North told the committee almost nothing. But he never said, "No Comment."

His handlers knew he would look bad. No Comment is very much like the Fifth Amendment. The Fifth Amendment is a perfectly valid Constitutional right guaranteed every person in this country. But because so many shady characters have used it in appearances before Congressional committees, it has fallen on hard times. Like "No Comment," we hear something else.

I Wish I Could Help You

North took a different posture. When he did not — or could not — answer a question, his response was, "Senator, I wish I could tell you what really happened. ... People in America would feel safer tonight if I could disclose the truth and put those rumors to rest." His stance appeared to be trustworthy, helpful, friendly, courteous, kind, cooperative, humble. A true Boy Scout.

Explain Why You Can't

If you can take that posture and be truthful about it, you avoid the negative message that "No Comment" sends. But you must follow it with a complete explanation of why you can't answer the question. "Because my lawyer won't let me," is not good enough.

North frequently based his failure to answer questions on national security. That probably won't work for you.

Sometimes you will not be able to answer because the law forbids it. Explain the law. Give the reporter a copy of the law.

Truth, Fairness, Public Good

Media Morality values truth, fairness, the public good. Use those values in your response. Explain that because so little is known at this time, you don't want to be inaccurate or unfair.

Explain in great detail how you plan to investigate and find the truth. How partial facts can lead to terribly unfair impressions. How great public harm can result if too much is released now.

I'd love to tell you more about the negotiations, but if I do, this city could lose its NFL football team.

I'll Get Back to You

Close the conversation with a promise that you'll get back to the reporter with a full answer just as soon as you can — as soon as the investigation is completed; the negotiations finished; the arrest made; the trial over; the contract signed. ***Be sure you keep that promise.*** In real life, if you are successful at the media game, you will also learn how to talk to reporters in confidence. (See **SKILLS/Off-the-Record**)

7 - It's OK to Say 'I Don't Know'

If you don't know the answer to a reporter's question, don't try to fake it. Don't assume your employees did what they were trained to do. Don't use statistics unless you're absolutely sure of the numbers.

Reporters don't expect you to have the Library of Congress in your head. But they do expect you to know where the information is, and to be able to retrieve it quickly.

But I Can Get It For You

I recommend that you include one or more staff members in any complicated interview or news conference. (See **SKILLS/Interviews** and **News Conferences**) It is the staffers' job to answer complicated technical questions in their area of expertise. Or to fetch the records that can answer the reporter's question.

"I can't remember the exact figure," you tell the reporter.

(Then to the staffer) "But Bill, if you'll get the 1996 committee report, that'll have it. (Back to the reporter) We can give you those numbers before you leave the building."

In this way, you appear helpful, open, cooperative.

8 - Confess & Repent

There is another attitude deeply rooted in our tribal psyche. We respect those who take responsibility for their mistakes.

We will forgive them if they admit it, say they're sorry, and do whatever they can to make things right.

How different our heritage would be if George Washington had said to his father, "Cherry tree? What cherry tree?" In deciding who is the good guy and who the bad guy, the lie, the cover-up, the insensitivity are greater sins than the crime itself. (See **SKILLS/Good Guys/Bad Guys**)

Presidential Confessions

Richard Nixon was disgraced and lost the presidency because of the Watergate cover-up, not the original crime. No evidence has ever surfaced that he was involved in planning the burglary itself.

Bill Clinton denied "having sexual relations with that woman" for almost a year before he finally confessed an improper relationship with Monica Lewinsky. But that still did not get him off the hook. *He failed to say he was sorry* for what he did.

Five days before the election in 2000, the story surfaced that George W. Bush had been arrested for drunk driving in 1976. His confession and repentance within hours was a classic.

"I've told the people I made mistakes in the past," Bush told a news conference. "And this was a mistake. What I did was wrong, and I've corrected that." He detailed once more his 1986 decision to become a teetotaler. He talked about counseling his children to never drink and drive.

Bush said he admitted he had been drinking to the Kennebunkport officer who stopped him, then paid a $150 fine the same night. His Maine driving privileges were revoked for a short time.

The classic formula: Confess, repent, accept your punishment, say you're sorry, do what you can to make things right.

Follow-Up Questions

After "How to you feel about ..." Reporters have a guaranteed follow-up question:

"What are you going to do (have you done) about it?"

One of my favorite training hypotheticals involves a fictitious construction company. The company has a multi-million-dollar contract to build a new civic center downtown. Today is a major event in the construction project. They finished clearing the site this morning. There is one nagging problem, however.

We Destroyed the Wrong House

One of the houses bulldozed this morning was not on the site. It was just over the line. There was nobody at home to stop them. The elderly widow who lives in the house was at the hospital, visiting her sister, who is dying of cancer.

And now, the widow (who scrapes by on Social Security) is digging through the rubble, looking for the only picture she has of her only son. He was the famous marine who died in Vietnam and was awarded the Medal of Honor (posthumously) for heroism.

What Do You Do Now?

What do you do now? I ask my audience.

"Take a six-month vacation in Hawaii," one man suggested.

NO. I tell them to confess they made a terrible mistake.

This drives attorneys crazy. We all carry in our wallets the little card our auto insurance company mailed us. *If you have an accident,* it says, *Do Not Admit Fault.*

Look, I tell the lawyers in the audience. I don't care where you try this case — who the judge is — who the jurors are — who the opposing attorney is — they're going to find out you knocked down the wrong house. *Never confess a sin you didn't commit.* But if you did it, say so. And in the same breath, do your penance.

Do Your Penance

What are you going to do about it? Build her a new house. Does she want it here? In the mountains? By the seashore?

"Just tell me where, and we'll start that new house tomorrow morning. You'll need a place to stay during construction. My American Express card will take care of everything at the Hyatt Regency. Meals, too.

"It looks like we tore up your furniture and clothes. That same credit card is good at Saks Fifth Avenue. When the house is finished, I'll pay to furnish it any way you like."

She will still sue. Any juror who hears about your confession and penance will get angry. But not at you. "That greedy bitch," the juror will say. "And she wants $20 million? Get out of here."

9 - Use the Big Dump

When you have bad news to dump, dump it all at once.

Don't let it dribble out. That prolongs the stories and multiplies the damage. Once you decide to confess and repent, you may be tempted to confess only part of your sins. That's human nature.

But then the media will find follow-up stories and repeat the original allegations as they add tiny bits of new information. With each new story, the damage increases.

Months or years from now, a tiny detail that has not previously surfaced will be discovered by an enterprising reporter. **New Evidence Uncovered**, the headline screams. You appear to have hidden evidence of your guilt. Obstructed justice.

Tear Gas at Waco

Before the FBI's final assault on the Branch Dividian compound near Waco, Texas, in 1993, agents fired three rounds of tear gas at a bunker about 75 yards from the living quarters. Hours later, the compound burned to the ground, killing about 80 people. In the investigations that followed, the FBI did not reveal the gas.

Six years later, the failure to disclose was discovered. That led to the appointment of Special Counsel John Danforth, who ruled in 2000 that the tear gas did not start the fire. He concluded:

Although the government did nothing evil on April 19, 1993, the failure of some of its employees to fully and openly disclose to the American people the use of pyrotechnic devices undermined public confidence in government and caused real damage to our country.

No Time or Space

Often, much of what you dump will not even be written if you dump it immediately. Its news value expands if you wait.

In breaking coverage, there will not be time on the air or space in print to cover everything. The leftovers become old, stale, insignificant. You can move on past the problem. As a consultant, I have had remarkable success with clients who used this technique.

Dirt that you disclose is always less newsworthy than dirt reporters dig themselves. So long as the news media believe there is more to be mined, they will continue to dig. That's their job.

10 - Prepare, Prepare, Prepare

Most organizations have carefully-prepared disaster plans. They conduct fire drills, tornado drills, earthquake drills, hurricane drills. They buy insurance and prepare for the worst.

It is much more likely that you or your organization will experience a media disaster before you have a fire or an earthquake or a tornado. Yet few companies or government agencies have prepared for that more likely hazard.

A first step is a written media policy. (See **STRATEGY/Media Policy**) Key spokespeople ought to be trained to deal with the media. They need to practice those skills often. Otherwise they get rusty. They lose their reflexes. (See **STRATEGY/PIOs**)

Rehearse Major Interviews

All major interviews should be rehearsed, preferably on videotape. Get staff or friends to play the role of reporters.

You need to see and hear your responses to the tough questions. And honest critiques of your performance.

Never, never do a news conference without a rehearsal. (See **SKILLS/News Conferences**)

What Would We Do If?

To prepare for future, predictable media crises, hypothetical incidents should be created and studied by your command staff. What if we suddenly discovered a major internal embezzlement?

How will our police department react if one of our officers makes a major mistake and kills an innocent person? What will the hospital say if a major slip-up occurs and a famous patient dies?

How will the bank explain an employee who helped a drug smuggler launder money? What will the judge say when he releases a career criminal and that criminal murders a little girl within a week?

How will we cope with hundreds of reporters and photographers if an employee we fired returns with an assault rifle and slaughters his co-workers?

All these things happen with some regularity. We are human. Our systems are imperfect. If we have not prepared for disaster, it can easily destroy us.

That Won't Happen Here

You may believe that you live far from the madding crowd. That you will never have to go through the torment of being at the center of an international story.

I'm sure that's what the sheriff in Union, South Carolina thought before Susan Smith strapped her kids in their car seats and pushed the automobile down the boat ramp.

With today's mobility, no matter where you live, several hundred reporters, photographers and technicians could be on your doorstep within about three hours.

They come by helicopter, by chartered jet, by boat. They use disguises to get in close.

"I don't think they've arrived by parachute yet," I told a seminar group.

"Wrong," a woman in the class said. "A photographer tried to parachute into Madonna's wedding to shoot pictures for the tabloids."

I stand corrected.

Section Two

SKILLS

Defending Yourself
Good Guys/Bad Guys
Interviews-Broadcast
Interviews-General
Interviews-Print
News Conferences
News Releases
Off-the-Record
Speeches
Talk Shows

SKILLS

Defending Yourself

Ambush Interviews
And Other Traps

It may be a bright spring morning. You will have no warning, no inclination to be cautious. As you leave your house and unlock the car in the driveway, you probably will not notice the van parked halfway up the block. Even if you are wary, you will not see the hidden camera videotaping everything you do. As you come out of the driveway, the van follows, a discreet half-block behind.

You Will Not Suspect

You drive to your usual parking spot, a block from your office. You do not notice the same van, double-parked. Two men jump out the rear door. One is shouldering a video camera. From behind, they come at a trot. You never hear them.

The reporter steps out in front of you, blocking the sidewalk. At that instant, the cameraman bursts ahead. With a start, you see them for the first time. The reporter says, "Good morning, I'm Mike Wallette from Channel Seven. I'd like to talk to you about your company's financial crisis."

A Difficult Time —

It is a difficult time, no matter how cool you are. The surprise of the ambush is a jolt. You look frightened. Pulse racing. Breathing short and hard. You have only an instant to decide what to do. You may act reflexively. Five options:

Ambush Options

1. **Punch out the reporter,** swing your briefcase at the camera, and run like crazy to get away.

2. **Keep walking,** but duck your head and put your hand in front of the camera lens. The photographer will stick with you, the reporter firing non-stop questions, into the lobby, all the way up the elevator, into the reception area of your office. Somewhere along the way, you will probably utter a "No comment" as you grit your teeth and stare straight ahead.

3. **Stop dead in your tracks.** "I have no idea what you're talking about. Now if you'll excuse me, I have to get to work."

4. **Say: "Good morning, Mike.** Gee, if you wanta talk to me, come on up and I'll see when I can squeeze you in today. If you'd called, I woulda been glad to give you an appointment." In this scenario, the reporter will still keep the camera rolling, and fire questions all the way to the office. He is afraid you will renege on the appointment.

5. **Say: "I'll be very glad to give you an interview,** but let's talk first, off camera. If you're sincere in wanting to talk to me — in doing a fair, accurate story — and not trying to make me look like some kind of criminal, turn off the camera and come on up. I'll get us a cup of coffee."

They Win, You Lose

The ambush technique has been used, and abused, throughout the history of investigative reporting on television. Radio and print reporters ambush their targets, too. On radio, we can hear the fear in your voice. We can't see your terror in those media. The reporters tell us, in their own words, how frightened and guilty you looked, then give us your response.

Reporters know they can usually count on the ambush to make the target of their story look bad. At the same time, they're carrying out their obligation to get your side of the issue. It's heads they win, tails you lose.

Some veteran reporters who ambushed their targets for years now question the fairness of the technique. Mike Wallace of *60 Minutes* (probably the most-feared reporter in America) says he now uses the ambush technique only if the target refuses to give him an interview.

The audience has become more sophisticated. Part of the re-thinking involves not wanting to look like a TV bully picking on a defenseless little guy. The audience believes television has enormous power. If reporters and camera crews abuse that power the audience will side with the target.

They Will Persist

Television is words and pictures — mostly pictures. If they are to write words about you, they must have your picture. Good investigative reporters take great pride in their persistence. If they truly want your picture, they will get it. Unless you lock yourself in your basement for the next year. Even then, there are ways to get to you, or smoke you out. So the only question is, what do you say when they catch up with you?

Let's go back and examine your options in an ambush.

- **Punch out the reporter** — This makes great video. You can be sure every moment will be played on the air. At least three or four times. You will enhance your reputation as a hoodlum. Few people will side with you. They will decide you are guilty, as charged. If there is another side to the story, it won't be told. The reporter can have you arrested for assault and battery. There are excellent grounds for a civil suit. The proof for both criminal and civil action is all on videotape. You will boost the reporter's career immeasurably.

- **Refuse to talk, keep walking** — In most cases, this will also make you look like a nasty guy with something to hide. Remember — television, like politics, is often a matter of impressions, not exact words.

- **"Excuse me, I have to get to work"** — Here, you've said *something*. The audience knows you're human. But you're still cold, elusive, probably guilty. This option has many modifications. If you don't want to give a full interview or answer questions, you can take this opportunity to get at least a brief statement on the air. "No comment" is like taking the Fifth Amendment. Many people will assume you're guilty. Otherwise, why not talk to the reporter? (See **STRATEGY/Ten Commandments**)

His question has suggested there are financial problems in your company. You can say something like, "We've become concerned about a cash flow problem in the last week or so, and we're working on it. I'm confident the company is not in danger. We're negotiating now with some new investors, and I'm sure we'll work it out. But that is a delicate thing. I really can't say very much about it. If you'll give me your name and phone number, I'll be glad to call you when we come to an agreement."

This answer will guarantee a string of questions, that you can politely refuse to answer, repeating your reason for declining. You may want to answer some of them.

- **Make an interview appointment** — If you're polite, the reporter tends to return the courtesy. In making the appointment, try to find out as much as you can about the story. You may have to do some research to answer some of the questions. Delaying for several hours will give you time to prepare. (See **SKILLS/Interviews-General**)

- **Let's talk first, off-camera or off-the-record** — This is usually the best choice if you're concerned about getting a fair shake from the reporter. News people work a lot on instinct. From experience, they tend to be suspicious. Anything you do that appears to evade, to delay, to deceive or cover up will feed their suspicion you're a bad guy, and probably will be reflected in their copy. (See **SKILLS/Off-the-Record**)

Lay It All Out

During that off-camera or off-the-record talk, if you're not guilty, lay all your cards on the table. That may be the end of the interview, and the story. The off-camera interview gives you a better opportunity to fully explain your side of the issue. The reporter may not have all the facts. Collect documents and bring in staff, if that's necessary for a full presentation.

There is another element of self-defense that you should keep in mind. If you are a public official or public figure you cannot collect in a libel suit unless the media publish or broadcast something false about you with malice. The U.S. Supreme Court says you must prove they had "reckless disregard for truth." (See **INSIDE THE MEDIA/Libel**)

Libel Suit Strategy

You must not only prove it was false — you must prove the reporter did a sloppy job; had information showing the story was false, but ignored it. If you meet with reporters or editors to refute their suspicions, make sure you can prove what you told them. Tape record the meeting. Have a reliable witness present. Get a signed receipt for any documents you provide.

Keeping Reporters Honest

If you are concerned about the integrity of the reporter who asks for an interview, it might be a good idea to take the same precautions. Have a staff member sit in on the interview. Keep track of the records you provide. Make your own audio or video recording of the entire interview.

Let the reporter know you're recording it. Reporters who know you have the tape are much more careful in quoting you. With a transcript of the entire interview, you can make a major dent in the reporter's career if the story is not fair and accurate.

Editors are very concerned these days about reporters who can't write truthfully. They're a $20 million lawsuit, just waiting for the right assignment. (See **INSIDE THE MEDIA/Libel** and **STRATEGY/Fighting Back**)

If, in asking for the off-camera or off-the-record conversation, you say you'll talk later on camera, or for quotes, don't back out. If you'll lie about giving an interview, surely you'll lie about more important things.

Reporters are always afraid to delay on-camera and on-the-record interviews. Too many people change their minds.

The Lie Will Never Die

Remember: Reporters and cameras are excellent lie detectors. Like the polygraph, the camera can sometimes be fooled. But if you're caught in a tape-recorded lie, television and radio will never forget. It will be played over and over again. You can't say you were misquoted. The lie is there, on tape, to haunt you forever.

The audience is also smart enough to know when you're blatantly evading a question. In many cases, it's better to say you can't answer — and why — than to sidestep the question.

A good reporter, like a good courtroom lawyer, usually knows the answer before the question is asked. Police investigators go to school to learn how to decipher body English so they'll know when suspects are lying, or when they have guilty knowledge of a crime. Reporters learn the same skills through experience.

Human Polygraphs

Almost unconsciously, they constantly monitor your fidgets and eye-blinks; what you're doing with your hands; whether your breathing is relaxed or shallow; whether you're sweating more than the temperature calls for; how tightly your legs are crossed; whether you avoid eye contact.

A real problem for TV interviews is fear of the camera. Stage fright gives the same physical symptoms as guilt and deception. You may be signaling that you're Public Enemy Number One, when you've really just got a bad case of stage fright.

The Camera Monster

Interestingly, most people are not as afraid of a newspaper reporter with a shorthand pad. The camera is the monster they fear. I believe that fear is badly misplaced.

Newspapers do much more investigative reporting than television. Their investigative teams spend months — sometimes years — on one story. Newspaper investigations are much more tenacious and persistent than those in radio and TV.

The wire services pick up the stories. They go all over the world. Congressional committees and federal prosecutors read them and begin major investigations.

Hidden Cameras

Newspaper reporters usually don't have a camera in their hands as they conduct the interview. But they have a camera in their heads.

As they sit there, making notes, they're often not writing what you're *saying*. They're writing what you're *showing*. Body English. Eye contact or movement. Fidgets. Sweat. How you reacted to that last question.

They will go back to their newsroom and create a picture of you with *words*. And that can be more distorted than videotape.

Take More Control

I urge clients to take more control of the interview — print or broadcast. If the room is hot and you're sweating, suggest that you take a break, turn off the TV lights, and let the air conditioner catch up. If you realize you made a mistake in something you said several sentences back, tell the reporter:

You know, I told you a couple of minutes ago we're planning to spend $54 million on that project next year. My memory was bad. Ask me that question again and I'll give you the correct figure. Or —

I told you we are planning to spend $54 million on that project next year. I'm not sure of that figure. Let's stop a minute while I check the numbers. Or —

My answer to that question you asked about next year's budget was awfully wordy and convoluted. If you ask me that question again, I'll try to give you a much better, shorter answer.

Deciding whether to talk to an investigative reporter is very complex unless the charges are absolutely false. If the reporter has been misled — if an understandably false conclusion has been drawn from the evidence — then you should definitely talk.

Not Guilty: A True Story

A real-life example:

An anonymous caller once told me I should investigate why a government agency paid the city attorney twice as much for his house as it paid the owners of other, identical houses that were condemned on the same block.

I went to property records at the courthouse and discovered the tip was accurate. The lots on the block were all the same size. The houses were all similar, built at the same time, carried on the tax assessor's rolls at virtually the same value.

Yet, when the government agency bought the entire block, it paid the city attorney — who had good political connections — twice as much as anybody else. Apparently an open-and-shut case.

I went to the city attorney to get his response — the last step before broadcasting the story.

The Target's Response

"Yeah, they paid me twice as much," the city attorney said. "But I didn't get the money. You see, I'd leased the house to a color photo processing company. The lease said if they ever had to move for any reason during the term of the lease, I would have to pay for their relocation and build them another processing plant. I've got a copy of the lease in my file, if you'd like to read it."

Oh. Three days of research down the tubes. No story.

When You've Goofed

If the story the reporter is pursuing involves your making an honest mistake, it's almost always best to say so. (See **STRA-TEGY/Ten Commandments**)

Past the point of admitting an honest mistake, the decision on whether to be interviewed for quotes or on camera gets stickier. It depends on how serious the accusation, and your involvement in it. In a sense, you're on trial.

The reporter will present the charges, and the evidence against you, to the readers/audience who serve as the jury. If the defense decides to rest with no evidence, no witnesses, we have been conditioned to believe that is a concession of guilt.

Conning the Reporter

Looking guilty by refusing to talk to a reporter may be better than taking the stand and convincing the audience you're not only guilty, you're a liar as well.

Career con men often amazed me by agreeing to a sit-down interview. It is a heady challenge, to see if you can out-smart, out-talk the reporter. You rarely win. Reporters have the last word.

If there are people and documents that support your side of the controversy, the reporter may not know about them unless you disclose them. Refusing to talk will ensure a one-sided story.

What Are You Hiding?

It's hard to draw lines for every situation. But generally, reporters believe people have something to hide if they try to keep them out of offices, or meetings, or records. The more open you can be with reporters, the more honest and fair they tend to be with you. (See **STRATEGY/Ten Commandments**)

Remember — whatever the reporter does that is underhanded, or belligerent — behavior that might raise eyebrows — will never be broadcast or written. Anything you do that is less than flattering will be preserved for all the world to see. We will see it, hear it, read about it many, many times.

There are other kinds of surprises reporters spring. They call and ask permission to shoot videotape in your business or office. "Just general footage to go with a story we're doing." Or reporters who say they need a general briefing on a benign subject. Once inside, you discover they have entered by subterfuge.

Sandbag Questions

In the middle of what you thought would be a friendly interview, the reporter gets nasty. Springs a completely different subject on you. A sort of verbal ambush. The sandbag question.

"Didn't your corporation fire four women in 1995 simply because they were pregnant?" the reporter snarls. You may not have the foggiest idea.

Too often, people who don't know the answer to a surprise question will try to answer it anyhow, saying what they assume or hope is true. Later, when it turns out they're wrong, it looks like they were lying or trying to cover up. If you don't know, say so. And tell the reporter you'll get the answer.

Become More Aggressive

If the reporter's question is a complete fishing expedition that unfairly or inaccurately impugns your character or motives, you should become very aggressive and adamant in your response.

If you're not insulted by a false, damaging suggestion, the reporter will believe the allegation is true. *Controlled* anger is the key here. Never give an interview when you're truly in a rage. You'll say something you'll later regret. Let us see a seething resentment that the reporter would stoop so low. A clear, positive statement, delivered with great intensity —

This company is not a sexist company, and I defy you to find a single shred of evidence that would even suggest such a thing. Or —

I have never beaten my wife. I have never abused my wife, either physically or mentally, and I resent your throwing that kind of question into this interview. You are completely off-base, and I'm sure your viewers/readers/listeners will come to the same conclusion if you report such a scurrilous question — and have the integrity to include my answer.

How Are Things Going?

If a reporter asks you how things are going in your company or department, be careful. The landscape is littered with the carcasses of executives who proudly said everything was hunky-dory, not knowing the reporter already had proof of a massive problem, getting worse by the minute.

Typical of this kind of mousetrap was a TV interview with a hospital administrator, bragging that his institution ran a model program to deal with infectious waste.

In his office, he gave a lengthy lecture, telling how waste was carefully controlled within the hospital until it was incinerated at another site. The temperatures there, he said, would destroy any infectious virus or bacteria. Nobody could possibly be harmed.

The TV reporter asked him to do the videotaped interview on the loading dock outside the receiving department because the light was better there. On the loading dock, as the administrator was talking, he was unaware the camera was zooming over his shoulder to a red bag of bloody waste, lying untended in the open.

They Could Be Better

If the question is a general one, about how things are going, the best answer is, "Pretty good, but I'm always trying to make them better. Do you have any specific area in mind?" That will make the reporter, who knows something you don't, re-phrase the question, getting closer to the real issue.

If a reporter surprises you with an allegation that is news to you, your answer should be something like:

I'm not aware of that, but if that were true, I'd be very concerned about it. If you know something I don't, please tell me, so I can do something about it.

Unload Everything

If you knew about the problem and have been quietly working on it, this is the time to unload everything you've done. There aren't any secrets now, so you might as well look impressive as a manager or executive who makes things right.

If you say you're working on it, but don't say how, the reporter will suspect you're lying. An accurate statement of your position can be written that telegraphs the reporter's suspicion —

The CEO said he's been investigating the allegation for two months, but refused to say who is conducting the probe; how they're doing it, or what they've found.

You may want to make a deal with the reporter, to keep things quiet a little longer. This will involve a confidential agreement, in which you persuade the reporter to delay the story.

To do this, you'll have to trade something. The price will usually be information that would not be available without this special agreement. (See **SKILLS/Off-the-Record**)

Beat Them to the Punch

Once you know you have a problem, you may be able to solve it before the story is published or broadcast. The story is not nearly as damaging if the problem has already been solved.

Call the reporter and announce what you've done, with thanks for bringing the problem to your attention.

If you really want to zap the reporter, hold a news conference and give the entire story — problem and solution — to the competition before the investigative report can be printed or aired. I call this counter-punching. (See **SKILLS/News Conferences**)

Air Your Own Dirty Linen

You will almost always look better announcing internal problems before the media find them. If they find them, they tend to make the story bigger and more sensational. It's a way to pat themselves on the back.

If you announce it, they are inclined to downplay it because they should have found it themselves. It makes them look slow or incompetent.

Answering Allegations

When there is an allegation that is damaging to you or your organization, here is a generic response that can be modified to fit almost any situation. This should be done quickly, to include your point of view in the first story. You need to tell the media:

- **Your concern about the allegation**. You try to run a first-class operation here. Any complaint or allegation is a major concern.

- **What you're going to do about it**. Here, I suggest you give as much detail as possible. If you're launching an immediate investigation, tell us how many people will be involved. How will they conduct their investigation? Will outside investigators be brought in?

- **A general timetable**. If you can't be sure how long the investigation will take, make it clear that this is only an estimate. You may find more to investigate than you expect. If you see you won't finish by that time, tell the news media well in advance, with a clear explanation of why it's taking longer than you expected.

- **Your personal investment in finding the truth**. Here, your reputation for being open and fair with the media is critical if you are to be credible.

- **A reminder that the allegation may be false**. Unfortunately, the reporting of allegations in the media are often heard and read as a conviction. The reputations and lives of innocent people can be destroyed.

- **You will disclose the truth when you find it**. Investigations are meaningless if the public never knows what you found.

- **You will see that justice is done; any problems corrected**. If the allegation is false, the suspended employee will be reinstated. If it is true, you will personally help the prosecutor.

- **You will review procedure and training.** Sometimes the system is at fault, not the people in it. Sometimes they have not been trained to handle a crisis. The system should be blamed, not those who were caught up in it.

SKILLS

Good Guys/Bad Guys

Saints and Sinners
As the Media See Them

I often tell my seminar audiences I teach human relations more than news media relations. How you deal with a reporter in the first few minutes will have enormous impact on how you are portrayed. Reporters claim to be unbiased and objective. But no matter how hard they try to meet that goal, they are inevitably affected by personal experience and first impressions.

Morality Plays

Since the morality plays of ancient Greece, the central theme of drama in most cultures has been: Good Guys vs. Bad Guys.

The news media in modern America have developed their own version of the morality play. The story may not say outright that you're a Saint or Sinner. But the trivia that is noted, in words or pictures, will make the point very clearly.

A lot that is communicated in news stories is written between the lines; in the cutaway shots of television.

Reporters' Radar

Reporters develop a kind of personality radar. A sixth sense that quickly judges you and casts you on one side or the other. Some media consultants claim reporters make that critical assessment less than a minute after first contact with an interview subject.

They already know something about you before they arrive. From research, they may know a great deal about you. So they arrive with a preconceived attitude. Then they watch you very closely. Your facial expressions, your body language, the words you choose can quickly confirm their suspicions.

The Snowball Effect

Of course, they're sometimes wrong. But that first impression will be passed on to their readers, viewers and listeners. Other journalists see the story, or dig it up as part of their preparation for your next interview. They arrive, already believing that you are who the previous stories said you were.

The snowball gathers speed. Can the political candidate really be as dumb as the media make him out to be? Is this movie star really as difficult on the set as the tabloids say? Is this mutual fund manager as brilliant as *Business Week* reports? This rock star as promiscuous?

Once something has been written about you, other reporters observe and listen to you very closely, looking for some nuance that will corroborate what has already been reported.

Perception Becomes Reality

In a media-driven society, the first reporter's perception can rapidly become reality. Conventional wisdom.

In the cowboy movies of the 30s and 40s, Good Guys wore white hats; Bad Guys, black hats. No shades of gray. Good Guys did not smoke, drink or swear. They were chivalrous, brave, honest, idealistic. No matter how dusty the trail, their rhinestone-studded outfits looked like they'd just came from the cleaners.

Bad Guys smoked foul cigars, slugged down rot-guy whisky and muttered oaths behind scowling eyebrows. They slapped women around, were bullies and cowards (it always took two or three to duke it out with one Good Guy), cheated and stole from their partners and their mothers.

You knew immediately, who was a Good Guy or a Bad Guy.

The news media have set up a very similar morality play. I've isolated eight traits — good and bad — that reporters will look for, and judge you by. There are others, but these are the basics.

The Media Morality Scale

GOOD GUYS	BAD GUYS
Caring, sensitive to family/ human values, quality of life	Lust after money and power — insensitive to human needs
David vs. Goliath — underdogs willing to challenge authority, power against the odds	Bullies who enjoy hurting little people (common perception of large organization CEOs)
Brave risk-takers, particularly if the risk is their job, financial security, or social status	Cowards afraid to risk their job, financial security, or social status
Rugged individualists — eccentrics, to the point of not being tightly wrapped	Conformists with no common sense who worship red tape and rules, are intellectually limited
Conscientious idealists with strong convictions who will stick to those beliefs	No conscience or conviction, will follow the party line or boss's orders without question
Candid, open, willing to take responsibility for mistakes	Secretive, evasive, blame others when things go wrong
A sense of humor, with a humble ability to laugh at themselves	Pompous, arrogant, full of them- selves & their own importance
Fierce competitors who expect to win against all odds	Wimps who give up easily and think of themselves as losers

Let's look more closely at these perceptions that can brand you Good Guy or Bad Guy in the first few moments with a reporter.

 # 1 - Sensitive and Caring

Good Guys care about people. They forget costs when human pain and suffering are involved. They are sensitive to human needs and place them above profits or career. Men who show these traits are especially valued.

Bad Guys love money and power. When was the last time an American movie or novel portrayed the president of a multinational corporation as a warm, loving, sensitive individual who cares about staff, children, puppies, clean air and water? American mythology says CEOs care only about self/power/career/company/money.

Michael Douglas' role in the movie *Wall Street* is the stereotype. CEOs like this reach the top by stabbing colleagues in the back, climbing up the pyramid of dead bodies to the executive suite. This is one of the myths that can be easily reinforced by news media stories. In television, it can be done without saying a word. The edited videotape speaks eloquently.

Isolated Executives Out of Touch

In the 1989 documentary *Roger and Me,* reporter Michael Moore intercuts video of General Motors CEO Roger Smith celebrating at a company Christmas Party while GM employees who have been laid off are being evicted from their homes.

A *60 Minutes* story about hotel magnate Leona Helmsley (before she went to prison for tax evasion) pointedly included a clip in which Helmsley interrupts the interview with Mike Wallace to viciously reprimand a hotel housekeeper.

A network news story in 1998 featured two congressmen who had flown to the Midwest to survey flood damage. They were interviewed in the rain, somebody holding an umbrella over them. Around them were people who had been working the sandbag levees for days. Depressed, muddy, wet, bone-weary people. The congressmen in their suits and ties had not even a fleck of rain on their immaculate clothes. Phonies! the videotape screamed.

Reporters Side With Victims

Are most reporters liberals? Yes. Why?

Reporters tend to identify with society's victims. Victims are news. Victims of natural disasters, medical malpractice, corporate policy, government bumbling. They cooperate with reporters, because the story may help them. Young reporters spend time with them, get to know them as human beings. Imprinting takes place.

Their vision of the world is formed in those early years. Most young reporters have never spent even an hour with a corporate CEO, a general, a governor, the director of the CIA.

Power people are distant, two-dimensional figures. They think they're too busy to make themselves accessible to the media. Reporters never see their human side. They become easy targets. Nothing happens to displace society's myths about them.

2 - David vs. Goliath

The David vs. Goliath story appeals to most Americans. That was the theme of the *Rocky* movies. We admire the town marshal who will go out alone to face the outlaw gang in the street. We love the housewife who fights City Hall. The dark horse who wins the Kentucky Derby or the political campaign. Show me two kids whose lemonade stand is shut down by the Health Department and I will show you an international news story.

Bad Guys are bullies. They take advantage of little people. They abuse their power and get great pleasure doing it. They boast about their position and wealth. Too much money, too much power are never enough.

Ralph Nader - Media Saint

Ralph Nader is probably our most revered media saint. Nader, the poor, young, bright eccentric who does not have a car or a driver's license writes *Unsafe at Any Speed* in 1965 — a book attacking General Motors. The book contends that GM produces cars with deadly design flaws; that the company is more interested in shaving costs than saving lives (Moral # 1).

He is David, choosing the stones for his slingshot while Goliath GM sets out to destroy him and discredit his book. With help from the news media, Nader hits GM between the eyes. The corporate giant is staggered. Corvairs go out of production. Seat belts and head rests become standard equipment.

The bigger they are, the harder they fall.

3 - Risk-Takers

Good Guys are risk-takers. Adventurers. They live on the edge. They thumb their nose at the boss, or company policy, if it feels good. They are particularly valued by the media if they are willing to risk their own job security to help someone else (Moral # 1 again). They are not afraid to fail. They are confident they can find another job if they lose this one.

Bad Guys will sit silently and watch terrible atrocities take place. This is a side effect of Moral # 1. Bad Guys are security-centered. More interested in keeping job, power, money, status than in doing good. They are job cowards.

Fire Me, I Don't Care

Newspaper reporters are paid so little they have very little fear of losing their jobs. At an early age, they become fiercely independent. They have great contempt for the executive who puts job above convictions, whether in government or the private sector.

Looking forward to retirement is not a part of most reporters' personal value system. People who do, in their thinking, are burned out or incompetent. If you work in government, reporters will walk in with a bias.

In TV, Firing is No Disgrace

Television news is one of the few professions where being fired is not a disgrace. It comes with the territory. When ratings stall or begin to slip, management shuffles people, looking for a winning combination. The shuffling is constant. Television people, unlike those in newspapers, work on short-term contracts. Some of television's brightest, most successful stars were fired from TV jobs early in their careers.

4 - Rugged Individualists

Good Guys are rugged individualists who do things their way. They are rebels with glorious causes. They hate red tape, and will find ingenious ways to short-circuit the system to get things done. They love to tweak the nose of pompous authority.

Eccentrics who run for public office or inventors working on the Original Perpetual Motion Machine often get warm, amused, but-you-have-to-admire-them coverage.

Reporters identify with them because good reporting requires a lot of individualism. Reporters develop tough skins. If they are hated and despised, they consider the source and wear it as a badge of honor. Reporters in the field have very little close supervision.

Good reporters are self-starters. Those who are innovative, willing to try anything, often get the story. They leave their habit-bound competitors in the dust.

Bad Guys Are Conformists

This is a side effect of Morals # 1 and # 3. Bad Guys do things by the rules, no matter what the cost in human terms. They believe that one broken rule can lead to the breakdown of the entire system. They are anal. Obsessively cautious.

Bad Guys wallow in red tape. During the Cold War, this part of life in the Soviet Union was frequently reported as a way to deride communism. It is still popular in reporting about new, inexperienced officials in Third World countries.

Journalists sneer at this value system. They believe that those who follow it are corporate drones, cannon fodder, bumbling bureaucrats. Bad Guys slavishly follow the rules because they are not bright enough to turn out the lights without a company manual.

This journalistic prejudice often appears between the lines in stories dealing with religious zealots, union organizers, law enforcement and military officers.

 # 5 - Idealists

Good Guys are idealists who sight on a personal star and never waver. They are persistent. Dedicated. To get gold stars in media coverage, the reporter does not have to agree with your ideals, so long as you truly believe them.

Bad Guys have no real conscience or moral value. They do whatever the job, the boss, the party require. They swing from one position to another, twisting in the political or corporate winds. They don't seem to notice that the position they embrace today was yesterday's anathema.

 # 6 - Candid and Open

Good Guys are candid and open. They have nothing to hide. Their lives and organizations are open books. One of the most disarming tactics you can take with a reporter who seems antagonistic is to offer access to everything. It jams the media morality radar.

Good Guys sometimes make mistakes, but they're big enough to take responsibility for the mistake and put it right. Rather than blame somebody, or invent an alibi, the Good Guy boss takes responsibility for the errors of those he leads.

Bad Guys are secretive and evasive. They do not want their pictures taken. They run. They refuse to disclose information about themselves or their organization. They sic their bodyguards or attack dogs on journalists.

To be truly memorialized as a Bad Guy, put your hand over the camera lens and throw the photographer out of your office.

Bad Guys try to cover their mistakes and blame somebody else when things go wrong.

7 - A Sense of Humor

Good Guys take things in stride. They can laugh at their own mistakes. They tell the uptight people around them to chill out. Good Guys can take a ribbing. It means somebody likes them.

Bad Guys are so full of themselves they can hardly fit in the thrones they've built to make sure the world understands how important they are. Their employees are afraid to tell them the truth about anything that would challenge the boss' self-serving perceptions. A joke about the boss is a firing offense.

8 - Expect to Win

Good Guys are fierce competitors, even when they're at a severe disadvantage. They pick themselves up and charge once more against enormous odds. They expect to win. They never give up.

Bad Guys see themselves as losers. Wimps. They're burned out. They don't even try any more. Reporters believe it is their duty to put losers out of their misery.

Journalists also feel some responsibility to praise winners. The story will have much more appeal if the underdog wins through sheer force of will and determination.

Most reporters are fierce competitors themselves. The business is so competitive, they don't last very long if winning is not a priority. (My analysis of Media Morality fits closely with **STRATEGY/Ten Commandments of Media Relations**)

Seven Deadly Sins

The seven deadly sins enunciated by the Catholic Church in the Middle Ages were pride, covetousness, lust, anger, gluttony, envy and sloth. These sins prevented sinners from reaching a state of grace with God. Until they were conquered, salvation was out of reach.

Modern-day media mavens have created a new list of deadly sins. Acts so heinous, it is the media's divine calling to destroy those who commit them.

The deadly sin is considered a greater offense than the crime it covers. Particularly if the sin is committed by a public official or large corporation. A personal weakness that will always be lurking, and therefore, almost impossible to forgive.

The Deadly Sins are examples of acts committed by Bad Guys; the kinds of things they do because of their character defects.

Today's Deadly Sins

This is my reading of the current deadly sins that can doom you in the media:

- **Hypocrisy**
- **Deception**
- **Insensitivity**
- **Abuse of power**
- **Waste**
- **Incompetence**
- **Cowardice**

Sin # 1 - Hypocrisy

Hypocrisy is by far the worst of the deadly sins as the media see them. Reporters and editors are powerfully driven to unmask those who claim to be virtuous.

The media tend to admire unabashed rascals. Politicians who openly admit playing around and using their office to help their friends. At least they're honest about themselves, if nothing else.

Gary Hart & 'Monkey Business'

Former U. S. Sen. Gary Hart's extra-marital affairs were common gossip among reporters who covered Washington. His womanizing did not become a hanging offense until he claimed to lead a dull, chaste life. When he suggested that reporters follow him around, they did. After they caught him with Donna Rice — and published a picture of the model on Hart's lap aboard the boat "Monkey Business" — his presidential aspirations and his congressional career were over.

The media's rapacious thirst for defrocking hypocrites sometimes becomes absurd. Jimmy Carter portrayed himself as a deeply religious man of strait-laced morality. When he admitted, in a *Playboy* interview, that he had occasionally looked lustfully at women who were not his wife, the admission became a major news story. (See more about hypocrites in the Stereotypical Stories section of **STRATEGY/Selling Your Story**)

Sin # 2 - Deception

Deception is closely linked to hypocrisy. Here, the sinner may not have professed virtue, but because of the sinner's position, we *expect* a higher standard. Deception can be an outright lie. Or less than total honesty. Or a major effort to hide the truth.

Deception was the deadly sin that destroyed Richard Nixon's presidency and forever changed his place in history. There has never been a shred of evidence to suggest that Nixon participated in the plot to break into the Democratic Party office in the Watergate Building, or knew about it in advance.

The cover-up *after* the burglary was the deadly sin Nixon committed that could not be forgiven.

The investigation of Bill and Hillary Clinton by Independent Prosecutor Kenneth Starr quickly switched from the finances at a failed savings and loan association. The major thrust was to find them guilty of perjury or obstruction of justice.

The Monica Lewinsky scandal had sex to make it interesting, but the real sin being pursued by both Starr and the news media was anything Clinton might have done to cover his trail. In this value system, deceiving the public is much worse than adultery.

Sin # 3 - Insensitivity

Insensitivity is the sin of not caring what happens to a helpless victim. Particularly to a child or an animal. The lack of human compassion. Some of history's worst monsters were portrayed in the media as having no sympathy for those who were suffering.

War criminals are guilty of insensitivity. Otherwise, they could not participate in the atrocities. The media portray them as evil personified — the Nazis during World War II; the slaughter of civilians in Viet Nam; the "ethnic cleansing" in Bosnia in the early 1990s; the continuing waves of tribal bloodshed in Africa.

Civil disobedience, as practiced by Martin Luther King Jr. and Mahatma Gandhi, goaded government and police forces to act harshly against their demonstrators. Both King and Gandhi understood that media coverage would portray the authorities as brutal and insensitive. They knew they would eventually defeat their enemies if they could set up situations that showed their enemies' deadly sin - insensitivity.

It is a powerful, perennial human interest story to show wealthy, powerful people who do not seem to care about the poor and hungry. Police brutality is another form of insensitivity often spotlighted by the media.

Sin # 4 - Abuse of Power

Power can be abused in many ways. It is a wonderful media story because it often combines hypocrisy, deception, insensitivity.

By definition, this is a venal act of the powerful. Those in public office. In the public eye. The wealthy. Those we trust. Those who run a large organization, like a church or a charity.

The sexual molestation of children in their parishes by Catholic priests became a major media story in the 1990s.

Sometimes the story is the bribery of public officials. Sometimes it is misuse of semi-public money. The conviction of William Arimony for misusing United Way funds was that kind of case, where he spent money donated for the poor on luxurious travel and girlfriends.

Reporters are especially sensitive to influence peddling. Special treatment for friends of the powerful. It brings out a sense of outrage in readers, viewers and listeners. The reporter who uncovers the abuse of power becomes a very powerful figure. A folk hero of sorts. A slayer of dragons.

Sin # 5 - Waste

Waste also involves a kind of power abuse. Usually the waste of money, resources, or human lives is done by someone in power. Damage to environmental resources that belong to the public and cannot be recovered is now a deadly media sin.

Stories about government and military purchasing often involve this sin. Five-hundred-dollar hammers. Expensive, ergonomic paper clips designed by industrial engineers and consulting firms will always get massive coverage in prime time.

Former U.S. Sen. William Proxmire became a major media figure by periodically giving a cynical "Golden Fleece" award for wasteful government projects. After Proxmire's retirement, *NBC Nightly News* took up the cause with a series of regular stories on "The Fleecing of America." Anchor Tom Brokaw introduced these stories with a sigh and shake of his head.

Sin # 6 - Incompetence

The media love to show how stupid the people and procedures in large organizations can be. Government and the military are favorite targets for stories that show bumbling bureaucrats.

Once the media focus on an agency that has stumbled badly, the system demands a scapegoat — a sacrificial lamb to appease the angry media gods. The media get credit for the kill; politicians get credit for cleaning up the mess; but the basic problem is still there, waiting for someone else to make the same mistake.

Sin # 7 - Cowardice

Bravery under fire has always been the highest value within the military. To run from battle during most recorded military history was considered a capital offense. In the past, many military codes of conduct gave superior officers the power to shoot cowards who refused to fight.

In the same way, the media code of honor makes heroes of those who risk their careers to gain the high ground in government or a large corporation. Whistle blowers are sometimes awarded the Media Medal of Honor.

Those who cower and refuse to do battle for truth and justice are tried on the front pages or the network news magazines. If the media find them guilty, their careers are summarily shot.

SKILLS

Interviews-Broadcast

It's a Conversation While The Camera Eavesdrops

Listening to one end of a telephone conversation, you can usually tell who's on the other end. If it's long distance, most people tend to talk louder. Subconsciously, they think they have to speak up to be heard clearly a thousand miles away. We slow down if we sense that the person at the other end of the line is old, or has a foreign accent. We change the tone of our voice if we're talking to a child, or a lover. The same kind of subtle changes take place when people talk in front of cameras and microphones.

An Audience of One or Two

If they know they're being taped, many people reflexively talk as if they're making a speech at a civic club. There may be half a million people — perhaps more — out there listening. With a crowd that large, you want to make sure the people in the back row hear what you have to say.

But they're not all in one, humongous auditorium.

The broadcast audience is one or two people. It is Joe Six-pack and Aunt Millie, sitting in the living room or kitchen, six or eight feet from the TV set. The radio listener is even closer. Probably in a car. One of the secrets of broadcast interviews is to keep *that* audience in mind.

Radio and television are very intimate. The zoom lens on a camera invades your zone of privacy, moving even closer than a person would, to focus on a drop of sweat, the flared nostrils, the gritted teeth. Radio's microphone puts the person speaking at our shoulder. Sometimes, it whispers in our ear. In the best radio and TV interviews, the people talking seem unaware that we are eavesdropping.

Think of the Living Room

To prepare for a radio or TV interview, change your mind-set so you're talking to that small, intimate audience. It may help you to think of a real living room, and real people. In your mind, think of the reporter as someone else, and that may help. Your spouse, a neighbor, the cashier at the restaurant where you have lunch, the bartender who knows you well enough that you no longer have to order.

Changing your mind-set will change your body language. In the noise and confusion of a political rally, a candidate holds up his arms and flashes a big grin to communicate warmth and charm as he tries to woo the crowd. He uses a very different kind of smile and body language if he's trying to seduce a beautiful woman sitting across the table in a quiet restaurant.

If you think of the large broadcast audience, you will instinctively project your voice to reach them. You don't need to do that. But it takes a lot of practice to squelch that natural inclination. Today's microphones are so sensitive they can pick up a whisper across a room.

Bush's Inaugural Speech

I remember how fascinated I was, watching George Bush (the father) deliver his inaugural address on the steps of the Capitol in Washington. The entire world was watching and listening, via radio and television. There was a live audience of several hundred thousand.

Without training, most of us would have delivered the speech as shouted oratory. Yet Bush never raised his voice.

If Bush *had* raised his voice, it would have been squeaky. Wimpy. So his media trainer, I'm sure, taught him to let the microphone do the amplifying.

For television and radio, the most powerful message is delivered with a whispered shout. It is emotional emphasis and intensity — not loudness — that will get your point across most effectively.

Clinton's Town Meetings

Bill Clinton's best style for TV has always been town meetings. He is at his best talking to a specific person, not the entire crowd. Watch how he does it. A step or two toward the person who asked the question. Intense eye contact to enhance our perception that this is a personal conversation, not a performance.

During interviews and speeches, he is much more wooden. We wonder if he, or a speechwriter, crafted those phrases.

Remember, the camera or microphone is not one of your professional colleagues. It's somebody you just met at a dinner party, who knows absolutely nothing about your job and won't understand its jargon. The camera and microphone are eavesdroppers, not participants in your dialogue with the reporter.

The Camera Spots Phonies

The camera detects phonies. Bring to the conversation the real person inside you, not a front. Let your emotions show, if they're real. You can be angry, or sad, pleased with yourself or your organization, shocked or dismayed at what you've just learned.

The radio or TV reporter does not want many facts or figures when you are being taped.

There is not enough time. You probably don't have the skill to boil down the facts extemporaneously. Even experienced reporters have trouble doing that. To condense them to 20 or 30 seconds may require a half-hour at the keyboard, eliminating a word, rewriting a phrase to save another three or four seconds.

A famous quote, attributed to several people: "I'm writing you a long letter because I didn't have time to write a short one."

The Sony Sandwich

If your interview is taped in the field, it is probably going to be the meat in a Sony Sandwich. What you say in the story — the "sound bite" — will be sandwiched between a reporter's introduction and the reporter's summary or conclusion.

The purpose of the interview is to add the personal, human perspective. In virtually every interview, the reporter at some point will ask you how you feel about the issue or event. The trite "How do you feel?" question is used to get to: What is your reaction?

How you are coping? (See the list of feeling words for interviews in **SKILLS/Interviews-General**)

The Story Comes Alive

Let's diagram the Sony Sandwich. (Next page)

The beginning of the Sony Sandwich is the bottom half of the bun. The reporter quickly sketches the scenario. It is like a line drawing, stark and two-dimensional. When I lecture, I tell my audience the story, at this point, is like a stick drawing of a human figure. We cannot tell whether the person is old or young, tall or short, happy or sad, proud or afraid.

The meat of the sandwich — the interview — gives the stick figure warmth and personality, emotion and flavor, color and dimension. The story comes alive.

The reporter may edit a series of interviews together — different people giving their reactions to, or perspectives on, the same incident. Or the interviews may pit one point of view against another.

A tenant says the landlord refuses to fix the plumbing. Without a pause, the landlord angrily says he's spent $5,000 in the last month on repairs, but the kids in the building tear it up faster than he can fix it. Then the story bounces back to the kids' response.

Editing Distills Conflict

When sound bites are edited against each other, the conflict is distilled quickly and effectively. Instead of watching a ten-round boxing match — mostly dancing, feinting and clinches — we get to see and hear just the knockdowns.

Occasionally, if the sound bite is very strong, it will be placed at the beginning of the reporter's story. In this position, it is usually very short. Then a longer portion of the interview, expanding that opening bite, goes in the middle of the story.

Job Conditioning

People in certain professions are interviewed more often than others. The ones who get the hang of it find reporters coming back to them on future stories. They make the reporter's job so much easier. Unfortunately, the experience and training for some careers tend to make some people poor interviewees.

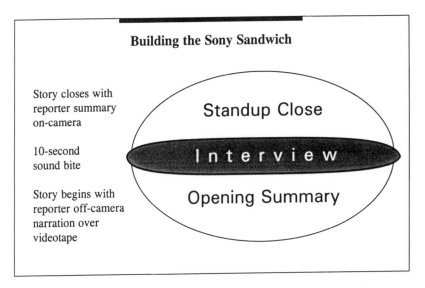

Building the Sony Sandwich

Story closes with
reporter summary
on-camera

10-second
sound bite

Story begins with
reporter off-camera
narration over
videotape

Standup Close

Interview

Opening Summary

Doctors, lawyers, scientists and accountants are often terrible on camera. They speak their own, professional jargon, as though we, too, had Ph.Ds in their specialty.

They provide dry, lengthy, logical, step-by-step reasoning, with lots of footnotes. The subject matter is complicated. The simplest question takes three minutes to answer.

This kind of interview is a horror to edit. The people interviewed call the next day to complain that they were quoted out of context. (See **INSIDE THE MEDIA/Editing**)

Human Synthesizers

On-camera, police and military officers often become voice synthesizers spouting official reports.

The cop who just caught two armed robbers after a shoot-out speaks very normally until the camera comes. Then he says something like:

> *My unit was dispatched to 4481 Ocean Street at nineteen hundred hours. As I approached, Code Three, I observed two white males rapidly exiting the dispatched location in an easterly direction with weapons drawn. When the perpetrators observed my vehicle, they commenced firing. One projectile impacted my vehicle. I then returned fire.*

What Did He Say?

What did he say? I think he said:

"As I rolled up, these two guys with guns were running out of the jewelry store. They saw the patrol car and started shooting. When the first bullet hit the windshield, I jumped out and shot back."

Which leads to the reporter's question:

"You ever been shot at before?"

"Nope."

"How did it feel?"

"Scared the hell out of me."

Guess which section of the interview is certain to be included in the Sony Sandwich. Police officers, doctors, lawyers, accountants have been conditioned to talk like robots by writing too many reports, and by testifying in court. On the witness stand, you are not allowed to express how you feel. Just the facts, please.

What Are We Afraid Of?

Survey after survey has shown that stage fright is America's biggest fear. Bigger than war, cancer, divorce, dying in a plane crash. What are we so afraid of onstage?

I think we're afraid of looking stupid.

People in front of a camera often talk non-conversation because they're afraid they'll make a mistake and look dumb. They're not sure the boss will like the idea of their talking to a TV reporter. So they cram and memorize, to avoid mistakes. They want to be walking encyclopedias. Instead, they look like stupid drones. The one thing they most fear.

Other people deal with the stress by drawing themselves into tight little knots, making their voices small and flat, and saying every word very carefully. They pause a lot. On TV or radio, they are deadly. More than five seconds, and everybody in the audience will be snoring.

What Does It All Mean?

The closing section of the Sony Sandwich is also formularized. The reporter sums up the story. Tells us what to expect next. Here's the form:

What does it all mean? Only time will tell. I'm Tom Trite,
Channel Four, Action News.

Listen to how TV reporters almost always build their closing
standups around this basic blueprint. The close to an interview with
the Speaker of the House:

Does this mean the tax bill is dead? We won't know until
the conference committee issues its final report — probably
tomorrow. I'm Claudia Cliche ... yada, yada.

Or the close to a story about an airline crash:

Was the explosion aboard the plane caused by a bomb, or
was it mechanical failure? Safety Board sources say it will
take months of meticulous detective work before they know
for sure. I'm Bill Bromide ... yada, yada.

Inverted Pyramid Formula

The old news story formula — developed by newspapers in the
1800s — was called the inverted pyramid. At the beginning of the
story — into the first paragraph, if possible — the reporter tried to
cram all the important facts. Who, What, When, Where, Why.

From that broad beginning, the story narrowed down to a point
at the bottom where unimportant details were thrown in. Pure
trivia. The inverted pyramid had several practical purposes. Correspondents in far away places (St. Louis was the edge of civilization
in those days) sent their stories to New York or Washington by
telegraph.

The telegraph was not very reliable. So if it failed sometime
during transmission, the home office would at least have the important stuff. If the entire story reached the newspaper, readers knew
they could drop off in mid-story and not miss anything critical.

In those days, newspaper stories were set in lead type. Down
in the composing room, they had to fit each line of type into a page
form. If they didn't fit, the employees in the composing room were
told to cut from the bottom until they did fit. Just throw away the
last paragraph. Maybe two paragraphs. There were huge barrels
where the lead type was thrown to be recycled.

They were not editors. They were craftsmen. As a result, stories sometimes seemed to have been edited with a meat ax.

The Sandwich Spreads

Because the Sony Sandwich works so well, both radio and newspapers have adopted it for their own use. Almost all radio stories that include an interview will be in Sony Sandwich form.

Newspaper stories have become much shorter, and the Sony Sandwich has been adopted by newspapers, too. Examine the stories in *USA Today*. A quick summary of the facts in the first paragraph or two, setting up the quotes of the person interviewed in paragraphs three and four. Then two or three paragraphs to tell us what it all means, and only time will tell.

> **The Sony Sandwich formula will help you craft a quote that will be used exactly as you said it — without editing — in newspapers, radio or TV.**

If you can learn to do this, you'll seldom be misquoted or taken out of context. You'll find your interviews go very quickly. As soon as the reporter hears the magic, formula quote, it's time to pack up and move on to the next assignment.

My FACE Formula

I invented the FACE Formula to help you remember what kind of quotes the reporter is looking for. If you're the subject of the interview, we're going to see your face on TV, and probably your picture in the newspaper. In radio, we'll imagine what you look like. Keep these factors in mind:

- **F** eelings
- **A** nalysis
- **C** ompelling C's
- **E** nergy

Reporters are going to ask you about the facts, but the facts will usually not appear in quotes. What appears in quotes in newspapers — and what we hear you say in radio and TV — will *almost always* be your response to "How do you feel about ... ?"

In a few stories, your analysis of something will appear in quotes or the sound bite. Let's look at each factor in the formula:

F — Feelings. Let the audience know what you're feeling. Go back from time to time and review the Sony Sandwich formula to help you reflexively craft quotes that begin with how you feel. (More about this in **SKILLS/Interviews-General**)

A — Analysis. Give them your assessment of the situation. In one phrase or sentence, tell them what the bottom line is. The audience wants your expert opinion on the subject. That's why the reporter is talking to you. But to avoid the cutting room floor, the expert must be able to translate into everyday language.

> **If you use numbers, they are meaningless unless you put the numbers in perspective.**

Many experts speak in strange tongues. After the reporter has said there seems to be no danger from the accident within the nuclear power plant, an internationally recognized expert says on camera:

We've put the effluent through exhaustive electron microscopy plus radiofluorocarbon laser analysis and we come up with a count of point four, seven, zero micro-mini roentgens.

Translated, with perspective:

You'd get more radiation sitting in front of a television set for two hours than you would if you took a bath in the water that leaked out.

C — The Compelling C's. Most news stories revolve around at least one of these basic elements. Notice the feeling words:

- **Catastrophe** — "I'm afraid. We're facing a global disaster if we don't change the way we dispose of toxic waste."

- **Crisis** — "I'm astounded by their stupidity. The tidal surge will sweep across the highway and cut off their escape route if they don't leave now."

- **Conflict** — "I hate him and everything he stands for. I'll fight him to my last breath."

- **Change** — "I'm confident things are going to be different around here when we control the Legislature."

- **Crime and Corruption** — "I grieve for the victims of this horrible crime. And I'm resolved to find who did it."

- **Color** — (We used to call it human interest.) "I'm really amused. Anyone who believes that also believes thunder curdles milk."

- **Celebrity-ness** — "I'm awed by his technical skill. He can manipulate that computer the way Michael Jordan controls a basketball."

E — Energy. There is one major difference in talking for television and talking to your friends in their living room. To be effective on camera, your conversation must project energy. Like a salesperson who must believe in the product, you must show that you truly believe what you're saying. Since so many stories for television news involve conflict and imminent danger, you must convince us — through the energy you invest in what you're saying — that we ought to be concerned, too.

Executive Cool = Dull

Some executives in high-pressure jobs adopt a cool, clinical personality that says to their employees, "I know exactly what I'm doing. If the building were on fire, I could lead you to safety." That deliberate, slow, calculating style can appear, on TV or radio, to be boredom, disinterest, or a mask for insecurity.

I constantly tell my clients that they need to see themselves on videotape to know what they really look like. In our minds, we have imbedded high school yearbook photos of ourselves. That image distorts our perception of ourselves. The mirror lies. The person I see when I shave is about 15 years and 15 pounds lighter than the person I see on videotape.

The TV Time Warp

There is a major distortion when we watch interviews played back on television. Time slows down.

Five seconds of dead air seems like a minute. Unless they inject energy into what they say, our perception of people talking on TV is that they are incredibly dull and boring.

Why does that happen? I think I have the answer. Have you ever been in a life-threatening crisis where everything seemed to go into slow motion? I've questioned hundreds of people in my workshops about these experiences. It seems to be universal. In the moments before the automobile accident, they watched the oncoming car spinning gracefully, edging closer, as they carefully analyzed whether it would hit them.

Life-Threatening Crises

A pilot told about losing an engine on takeoff. It seemed to take half a day to turn the plane and get it back on the ground. A scuba-diver ran out of air and made a desperate attempt to reach the surface. He drowned, but was rescued by his buddies and resuscitated. The time between his realizing the air tank was empty and unconsciousness seemed like hours.

A cop was shot. The bullet knocked him on his back. As he fell, he was able to pull his pistol and fire three times before he hit the ground. It was easy to do, he said, because it seemed like he was suspended in mid-air for about five minutes. One of his shots hit his assailant in the chest.

The technical name for the phenomenon is tachypsychia. Part of it is caused by the sudden dump of adrenaline into your bloodstream. And part is your total focus on the threat to your life.

Our Perception Changes Time

It is my theory that when we watch a television screen, we are focused just enough to change our perception of time.

I see this happen regularly in my seminars. I videotape an interview and then we have instant replay. The person who seemed to be speaking in a normal voice just a few seconds ago now seems — on tape — to have lost energy and conviction. I believe the tape is accurate. It is our perception that robs the interview of energy and passion.

By studying yourself on videotape, you can learn to inject just the right amount of energy to make our perception of you on videotape match what we see in real life.

Forget About Memorizing

In preparing for an interview, don't memorize, or write out what you intend to say when the camera or tape recorder is rolling. It makes the interview seem staged and rehearsed. Statements read at live presidential press conferences are about the only prepared statements that make the air, unedited.

Winning with the News Media

I recommend that before the interview, you go over in your mind the main points you'd like the story to include. You need to have a central theme in your head, and some sub-sections that connect to that central idea. No more than three. If you're afraid the stress of the interview will make you forget, write yourself a cheat sheet, the same way students cheat on exams.

Using a Cheat Sheet

The cheat sheet should be one-word cues — bullet points — that will refresh your memory if your mind goes blank. Put the cheat sheet where you can glance down at it if you need to.

For TV, the trick is to suddenly look thoughtful, pause and glance down as if you're thinking deeply, then look back at the reporter to finish the thought. This is a natural head movement in normal conversation. Nobody will know you cheated if you do it carefully. For radio, you don't even need to hide the cheat sheet.

Writing the key points helps you remember. Having the cheat sheet handy is an assuring psychological crutch. If it's there, you probably won't need it. Remember — unless it's a 30-minute talk show in the studio, you have to *condense, condense, condense*. In public speaking courses, the instructor gives you a subject and forces you to make an immediate, extemporaneous talk. The exercise teaches you to think and talk on your feet.

Some Training Exercises

To train yourself for broadcast interviews, try to say how you feel about a difficult subject — and three reasons why you feel that way — in 12 seconds or less. Pick tough, complicated subjects and practice with a tape recorder or video camera. In one sentence, say how you feel — and why — about difficult subjects like:

Legalized abortion	**Gun control**
Capital punishment	**Prayer in schools**
Ethnic job quotas	**The welfare system**

There is no quick miracle drug, no magic diet, no futuristic exercise machine to make you an instant success. It takes tough, conscientious mental calisthenics if you want to be truly good at it. This exercise, practiced regularly, will develop your mental agility for condensing what you know and feel about complicated subjects.

Congressional Pros

The real pros of TV interviewing are congressional leaders who've been interviewed several times a day for 20 years. They develop stopwatches in their heads. Before the camera rolls, they discuss the story with the reporter. They get some idea of how their quotes will be used.

"How much time do you need?" the congressman says, clearing his throat and brushing his hair aside.

"About 12 seconds," the reporter tells him.

"OK. Ready?"

"Rolling."

The congressman speaks for 12 seconds. Perhaps 11. Sometimes, 13. And then he stops. He has learned the language, and the game. He edits himself. There can be no distortion. He is rarely quoted out of context.

You Can Do It, Too

Most of those who've learned to speak in sound bites did it the hard way, through trial and error. For many, it became a self-defense tactic. The news media are kinder to some people than others. One person's slip is never aired. Another, similar stumble becomes the comedy element in tonight's news.

Watch and listen to TV and radio news. Make notes on the people who are effective in their interviews. Learn from the mistakes and blunders of other people.

Watch the Process

If you're in a position where you expect to be interviewed regularly, ask for a guided tour of the local newsroom and editing facilities. If you can, spend a day with a TV reporter and camera crew. Watch them shoot, write, and edit a story. The more familiar you become with the entire process, the easier it will be to adapt your speaking style to the medium.

Learning to speak Media Language requires some concentration and hard work. But it's a lot easier than Spanish or German.

You can do it.

Antagonistic interviews are covered in **SKILLS/Defending Yourself**. For now, let's assume the reporter is friendly, or at least neutral — neither warm nor cold. Most radio interviews, and many newspaper interviews, will be done by telephone. There are special hazards there. (See **SKILLS/Interviews-General**)

Do TV Interviews Early

If you set up an appointment for a TV interview, try to make it at least four hours before the newscast. The closer to air time, the more harried the crew. They'll do a better job of lighting, shooting and editing if they're not pressed against their deadline.

Choose Your Turf

Choose a place that's comfortable for you. If possible, one that fits the story. If you're a doctor, and you'll be talking about a new surgical technique, do the interview with a backdrop that says *medicine*. If you're a computer programmer, let us see a monitor and keyboard behind you. It's a real advantage if viewers who turn on their sets in the middle of the interview know at a glance this story has something to do with doctors or computers.

If you're more comfortable standing while you talk, suggest that to the TV crew. When some people sit down, it appears — on camera — as if they've let the air out. They go flat. Their entire speech pattern changes. You'll have to watch yourself on videotape to see if this happens to you.

Don't Cram

For the interview, you don't need to do any cramming. If you, the expert, can't remember, how do you expect viewers to retain what you say? The reporter doesn't want statistics on camera.

Go over the numbers before, or after, the interview. Most people can't absorb spoken statistics. They *do* remember analogies and perspective. "The money we'll spend this year treating this disease would buy everybody in the state a new Lexus."

Provide Graphs & Charts

If the audience is to retain numbers, the story will have to be told with graphs and charts that put them in perspective. Seeing the numbers on the screen helps people remember them. Most reporters in major cities would not think of printing or broadcasting a news release exactly as you wrote it. But they will often use your graphs or charts with no editing whatever. Every Windows word processing program has graph and charting capability. Your providing graphics will help the story immensely.

TV Crew Pecking Order

You should know there is a rigid pecking order within a TV news crew. In most places, the photographer works under the direction of the reporter. The sound technician or grip (rapidly becoming extinct with the advent of lighter, more compact equipment) is considered the photographer's assistant.

For network interviews, the story producer often accompanies the correspondent. The producer may come ahead of the correspondent to gather information, scout interviews and shooting locations.

The correspondent makes more money and technically has more authority than the producer. But the producer often does more reporting than the correspondent. For many stories, the producer even does some of the on-camera interviews. The producer and correspondent then work jointly later, editing it all together.

Help — Don't Push

If the reporter doesn't introduce the other crew members to you, introduce yourself. Remember, the photographer is the one with the power to make the shot flattering, or downright ugly. It never hurts to be on good terms.

You can suggest a place for the interview, but leave the final decision up to the crew. There may be some technical problem with the spot you've suggested. It will take about 15 minutes to set up the equipment. It helps if you know where the electrical panel is, in case their lights overload a circuit.

If the crew is using a small "peanut" mike that clips to your clothing, try to hide the cord. Run the wire inside your shirt or blouse to the waist, then inside your waistband to one side. (See **SKILLS/Talk Shows** for more ideas and illustrations)

There's always a clumsy moment when a male crew member tries to clip the mike to a woman's blouse. Help him, so he doesn't feel like he's groping you; and to prevent the clip on the mike from damaging your clothes.

Forget the Mike

If they're using a hand-held mike, the tendency is to lean down, or toward the mike. You don't have to do that. It makes you look stoop-shouldered. Forget about the mike. Picking up good sound is their job. If you're not speaking loudly enough, they'll tell you, or move the mike.

Talk to the Reporter

During the interview, talk to the reporter, not the camera. The camera is there, listening to the conversation, but it doesn't ask questions. If you answer into the camera, the audience reacts. The reporter asked the question — why are you giving *me* the answer?

Another fine point — look at the reporter's eye that is closest to the camera. In normal conversation, we switch back and forth between the eyes of the person we talk to. If the camera zooms in very tightly, we will see your eyes darting back and forth. You make us think you're shifty. Scared. Guilty.

By looking at the reporter's eye nearest the camera, we'll see more of your face, but you won't be looking at the camera.

Try not to blink too much. That can also be interpreted as a sign of stress or deception.

Swivel Chair Hazards

Swivel chairs are a real hazard. You'll want to rock. Stress makes you twist back and forth *while* you rock. They squeak. The viewer gets seasick as you bob up and down on the tube.

Avoid couches and overstuffed chairs where you sink so deeply your hands on the arms of the chair are at shoulder level. Looks like you're hanging from parallel bars.

Sit Up and Lean Forward

Don't lean back in the chair, whether it's hard or soft. Leaning back changes your body English. You tell us, without words, that you're not very enthusiastic about what you're saying.

To convey a sense of energy and interest, lean slightly forward. TV anchors sit on the edge of the chair with one leg extended. Straightens the spine. I teach witnesses in trials and legislative hearings to sit the same way. It adds authority. Try it.

There's No Hurry

Take your time. If you start a sentence that gets tangled and confused, start again. That's what editing is for.

If you don't understand the question, say so.

If you're nervous and your mouth is dry, stop for a drink of water. Keep thinking of the living room and the friend or neighbor you're talking to. That will relieve the nervousness. If the lights heat up the room and you begin to sweat, suggest that you take a break to let the air conditioner catch up. Once the camera is rolling, most people give up all control of their lives to the TV crew. Don't do that. Take more control. Like:

You know, I gave you an answer several minutes ago that took me much too long to get to the point. If you'll ask me that same question again, I think I can give you a better, shorter answer.

Short and Simple

Try to talk in short, simple sentences. Lawyers and professors have a tendency to speak in outlined, organized form — firstly, secondly, thirdly — or to label their points A, B and C. Suppose the reporter is only interested in your third point, and you've run the words together, so they can't edit out "thirdly." They may have to throw away the entire section.

Other common phrases like "first of all" and "as I said earlier" can create editing nightmares. There may not be enough time in a news story to let you say it twice, or to include your "first of all" point. If you drop the "as I said earlier" in the middle of a sentence, the entire sentence may have to be dumped.

Talk to the Jury

Some of the best on-camera interviews are with trial lawyers who've spent their entire careers summing up complicated cases for jurors.

They keep it short and simple, conversational and colorful. They're good at one-sentence conclusions jurors will remember and repeat to each other in the jury room.

For the main point, they let their feelings show. Jurors are very much like those people sitting in front of the television set after a hard day's work. They're easily bored. They want it simple. They want it interesting. They want to know what it was really like. How did it feel?

Eliminate Parentheticals

Any kind of parenthetical thought can make a sentence too long for radio and television.

Example:

I've come to believe, as most of my constituents do, who've had any experience with firearms, that every person in this country has the God-given right to own a gun.

It can be edited easier if the senator says:

I believe every person in this country has the God-given right to own a gun. I'm sure most of my constituents who have any experience with firearms feel the same way I do.

With this version, the reporter can use either sentence, or both. The two sentences can be separated to punctuate different points in different parts of the story.

Anticipate the Why

Another technique that can help the editing process:

QUESTION: Then you will not vote, Senator, to outlaw Saturday Night Specials?

ANSWER: No.

QUESTION: Why?

ANSWER: The Saturday Night Special is a phony issue.

QUESTION: Why do you say that?

ANSWER: Most police officers, and most store clerks are killed with expensive weapons. Why should the poor home-owner be denied a weapon he can afford to protect himself and his family?

If you give a "Yes" or "No" answer, it will almost always be followed by "Why?" Anticipate the Why. And if you repeat the question as part of your answer, it saves valuable response time between questions and answers. This answer will enable the reporter to cram the entire response into about two-thirds as much time:

QUESTION: Then you will not vote, Senator, to outlaw Saturday Night Specials?

ANSWER: I will never vote to outlaw Saturday Night Specials. They're a phony issue. Most police officers ... etc.

Incorporating the question into your answer allows the reporter to drop the sound bite into the story without having to set up what you were asked.

Don't Date What You Say

Try not to date what you're saying, particularly if the interview will not be used today. If you talk about something that happened today, or predict what will happen tomorrow, it won't be accurate if the story runs on the early morning news tomorrow, or next week.

Show Me While You Tell Me

What the audience *sees*, if you're genuine, may communicate more than what they *hear*.

Years ago, advertising agencies learned how to use visual signals in print. A lot can be said in a picture that doesn't require words. Because of television's time limitations, that technique has become a science. The real message is visual, not verbal.

Luxury car commercials tell us about the wonderful engineering or handling of the automobile. But the more powerful message is what we see. The owner is pulling up to a home that cost several million dollars. Sliding behind the wheel at the country club, or at the airport, with a corporate jet in the background. And, of course, there is a trophy wife or husband in the passenger seat. The key visual message: If you're rich, sophisticated, influential, sexually attractive, you'll drive this car.

Visual Shorthand

Politicians have learned to use visual symbolism to communicate with their constituents. After a flood or earthquake, it is now a tribal ritual for the governor — dressed in fatigues and combat boots — to survey the damage from a National Guard helicopter.

Is that really necessary? Can't governors get reports from experts who are better equipped to assess the damage? Yes, but we've come to expect a personal visit. If we don't see the governor, the president or the vice president at the scene of a major disaster, we think they don't care.

I do a lot of law enforcement training. Chiefs and sheriffs worry about what they will say the day an officer is killed in the line of duty. I tell them I'm much more concerned about what the public will *see* you doing, than in what you will *say*. You need to be seen at the scene, at the hospital, at the officer's home. And if you're not at the funeral, kiss the job good-bye. *Being there* speaks volumes. *Not being there* also delivers a powerful message.

The Great Communicator

Ronald Reagan's popularity was helped immeasurably by his understanding of the camera and the need to be seen *doing* something rather than talking about it. Do you think he really liked to chop wood on his ranch in California?

More likely, his media managers decided it would convey other, unspoken messages about him if he were photographed, early in his first term, clearing brush and chopping firewood. They frequently arranged for him to be photographed on horseback. The John Wayne image never hurt a politician.

Clothing Messages

The clothes you wear are part of the visual shorthand. When he was president, Jimmy Carter liked to be interviewed in a plaid shirt and sweater. To enhance his "just plain folks" image, Carter often carried a piece of luggage when he was embarking from a plane or helicopter — even though a small army of aides and Secret Service agents were there, empty-handed.

Richard Nixon wanted to suggest a more regal kind of presidency. You sometimes wondered if he slept in a coat and tie.

Retirement festivities for admirals and generals are normally a sea of dress uniforms, gold braid and ceremonial swords. At General Norman Schwarzkopf's retirement, the special guests were splendid in their spit-and-polish best.

But not the retiree. Schwarzkopf wore his desert fatigues and combat boots — the same uniform we had seen him wear all through the recent Gulf War.

There was a message there.

Coats and Ties

A CEO wearing his coat and tie behind an immaculate desk tells us, subliminally, that he is a figurehead who is aloof, unfamiliar with his employees, and rarely gets involved in the nuts and bolts of running the company. A paper-shuffler.

Let's design another scenario. The desktop has some papers scattered on it, with a computer at one side. That same CEO has his coat off, tie loosened, sleeves rolled up. Now we get the impression that he is hands-on, hard-working, personally involved.

I suggest to my clients that if they normally come to work in business clothes, they should also keep some more casual clothes at the office, for interviews in the field where office attire may be out of place.

Business Casual

In 2000, some studies showed 60 per cent of the offices in America have now extended "casual Friday" to casual dress every day. Even high-end law and accounting firms.

The Silicon Valley culture is partly responsible. Young, billionaire high-tech CEOs don't even own business suits. There is now a demeaning term for those who dress that way — "the suits."

If most Americans no longer wear the more formal business outfits to work, the message you give them if you're interviewed in that kind of clothing may be that you're old, out-of-date, uninvolved in the real work your company does.

In Early TV, Blue Was White

In the early days of television news, men were told to wear blue shirts. That's because they were shooting black-and-white film. A white shirt glowed in the harsh light and high-contrast film. A blue shirt *looked* white when the film was broadcast. With color cameras, white looks white, and blue looks blue.

Generally, your clothes for television should be subdued. Plain, solid colors are best. Stay away from stripes, checks and bold prints. Make the clothes fit the story and the place you're being interviewed. A power business suit for an interview in your living room will seems as ridiculous as a tuxedo or evening dress at Burger King.

> **If we remember what you were wearing, you wore the wrong thing.**

Don't Get a Haircut

If you know the camera is coming, don't go to the beauty salon or the barber shop. We will probably be able to tell that you spruced up for the interview. Remember, this is a spontaneous, unrehearsed conversation, not a portrait gallery.

Flashy Jewelry Distracts

The goal: Don't let anything about your appearance distract from what you're saying. Large, flashy jewelry is so distracting we may not pay attention to what you're saying.

Wear Your Eyeglasses

If you normally wear eyeglasses, wear them for the interview. Without them, your eyes will have to work harder. You'll squint. There will be a crease through your sideburns and depressions in your nose where the glasses were before the interview.

But don't wear dark glasses for TV interviews. In this culture, you're supposed to look people in the eye when you talk to them. The stereotyped movie hoodlum wears dark glasses during conversations — perhaps to hide the evil thoughts his eyes would reveal if we could see them.

Prescription glasses that darken in sunlight may also turn dark in TV lighting. If you have light-sensitive lenses, and know you'll be talking before a camera often, buy another pair with regular lenses. If you're going to do a lot of TV interviews, have your optician treat the lenses with the invisible, anti-reflective coating that television reporters and anchors use.

Squinting in Sunlight

If you're being interviewed in bright sunlight, it is almost impossible not to squint. Try this:

Just before the camera starts rolling, close your eyes and look up at the sun. Tell the reporter what you're doing. The bright light coming through your closed eyelids will contract your pupils. When the camera's rolling, bring your head back down and open your eyes. Because the pupils are already contracted, you won't sense the glare as much. If you have to talk very long, though, you'll start squinting again.

Modern-day cameras can shoot in the shade. The result is more flattering for most people. Some young, inexperienced photographers may not know that. Tell the camera person your eyes are unusually sensitive to bright light. Can we shoot in the shade?

In-Studio Makeup

A suntan makes you look healthier and younger. A *sunburn* makes your skin shiny and puffy. For field interviews, women should wear the same makeup they'd wear to work. In a TV studio, the light will be much brighter and harsher. Use heavier makeup, with eye shadow and cheek blush a little darker.

Outside the studio, men don't normally use makeup. If you're bald, use rubbing alcohol to wipe away the shiny forehead just before the interview. Give it time to evaporate, so you don't smell like you've been drinking it.

To look normal in the studio, you need to wipe pancake makeup across your beard area and the shiny places. The floor crew will have makeup and a communal sponge. You may want to bring your own. It's available in most drug stores, in different shades to match skin tone. To apply, wet a small sponge, rub it on the hard cake of makeup, and then wipe it on your face. It doesn't smell, and will wash off easily when the interview's over.

Receding hairlines and noses are particularly shiny in bright studio lights. Some men with dark beards look like they just left skid row, even if they shave just before they go to the TV station.

The idea is to apply just enough makeup to look normal through the eye of a studio camera. If it's done right, you can walk out of the studio and nobody will know you're wearing it.

In the TV Studio

Interviews in the studio use many of the same techniques as field interviews, but are also different in some ways. You need to understand the differences. Some field interview techniques used in a talk show will make you look like a wind-up toy. For a preview of what the TV studio is going to feel like and the difference in techniques, see **SKILLS/Talk Shows**.

Live Remotes

The most difficult of all TV interviews is the live remote. Most local stations have the ability to beam back to the studio audio and video that can be broadcast live during the newscast.

The toughest live interview format involves your having a conversation with an anchor, back in the studio, whom you can't see. In this format, you talk to the camera lens. To the audience, it looks like you're talking to the anchor.

You'll have to wear an earphone to hear the anchor. Television reporters have their earphones custom-molded, like a hearing aid, to improve the quality of the sound.

Get a Better Ear Bug

But they'll give you a clumsy ear "bug" with a bent wire that hangs it loosely over your ear. It will be hard to hear what the anchor is saying. You often see live shots where the person on the street has one hand pressing an ear, head tilted. They're pushing the earphone tighter, straining to hear.

If you know you're going to be interviewed regularly in live shots, it's a good investment to have a custom earphone. They're made at hearing aid shops. Call local news directors to get any special technical requirements used in your community.

Reading the Details

As a television reporter, I developed the technique of ad-libbing live remotes, but pausing to read exact words from an important document. It adds authority and credibility. If three legislators had been indicted, I'd be live, outside the courthouse, with the indictment in my hand.

After summarizing the breaking news, I'd say, "Let me read for you exactly what the grand jury said." I'd have a sentence marked; read it, then continue off-the-cuff until I reached another section where I wanted to use the grand jury's exact words.

If your interview is a live shot, the pressure to condense is greater than in any other interview form. There's no chance to edit, and very little opportunity to use cutaways and other video techniques that can keep viewers visually interested while you talk.

If you don't say it quickly, they'll cut you off.

SKILLS

Interviews-General

Quotable Quotes That Won't Be Misquoted

When reporters want an interview, the most basic rule is:

Give Yourself Time to Think Before You Talk.

The quotes that people regret are usually said reflexively, in the traumatic surge of anger or shock that follows a rude surprise or sudden loss. If you can stall for even five minutes, you'll do a better job of speaking for yourself or your organization.

If Your Pulse Races, Pause

The rule is especially critical if the reporter's first question makes your adrenaline surge or pulse rate jump. You won't think well in the fight-or-flee mode. You need a little time to get back to normal. To get your thoughts together.

If the reporter shows up unexpectedly, find an excuse to delay for a few minutes. If the reporter calls on the phone, say "I'm really busy." (Which is true. You've got a lot to do in the next few minutes.) "Can I call you back in about 10 minutes?"

In that brief conversation, get a grasp of what the story is about. Then hang up and spend 10 minutes getting ready.

Use the time to decide what you really want to say. Boil it down to one sentence you can speak without taking a breath. That one sentence will become the base of the interview. Other thoughts will branch out from it. You'll want to keep coming back to it. Explaining it. Expanding it.

Repeat The Central Idea

Always go into an interview with one central idea you want to get across. And repeat it often. In normal conversation, if you repeat yourself, we wonder if you're getting senile. But in a news interview, if you say it often enough, at least one of those quotes or sound bites that states the central idea is more likely to be used.

In normal conversation, we build up to our conclusion. We lay the groundwork first, before we get to the point.

In media interviews, the process is reversed.

Always give the conclusion first. Then tell us how you got there. This takes practice. It's like telling a joke, punch-line first.

Check With Staff

During that 10-minute reprieve before you call the reporter back, check with your staff. "A reporter just called. The lead they're pursuing caught me completely by surprise. Is there something I should know?"

The delay rule isn't necessary if the reporter's request is for simple information that poses no threat. But if you react viscerally, buy some time.

Telephone Interviews

Many of your routine interviews will be on the telephone. Reporters save time by gathering quotes and information this way. Be careful. A reporter on the telephone is less threatening than in person. Many people are less cautious when they can't see the reporter. They say things they later regret.

Try standing while you talk on the telephone. This keeps some people more alert and aware that anything they say may be quoted.

If the interview is critical to you or your organization, *do it in person, if possible*. It's much easier for you to get a handle on the reporter and the story angle if you're face-to-face.

If you don't recognize the name or voice of the reporter on the phone and the story is sensitive, use the delay tactic. When you return the call, look up the number in the phone book, to make sure the call is legitimate. The number the caller gave you may bypass the switchboard. Private eyes, insurance investigators, and business competitors sometimes pose as journalists.

Are You Being Taped?

You should know whether the reporter is recording the interview at the other end of the phone line. In some states, you don't have to tell the other party you're recording. In states with more restrictive laws, failure to notify the other person is a crime. (See **INSIDE THE MEDIA/Privacy**)

Ambushes on Radio

Radio talk show hosts delight in calling people — particularly public officials — for an instant, live interview. FCC regulations require them to tell you you're on the air. Which means instant stress. It's radio's version of the ambush interview.

Review the ambush interview portion of **SKILLS/Defending Yourself**. The suggestions for dealing with a TV ambush can easily be adapted for radio.

Once you begin a telephone or face-to-face interview, where you've had time to think about what you want to say, the next rule is: **Conduct a Pre-Interview-Interview.**

The Pre-Interview-Interview

From the first contact, where you arranged to delay the interview for a few minutes, you know generally what the story is about. When you call back, or the reporter arrives, expand that inquiry. Weave it into the social chat that begins most conversations. While a television photographer is setting up the lights and camera, talk to the reporter about the story at hand.

If you understand what the reporter is after, you can save a lot of time and anxiety. In this conversation before the shorthand pad or recorder is at work, you should learn some basics:

- What exactly is the story assignment, and who thought it up
- When the story will run, and the deadline for finishing it
- How much time or space the story will be given
- Who else the reporter has interviewed
- Any other research that's been done
- The reporter's knowledge and preconceptions on this subject
- Some idea of the reporter's intelligence and experience

What is the Story About?

This is a very important thing you need to know, so you can judge whether the reporter is working on a preconceived concept that may be misguided. If that's the case, you'll have to work very hard to swing the story in another direction.

Particularly if the misconception came from the reporter's editor. The reporter doesn't want to go back empty-handed. You'll have to work *very* hard to convince the reporter the story concept should be abandoned.

Are They Here To Hurt You?

Before the real interview begins, you should have a good idea about whether the reporter is here to gut you, or simply needs your quotes to fill out the story. To give it authority and credibility.

Young, inexperienced reporters are rarely given tough investigative assignments. If the reporter seems very sharp, that should be a warning flag.

As an investigative reporter, the interview with my target was the last stop before I wrote the story. I wanted to know as much as possible before the confrontation, so I'd know if my target was lying.

Good investigative reporters can also con you into believing they're dumb and innocent, so you'll talk a lot more freely.

You May Need More Data

You may learn in the pre-interview-interview that you need to gather some more written information to help you recall exact facts and figures.

If you discover the reporter knows very little about the subject matter, you have a great opportunity to steer the story your way. The way you structure the pre-interview-interview can strongly influence the questions when the real interview begins.

The room will sound like an echo chamber. The reporter will ask you questions that let you repeat what you said before the note-taking or recording began. That's all the reporter knows to ask. Avoid the temptation to educate the reporter too much. (See more on the pre-interview-interview and how to deflect pre-conceived story ideas in **STRATEGY/Accuracy**)

Pre-interview Ethics

It is considered unethical for a reporter to tell you exactly what the questions will be. The interview is supposed to be a spontaneous conversation. To rehearse either questions or answers is staging. But there is a fine line here.

Most reporters consider it proper to tell you the subject they're covering and broad areas they want to explore in the interview. Find out as much as you can.

Remember, the reporter will also be sizing you up. And the impression you give in those first few minutes will be critical to the slant on the story. (See **SKILLS/Good Guys/Bad Guys** for personality traits reporters look for)

Have Your Staff Handy

For stories that involve a lot of numbers or complicated, technical details, it's a good idea to have your staff experts sit in. They can hand you documents when you grope for the right number. You can ask them to fetch details the reporter needs for the story. Having a friend in your corner may also make you feel more at ease and less threatened.

The Certain Question

I estimate that about 35,000 people are interviewed by the news media in America every day.

This is hard to believe, but I already know *exactly* what the reporters are going to ask in the vast majority of those interviews. It doesn't matter where the interview takes place. Doesn't matter who the reporter is — who is being interviewed — doesn't even matter what the story is about. I know the key question:

How Do You Feel?

How do you feel?

The perennial question was institutionalized by a television news story formula — the Sony Sandwich. (See diagram and other details in **SKILLS/Interviews-Broadcast**) It has now spread to all news media.

The meat in the Sony Sandwich is the interview in the middle. It gives the story flavor, substance, emotion, humanity. It is sandwiched between the facts the reporter gives at the beginning, and the conclusion the reporter draws at the end.

The Sony Sandwich

The reporter sets up the basic facts for the reader, the viewer, the listener. Then we go to the central figure in the story.

- How did you feel when you learned you have terminal cancer?
- (On election night) How does it feel to lose after 24 years in the Senate?
- How does it feel to win the New York lottery?
- How do you feel about the Mayor's proposal?

The Top on the Sandwich

Then the reporter puts the top on the sandwich by drawing the conclusion, telling us where the story goes from here.

Print reporters once laughed and made fun of broadcast reporters who always asked, "How do you feel?" But you'll hear newspaper and magazine reporters asking it now, too.

Television has changed the format for all news media. Newspaper stories today are much shorter. They use more pictures and graphics. To compress their stories — just as broadcasters do — they've adapted the Sony Sandwich to print.

If you can learn how to speak media language, and give a formula response to the formula question, you almost guarantee they'll use what you said, exactly as you said it. No editing or taking out of context. It is the best self-defense technique to avoid being misquoted.

Disguising the Question

Reporters are so aware of their trite question, they try to disguise it. But it is still the search for the human perspective.

Tell me — what you were thinking when the section of the airplane just ahead of you blew out?

When the officer walked in the door with your baby in his arms, what was it like?

Someday, we may be in that same place, going through that same experience. How does it feel to do what you did … see what you saw ... hear what you heard? We want to know what it was like to be there.

What Was It Like to be There?

That has always been the essence of storytelling. If a ghost story is told skillfully, I shudder and look over my shoulder in the dark. Tell me the story of a blind child who can see for the first time, and I get a lump in my throat. When she tells me what she's feeling, I may cry.

Interviews inject the human perspective in news stories. Few people outside the news media understand this basic purpose for the question that will elicit the quote or the sound bite.

Verbal Shorthand

Words that express feeling tell us a lot very quickly. They are verbal shorthand — headline words that communicate like no others in our language. They set us up to hear your reasons for feeling that way.

When the reporter asks how you feel about something, it can mean, "What do you think about this? — What is your reaction to the situation? — What is your opinion?" But we will understand your reaction — your opinion — your conclusion — much more clearly if you tell us how you FEEL.

News stories are so formularized, it is almost a paint-by-numbers process. I've collected a list of words, from which at least one will fit virtually any news interview. Pick one.

Words That Say How You Feel

Abandoned	Abused
Aggravated	Afraid
Alienated	Alone
Amazed	Ambushed
Amused	Angry
Anxious	Ashamed
Astonished	Astounded
Besieged	Betrayed
Bored	Burned out
Caught in the middle	Certain
Chagrined	Cheated

Confident | Confused
Cozy | Crazy
Dazzled | Deceived

More Words To Convey Feeling

Delighted | Deserted
Disappointed | Dismayed
Disorganized | Elated
Embarrassed | Encouraged
Energized | Enthusiastic
Envious | Excited
Exhausted | Exposed
Fearful | Fed up
Frantic | Friendly
Frightened | Glad
Grateful | Great!
Grief-stricken | Guilty
Happy | Harried
Hate (I hate it!) | Helpless

Words for the Key Question

High | Homicidal
Hopeful | Hopeless
Horrendous | Horrible
Hounded | Humble
Humiliated | Hurt
Impatient | Impotent
Ineffective | Insecure
Inspired | Intrigued
Invaded | Isolated
Jaded | Jealous
Joyful | Jubilant
Justified | Livid
Lonely | Love (I love it!)
Loser (Like a loser) | Lucky
Mad | Marvelous
Mortified | Mystified
Naked | Nauseated
Offended | On top of the world

Optimistic
Outgunned
Outraged

Out of touch
Outnumbered
Overjoyed

Tell Me How You Feel

Overwhelmed
Parental
Pessimistic
Powerful
Prepared
Proud
Put out
Ready
Rejoice
Relieved
Responsive
Sad
Scared
Sick
Stupid
Sure
Surrounded
Terrible
Terrified
Torn
Under control
Unjustly accused
Unworthy
Victimized
Vulnerable
Weak
Weepy
Wonderful
Worn out

Paranoid
Peeved
Pleased
Powerless
Protected
Put down
Puzzled
Regret
Rejuvenated
Resentful
Rested
Satisfied
Secure
Skeptical
Supportive
Surprised
Sympathetic
Terrific
Tired
Uncertain
Undone
Unwanted
Used
Victorious
Warm
Weary
Winner (Like a winner)
Worried
Wounded

Condition Words

Some of the feeling words in the list above are not real feelings. They are *conditions* that convey several emotions or strong feelings. When you say, "I feel betrayed," you tell us —

with just one word — you feel angry, deceived, abandoned, vulnerable. If you feel surrounded, you are feeling insecure, outnumbered, overwhelmed.

When you say, "I feel disorganized," you tell us you're feeling guilty about the need to put things in order.

Interviews add flavor and spice to a story. Once the conflict, the catastrophe, the crisis is established, we want to hear the participants. We want to know how they feel about it.

Quotes they'll use for sure:

- "I'm embarrassed. The mayor has made a terrible mistake, and we're all going to suffer for it."

- "I'm serious about this. When I'm President, every animal in the country will be wearing clothes to hide its nudity."

- "It's frightening. This guy is completely bonkers."

- "Just before we hit the water, I wasn't afraid — I was terribly sad, that I'd never see my son again."

- "I feel like a kid again. After the surgery, I've got a whole new life ahead of me."

A Word of Caution:

There are a few rare times when showing too much emotion on camera can be hazardous to your career. We don't expect a homicide detective to break down at a murder scene. Unless the victim is his partner, or his own child.

Edmund Muskie may have lost his campaign for the Democratic presidential nomination in 1972 when he cried during a speech in the snow in New Hampshire, talking about a newspaper editorial that had defamed his wife. Tears might have been acceptable for some professions in those days, but we expected Presidents to be tougher than that.

The Rules Have Changed

Society's expectations have changed. During the televised 1988 presidential debates, Gov. Michael Dukakis — an opponent of capital punishment — was asked how he would feel on that issue if his wife was a rape or murder victim.

Dukakis showed no emotion. His answer was academic, distant, unfeeling. People in the audience thought to themselves:

What sort of man is this, who doesn't react to the idea of his wife being violated or killed?

One of his nicknames in the campaign was "Zorba the accountant."

A Kinder, Gentler President

In that same campaign, George Bush's media experts asked focus groups what kind of President they wanted. Using that research, Bush promised to be a "kinder, gentler President."

In television interviews, Bush began to talk about his family as sensitive, caring people. The Bushes, he said, show what they feel. Sometimes the men are not afraid to cry. His saying that drew a sharp contrast between himself and Dukakis.

During Thanksgiving dinner with the troops in Saudi Arabia in 1990 — before the ground war was launched in Kuwait — Bush talked about the young soldiers he would soon send into battle. Some of them would not come back. He became teary, thinking of their deaths. We would have thought less of him if he had not.

At a church service hours before his inauguration in 1993, a TV close-up showed tears running down the cheeks of President Bill Clinton. At the memorial service for Richard Nixon in 1994, Sen. Bob Dole cried.

Tough cops and firefighters cried as they carried young victims from the bombed-out Murrah Federal Building in Oklahoma City. Athletes who lose Super Bowls or World Series sob openly.

Schwarzkopf's Tears

One of the most dramatic demonstrations of how the rules have changed came during Barbara Walters' interview in Arabia with Gen. Norman Schwarzkopf shortly after the Persian Gulf War ended in 1991. "Stormin' Norman" talked about how much he missed his family, half a world away, and the tears welled in his eyes. When Walters asked about his dead father, who had also been a general, the tears came again. "I'm sure he'd be proud of me," Schwarzkopf said, his lower lip trembling.

There was a long pause in the interview. "You know," Walters said, "The old picture of generals — is that generals don't cry."

"Sure they do," Schwarzkopf shot back, listing names and places. Ulysses Grant after the battle of Shiloh. William Tecumseh

Sherman. "And these were the tough old guys. Lee cried at the loss of human life, the pressures that were brought to bear. Lincoln cried. And frankly, any man that doesn't cry scares me a little bit. I don't think I would like a man who was incapable of enough emotion to get tears in his eyes every now and then. That's not a human being."

Gender Conflicts

In their childhood, men who are now middle-aged or older were taught not to show their feelings. Men don't cry. Men don't show fear, or pain. In that old, cultural conditioning, they did not even show love.

Women are caught in a crossfire as the culture shifts. Cry at the office and the men in power are likely to invoke the old standards that said showing emotion was a sign of weakness. "Just like a woman," they mutter under their breath.

America still has many double standards for men and women. An angry man is called aggressive. Bold. An angry woman may be called shrill. Bitchy.

That's why seeing yourself on videotape is so important. Everybody has a different threshold in expressing how you feel without appearing to go overboard. Tape is the only way to find your individual line that shouldn't be crossed.

Show Your Humanity

I don't want you to cry in every interview. My goal for you is to show your humanity. If you do, by crafting quotes that tell us how you feel, those quotes will be used, and used *exactly* as you spoke them. In context. No misquotes.

The formula that reporters use is so predictable, I make a bet with my seminar groups:

Send me a transcript of your next media interview. Print, radio, television. Doesn't matter. I'll bet you a steak dinner I can pick the quote or sound bite the reporter uses.

It will always be the quote that tells us how you feel.

SKILLS

Interviews-Print

No, You Can't Talk
To My Psychiatrist

Compared to broadcasting, print interviews can be a very lengthy process. To compete with broadcasting's immediacy, newspapers and magazines go overboard with detail. Intimate, minute trivia is showcased. It is common for print stories to tell us what brand of cigarette the interviewee smokes and just how the smoke is inhaled. The designer of the dress. How many times the phone rang during lunch, and who called. Everything that was ordered. Whether it was eaten.

The Luxury of Time

Print reporters have a luxury that few broadcast reporters ever have — the luxury of time. Lots of time to research and write the story. Writers at newspapers like *The Wall Street Journal* and *The Washington Post* may work on one feature story for weeks. Investigative projects can take more than a year.

Another reason for this kind of trivia is an effort to draw pictures with words. Many newspaper editors are still not interested in pictures. They are word people. They simply don't understand the impact of pictures. When they have good photos, many of them don't know how to display them to their best advantage.

In television, the reporter and photographer work closely as a team. Without pictures, the reporter has no story. Every word the TV reporter writes must have a picture to go with it. The reporter and photographer map out ahead just what they'll need to illustrate the story. The pictures often tell us more than the words.

Separate Words, Pictures

In newspapers, the reporter and photographer generally work separately. Even at a breaking news story like a plane crash or building collapse, they go to the scene in separate cars and have little contact with each other. They bring their work to an editor independently. It is the editor's task to merge the words and pictures.

Print reporters' obsession with trivia can be a real pain. They may want to just hang around and watch everything you do for several days. They'll want to talk to your spouse, your children, your boss, your employees, your parents and your psychiatrist.

Drawing the Boundaries

You may have to decide just how much time and privacy you're willing to give up. Early in your contact with the reporter, you should diplomatically draw some boundaries. Celebrities often do this to protect their families.

Remember — barring a door often whets the appetite of a reporter to get inside. (See **STRATEGY/Ten Commandments of Media Relations**) But knowing very early how the reporter views the assignment — the talent and experience the reporter brings to the story — can help you make that decision. (See pre-interview-interviews in **SKILLS/Interviews-General**)

Print Is More Tenacious

Print reporters are often much more tenacious than broadcast reporters. The luxury of time permits them to doggedly stick with a rumor, trying to prove it's true. Broadcast reporters will usually be pulled off and sent to another story if they don't find what they're looking for quickly.

But in-depth reporting is an endangered species.

The profit margins at TV stations and newspapers are not nearly what they used to be. Owners are almost universally looking for ways to cut operating costs and restore their profit margins. Newsrooms are shorthanded. When people leave, the job is often left vacant for a long time. Maybe permanently.

So there's a real emphasis on pushing every employee to be as productive as possible. Too often, that rules out any serious investigative reporting or extensive research.

Experts With a Specialty

Reporters at larger newspapers are generally better educated and more experienced than their broadcast competition. They are experts who develop a specialty. Police reporters do nothing but crime and law enforcement stories. Reporters on the school beat may know more about schools than members of the School Board. The school beat is a full-time job at some newspapers. School Board members usually serve part-time.

When you know a print reporter will be interviewing you as part of a major assignment, it saves time if you can supply written material before the interview.

Collect data that will educate the reporter. Supply history and statistics. Arrange other interviews with staff who are technicians. When the reporter is ready to do your interview, this can save a lot of time.

Charming and Disarming

Good reporters — both print and broadcast — know how to be very charming and disarming. With the luxury of time, newspaper and magazine reporters will begin to seem like old friends. They'll hang around a lot. Have meals, drinks and coffee with you. Their goal may be to get your guard down. Don't get defensive. Just be aware. That's their job.

In a confrontation with a newspaper or magazine, a written statement can be effective. If we don't see you on TV or hear you on radio, it seems like you're hiding.

Quotes from a written statement in print don't telegraph that same message. Even if the story points it out, few readers will care that you gave a written statement rather than an interview.

Questions in Writing

If you refuse to be interviewed, you can offer to answer written questions in writing. This can avoid a slip of the tongue in a touchy situation.

You may want to grant an interview with certain restrictions. Remember, the ground rules must be agreed on by both parties in advance. You can't talk to a reporter, then ask that part of what you said be trashed. (See **SKILLS/Off-the-Record**)

Newspapers keep mug shots in their libraries. Often they're old and unflattering. If you don't like the picture they're using, send a newer, better one. The cover letter should say the old shot is out of date, and you're offering another. You can do the same with your organization's annual report. Send the latest one, just to keep in their files.

During an interview, if the reporter doesn't ask about shooting your picture, you may want to offer one. They're more likely to use a candid, informal shot, rather than a posed portrait.

While most daily newspapers won't print news releases verbatim, they'll often reproduce graphic material you give them. To emphasize your points in an interview, give the reporter copies of graphs and charts that illustrate your data. (See **STRATEGY/Selling Your Story**)

Print's Comfort Deceptive

Most people feel more comfortable with print reporters. At the moment, the interview seems less threatening. But print can often do a lot more damage.

When we know we're being taped for broadcast — both TV and radio — there is a much greater stage fright factor. As we speak, we think the entire world is listening and/or watching.

Not only are the print media more tenacious; newspapers and magazines have traditionally been much more vicious than broadcasting. Today's newspaper, or this week's edition of a magazine, are readily available to re-read and analyze. They're on file at the library. Clips of the story will come back to haunt you.

Broadcast News Fades

Television news, with its visual power, has more immediate impact. Some of its film and videotape are deeply burned into our tribal memory.

But most TV and radio stories quickly fade. The audience can't remember a few hours later what was in the newscast. Most people don't have a tape of today's broadcast news in their homes or offices. You can tell a friend what you saw or heard, but you normally can't show it to them.

SKILLS

News Conferences

Stage Productions
That Sing and Dance

News conferences are a necessary evil. Good reporters don't like them. Everybody will come away with the same story. Most reporters need to win. To beat the competition. Stand out from the pack.

But news conferences are efficient. It would take all day to give individual interviews to a dozen news outlets. So you do them all at once at a news conference.

News conferences are also a way for you to take advantage of the fierce competition between the media. If the story is marginal, they may all use it to prevent their competitors from having a story they don't.

Neat, Convenient Packages

News conferences offer some real advantages. You can provide, in one, convenient place, the people that reporters would like to talk to. Properly produced, a news conference provides all the elements needed for a story in one neat, convenient package.

News conferences, when done right, give reporters *everything they need to write the story you want*. They inspire them to write the story from your point of view.

Suppose you had to choose between a story that will take a lot of legwork and one that's easy. Both of them are fairly equal in news value. On most days, if you're the assignment editor or city editor, you'll take the easy one.

Now, the Disadvantages

News conferences also have some major disadvantages.

They're much less intimate. At a news conference, you never know who they'll send. If you call a specific reporter to suggest a story, you get to pick the reporter.

In a news conference crowd, you can't give reporters you trust confidential background material. If you're under attack, and the mob of reporters and photographers smell blood, it's easy to be overwhelmed and lose control.

News conferences should be called only for stories that all media will consider important. BEWARE false alarms. If you call news conferences for stories that don't merit them, you'll seem like the boy who cried, "Wolf." Next time you call a news conference to announce a cure for cancer, nobody will come.

A Theatrical Production

You should think of a news conference as a theatrical production. It needs a stage, a script, a cast, costumes, a director, a program, props, a rehearsal, an audience, and a final curtain.

Choosing The Stage

Where you hold the press conference can be very important. Think about the way television reporters shoot their standups. If the story involves a trial, we see the courthouse over the reporter's shoulder. Network correspondents who cover the President do their standups on the lawn of the White House. At space shots or political conventions, we see the launch pad or the banners in the background.

Place Gives You Credibility

It is a kind of visual shorthand that television has developed. It suggests, subliminally, that because you're there, you're a real authority on the subject.

If you're an officer in the longshoremen's union, hold your news conference on the docks, so we can see the ships at the wharf behind you. If you're a school administrator, let us see a school in the background. If you're a cop, talking about street crime, go to the most violent neighborhood in your community, where it happens. It tells viewers you know what you're talking about.

That kind of field location is not always possible. TV cameras are magnets for kids, who swarm in front of the lens. Grinning, jumping, waving, yelling "Hi, Mom. Am I gonna be on TV?"

If it's indoors, the room needs to be big enough to hold everyone you invite, and all their equipment. It needs electrical outlets with circuit breakers that can withstand the heavy loads of TV lights. The room should have a good air conditioning system.

If the topic is truly newsworthy, reporters will need telephones as soon as the news conference ends.

Write a Script

Decide what you want to say. Not a word-for-word script. A bullet-point outline.

Somewhere in Media Class 101, they told you all news conferences should begin with the boss reading a statement. Dull. Deadly dull. Presidents do this, but their news conferences are carried live. The audience HAS to sit through the entire statement. Or switch to the movie channel.

Openings We'll Never Hear

In working with clients, I try to avoid having them read prepared statements at news conferences. Most executives do not read statements well. It's obvious they're reading something somebody else wrote, not expressing their own convictions.

You may want to distribute a statement as part of your handout material. Newspaper reporters don't need to hear you read it. If you *must* read, limit it to one or two sentences. But it would be a lot better if you made that summary without looking at a script.

The electronic media will summarize the gist of the news conference and then look for two or three short sound bites. The sound bites will almost always be your off-the-cuff answers to questions.

Casting the Play

Movies, plays and TV shows have a cast of characters. Each is necessary to tell the audience what the author wants them to hear and understand. To move the plot along. Each member of the cast is chosen carefully for talent, experience, and audience appeal.

In most organizations, protocol requires that certain people be featured at news conferences. They'll get their feelings hurt if they're not invited. If they're good spokespeople, that's great.

But they may not be.

The Boss May Not Know

It's embarrassing when the boss doesn't know the answer, fakes it, and someone on staff has to correct the error.

Generally, the boss needs to be there to speak about policy. But you also need someone there who is intimately familiar with the equipment or process. A technician.

If you're talking about a major event, where someone has made a breakthrough in research or saved a life, that person should be there to tell the world how it felt at the moment of triumph.

The boss can't tell us how it felt.

Don't Do It Alone

For most news conferences, use two to three people, if possible. I recommend no more than four.

Never do it alone. One person rarely knows everything. If you're by yourself you'll feel terribly outnumbered in a room full of aggressive reporters. You can easily be overwhelmed. More than three or four can get clumsy.

It works this way: If you're overwhelmed by questions, one of the other members of the cast steps in for the rescue. "Let me answer that question," the relief catcher says, "That's my area of responsibility." That gives you time to catch your breath.

Costumes

Decide what the cast of the news conference will wear. Their clothes should fit the story. Business suits are out of place at a news conference that gives details about a disaster or an ongoing search and rescue operation.

Most Americans no longer wear "business" clothes to work. Factory workers never did. Casual Friday at the office has expanded to the entire week. The visual message of more formal clothing may be that you don't really work — you preside. Watch Presidential candidates. They have good market research to guide them. In most appearances, they no longer wear coats and ties.

The Director's Role

Like plays, good news conferences need a director. A stage manager who supervises the production. Shapes both the content and the style. Coaches the actors.

The director of a news conference is usually the public relations director or public information officer. The director's job also includes: notifying the media, preparing the room, distributing the handouts, establishing the ground rules, introducing the cast, and closing the news conference. (See **STRATEGY/PIOs**)

The Press Package

When you walk into a theater, you hand the usher your ticket and the usher gives you a playbill. A printed program. The playbill has a very specific purpose. It educates you about the history of the play, its author, and the cast. It gets you ready for what you're about to see and hear.

You should do the same thing for reporters as they arrive at your news conference. Give them a press package.

Avoiding Stupid Questions

Editors often send new, less talented reporters, believing news conferences don't require much skill or experience. You'll get some really stupid questions. The press package will educate them and, hopefully, avoid some of those dumb questions.

Include in the package the names and titles of those who'll be taking questions. That way, the names will be spelled right. Give reporters time to read and digest the information before you begin.

The press package should also include copies of things you're going to show and tell the audience. A copy of your formal statement. Graphs, charts, pictures — which the media can include in their stories — are powerful tools in shaping the story.

Good Props Are Vital

Trial lawyers have learned that juries are more convinced by evidence than by witnesses. The best witnesses for details and statistics may have personalities that irritate some jurors.

Witnesses have faulty memories. No matter how sharp, under tough cross-examination, witnesses can become confused. They can be sandbagged with the nitty-gritty of what they said earlier that appears to conflict with their testimony today. And if two witnesses contradict each other, who's telling the truth?

But hard evidence — documents, pictures, the murder weapon — can be touched and studied by the jurors. Evidence can be carried back into the jury room during deliberations for closer examination.

Reporters Are Like Jurors

If you're under attack, the reporters at a news conference are very much like jurors at a trial. They've already heard the plaintiff's or prosecutor's side. Now they're ready to hear your side. Persuade them with the right witnesses **and especially the right evidence.**

You need to use props all through the news conference. Refer to the charts and graphs. Hold up the broken part that caused the accident so all the world can see it.

One of my favorite props is a poster board that summarizes with large type the points you want to make. You need to stand near it from time to time, pointing to the next item you want to discuss.

Use Poster Boards

The poster board is a visual element for the story which also serves as a cheat sheet to keep you organized and on track. With it, you don't even need a script. Newspaper editors will always choose the picture of you at the chart over the shot of you at a podium. The reporter may not get into the story all the points you wanted to make. The picture of you at the chart can do that.

As you design a news conference, you should create the picture for tomorrow's front page and tonight's newscast. What we see will be much more memorable than what we hear.

When you hold a news conference to announce the introduction of a new product or service, I believe it's important to let reporters play with that product. If your new copier or computer is faster than the competition, have both at the news conference.

When you've finished your presentation, invite reporters to test what you've just told them. Personal involvement by the reporters will *always* result in bigger, better stories.

A Cure for Broken Hearts

Suppose your company is announcing a major medical breakthrough. A small pump to replace an ailing human heart. A device so small it fits in the patient's chest, powered by an inexpensive battery. Show us the new artificial heart. Let reporters handle it. Bring the frisky German shepherd in whom the prototype was implanted three years ago. Let reporters pet him.

Make sure the cast includes the inventor who toiled in his garage for 20 years. Let us hear about the failures and disappointment, until the night the inventor woke out of a sound sleep, knowing immediately how to solve the critical problem.

He ran to his shop and tried it. It worked! Guaranteed question: "How did you feel at that moment?"

The answer is a guaranteed quote and sound bite.

The Rehearsal

No group of actors would think of going on-stage, in front of a live audience, without a rehearsal. Lawyers carefully rehearse their witnesses by asking them the questions they know the other side will ask on cross-examination.

But most people hold news conferences with no preparation at all. Standard procedure is to choose one or more knowledgeable people, throw them on stage, and let the audience of reporters cross-examine them.

When I'm hired to help a company plan a news conference, we hold two rehearsals, if there's time. The first rehearsal turns up graphs that are too complicated; cast members who are not as skillful as they should be. We rework the graphics. Sometimes replace a cast member.

Who Answers Which Questions?

Part of the rehearsal is designing who should answer which questions. Cast members should know when and how to hand off a question to someone else, who has more expertise.

Employees may be uncomfortable taking the ball away from the boss, unless the play has been carefully practiced.

My choice of timing for the dress rehearsal is late in the afternoon the day before the real performance. It seems fresher the next day. As with all rehearsals, don't over-do it. Remember, these people are not professional actors. To much rehearsing can make them appear insincere. Regurgitating a canned script. The audience/jury should get the impression that what they say just occurred to them.

Advertising Your Play

If possible, alert the **City Editor** at the newspaper and the **Assignment Editor** at radio and TV stations — in writing — a day or two in advance. Just a simple note. "We will hold a news conference at a certain time and place to discuss a certain topic." Say who will be there to answer reporters' questions.

Don't be vague or mysterious. There may not be enough staff to gamble on an unsure story idea. If your note clearly explains why this is a good story, they'll be there.

Call, fax or e-mail the assignment and city editors the day of the news conference, to remind and update them.

The Earlier, the Better

If you want the story to break on the noon news and in the afternoon newspaper, call your conference no later than 10 a.m. Nine or 9:30 is better.

If you want the story to break on the evening news and in tomorrow morning's newspaper, call your conference no later than 3 p.m. One-thirty or 2 p.m. is better.

The Timetable

Let's look at the timetable. If you begin at three, the television crew may not be able to break down their gear and get away before four. A 30-minute drive back to the station gets the writing started at 4:30.

Script finished and approved by 5:15 means only 45 minutes to edit, during the worst crush of the day in the editing booths. If other stories are breaking late, your news conference may have a tough time competing.

In a crunch, a daily, 90-second news story can be slapped together in 15 minutes. But it looks slap-dash. Since a news conference can be called at any time, the earlier you set it, the more care and attention the story will get.

Avoiding Musical Chairs

Many news conferences are a major technical problem for broadcasters. A common setup puts five or six people at a long table, facing the reporters and cameras.

That format was created for press conferences — the printed press — before radio and television were invented. It just doesn't work for the electronic media.

Where do you put the microphones?

The sound problem can be overcome, if each person participating has a microphone that feeds into a central sound system, and each broadcaster can plug into that system. That requires special equipment.

Do It Standing Up

If you don't have a sophisticated sound system, do your news conference standing up, with a podium for the microphones. Those participating in the conference stand close to the podium. Reporters can ask questions of specific people, and they can easily move to the mikes to answer, then step back.

Most people who don't have a lot of experience (and many who do) are much more effective standing than sitting. They invest more energy in what they're saying.

If you're expecting 100 reporters and photographers, you may need a sound system to be heard at the back of the room. As I said earlier, make sure there are enough electrical outlets, air conditioning, and telephones.

Have backup people there who can, hopefully, rush out and get material you may have overlooked, and supply it to the reporters before you adjourn. If you can't get it in time, tell the reporters how they can get the information later in the day.

Keeping It Under Control

Like dogs and horses, groups of reporters can smell fear. They sense it when you're losing control. Once it happens, the mob mentality takes over. The first drop of blood puts sharks into a feeding frenzy.

It's *your* news conference. They're there at your invitation, and they need to understand what the rules are. *In advance.*

When half a dozen reporters all shout questions at the same time, you need to be firm in saying you can only deal with one question at a time. Ask reporters to hold up their hands and be recognized before they ask a question.

The Final Curtain

If you're under attack and try to close the conference in midstream, you look like a coward who couldn't take the heat.

If you expect a stormy session, have a staffer announce in advance that you can only give the reporters X minutes. That staffer should then be the timekeeper who announces the time is up and gets you to your next appointment.

At that point, you can always be the good guy, if you choose. "I'll take just one more question." You can take one more question all afternoon. You're in control. If things are going badly, you can get out without the appearance of running away.

If you're briefing reporters in the middle of a breaking disaster, you may want to announce at the beginning that you will not answer questions. You should also say when you'll come back with more details and take questions.

Careful With the Names

In a one-on-one interview, it's usually a good idea to use the reporter's name in your answers. "I'm doing this, Sally, because I think the school system is in deep trouble."

In a news conference, your recognizing one television reporter by name may prevent the competing stations from using your answer. That's how competitive they are.

Don't Leave Too Soon

Good reporters who know a lot about the subject of the news conference may want to interview you privately after you finish. They don't want to disclose their exclusive by asking key questions that would tip their competitors.

So don't leave too soon, before those more knowledgeable reporters have a chance to buttonhole you, one-on-one.

Again, the theater analogy. It's nice to go backstage and talk to the actors after the play.

SKILLS

News Releases

Save the Forests — Stop PR Junk Mail

America would have more forests if public relations firms would stop cranking out so many news releases. Editors consider them an insidious form of junk mail. Most go straight to the trash can.

But PR people blanket the nation with news releases to justify their jobs or their fees. Look what I did, they tell the boss or the client. I've been churning them out, but those editors are really stupid. They wouldn't know a story if it hit them in the face.

The boss's name is in the release. Probably in the first sentence. Words written for the boss are quoted extensively. Good stuff, the boss thinks. *The PR people are right. Local editors are truly dense. They don't appreciate my golden words. Even if I never said them.*

Historical Artifacts

For most news coverage, the written news release *in news story form* is obsolete.

The news release was invented to cater to lazy newspaper people. Since it was written in newspaper style, a sluggish editor or reporter could retype it, word-for-word, and put it in the paper.

In the bad old days, some sleazy reporters would even put their own by-lines on the story. Public relations people loved it. They could not only plant stories, they could actually write them exactly as they appeared in print. It was better than free lunch in the old-time saloon.

Times have changed.

News Release Ethics

Most daily newspapers today consider it unethical to run an un-edited news release. Some weeklies, however — short on staff and budget — will run them just the way you send them.

The moral for people trying to get publicity:

If you can still get away with it, do it.

But if they don't run them the way you send them, you need to re-think the whole process of news releases.

The news release *written in news story form* takes a lot more time and paper than just a straightforward, quick summary telling an editor about a possible story.

Television news doesn't write a script until after the video is shot. The script has to fit the pictures. If the story has actualities, radio will write the script around them. So your effort to write a script for broadcasting can be a total waste of time.

Advance Notice for TV

What all editors — print and broadcast — DO need is advance notice by mail, phone, fax or e-mail so they can have a reporter and/or camera there. A simple, one-paragraph memo will do, addressed to the city editor (print) or assignment editor (TV and radio). Something like:

> *Mike Megawatt will speak to the Chum and Chowder Society next Tuesday at 12:30 p.m. in the Anthracite Hotel. He'll talk about the company's requested rate increase and the Power Company's petition to burn coal in the Smoky Hollow plant. We hope to have copies of the speech available for your reporter shortly before the meeting begins.*
> (See **STRATEGY/Selling Your Story**)

Fact Sheets

If you're opening a new plant, send both print and broadcast editors a fact sheet, not a flowery news story. Example:

> *The Wee Widget Company will open its new plant Monday. The new assembly line will be the most automated of its kind in the world. Robots will perform many of the jobs formerly done by humans. Production will increase by at*

*least 30 per cent. Brief opening ceremonies begin at
9:00 a.m. A special tour for the news media will begin at
9:30 a.m.*

Plant construction cost — $ 46.3 million.

Building contractor — Saw and Hammer Corp.

Construction time — 21 months.

Square feet — 92,500, all air-conditioned.

*Special features — Employees' cafeteria, child care center,
swimming pool, gymnasium, solar panels to heat water
and generate electricity.*

*Expected production capacity — 6.6 million widgets per year;
retail value, $134 million, to be sold throughout the world.*

Better Questions

If the editor decides to cover the opening, the fact sheet will go
to the reporter who's assigned the story. It will result in better
questions. It will help a photographer know what's available for
pictures.

Fact sheets are especially helpful if you have a news conference. I've covered news conferences where the only handout was a
release in news story form that ran several pages. The facts, names
and numbers I needed were hidden far down in the copy. Or simply weren't there. (See **SKILLS/News Conferences**)

Historic Relics

News releases churned out by government agencies often follow the rigid form J. Edgar Hoover designed in the 1930s. Every
press release began: "FBI Director J. Edgar Hoover announced in
Washington today ..."

The opening sentence changed for several years in the early
1960s when Bobby Kennedy was U.S. attorney general and, technically, Hoover's boss. They did not like each other, and were involved in a constant power struggle.

During those years, the releases began: "U.S. Attorney General Robert F. Kennedy announced in Washington today ..."

Bureaucrats and corporate executives love the format, because
their name is right up front. Those kinds of releases usually include

some stiff, wooden quotes from the boss that no respectable newspaper, radio or TV station would run.

Nobody seems to notice that the releases are not published or broadcast. It's done that way because that's the way it's always been done. It creates work for someone in the public affairs section.

TV Is Pictures and Sound

Television is pictures and sound. Radio needs actualities.

Some major corporations are beginning to catch on. There is a glimmer of understanding in many government agencies. The modern news release for television is a broadcast-quality videocassette, sometimes produced by a professional studio.

The print version of the release includes high-quality still pictures with cutlines taped to the print. In some situations, the newspaper or magazine will prefer color slides. You need to be aware of their technical requirements and preferences.

Today's fact sheet or news release is usually a fax or e-mail.

Photo as News Release

Automobile crashes videotaped and photographed in laboratory safety tests are a good example of photographic releases. The tests take place over months, or years. Knowing that someday you'll want news coverage, you photograph the tests as you go along.

When you're ready for publicity, you don't try to produce a television news story or a magazine photo layout. You supply videotape copies and still photographs of the crash tests, along with a fact sheet on the tests and what the pictures show. Perhaps some technical detail on how the pictures were shot.

Your fact sheet notifies editors that laboratory officials and engineers will be available for interviews. The reporter puts the story together, incorporating some of the crash pictures. On TV, the videotape can be used to cover part of the interviews with the technicians.

When a new airliner makes its inaugural flight, the manufacturer supplies videotape and pictures of engineers at the drawing board, a model in wind-tunnel tests, the assembly line, the cockpit instruments, the plane's interior, and finally, the plane in flight, outlined against a spectacular sunrise, with the company name prominent on the tail section. Hard to produce a story without using some of those pictures.

Video and Photo Libraries

The Pentagon has extensive photo and videotape libraries showing weapons systems, ships, planes, and troops in war maneuvers. When a reporter does a story that needs pictures, the public affairs office is happy to supply them. They make their people and their equipment look good. More corporations and government agencies need to build similar libraries.

Staff Photographers

Many police and fire departments now have broadcast-quality equipment and talented photographers who get to major disaster, fire and crime scenes before the news media do. They move in close, shoot pictures news photographers may not be able to shoot, then make them available to the media.

If the public is going to know who you are, and see you doing what you do best, it must be on film or videotape.

Medical Research

Major medical research facilities do the same thing. In some kinds of pioneering surgery, the risk to the patient is too great to invite a news camera. So the hospital photographs and videotapes the entire procedure. Once the procedure becomes less risky and is publicly announced, the tape is part of the announcement.

Sometimes, still pictures are shots from a video monitor. Newspaper editors don't like them. The quality is poor, and it shows that TV had a higher priority.

If at all possible, shoot both still pictures and videotape.

Videotaped Interviews

True story —

In a major city, two cars loaded with teenagers collide head-on at 2 a.m. A 16-year-old boy receives massive head injuries. The paramedics rush him to the nearest hospital. The hospital refuses to treat him. The emergency room does not have a neurosurgeon on duty.

After a heated argument, the paramedics take the boy to an-other hospital, where he dies. The first hospital's failure to treat the youngster is leaked to a reporter and becomes a major news story. Day after day, the ethics of refusing medical treatment are debated in the media. You can smell the lawsuit coming.

Sure enough, a prominent attorney calls a news conference to announce that he represents the parents of the dead boy, and has just filed a multi-million-dollar suit against the hospital.

Control Over What is Said

He explains the basis of the suit and how he plans to pursue it. In closing, he says, "I know you would like to interview my clients, the parents. But they have been through so much pain and suffering, I just couldn't put them through that ordeal.

"But — knowing you would want to hear their story — I video-taped an interview with them. I have copies here, for each of you."

In this real case, every local TV station used portions of the taped interview. By making his own videotape, the lawyer was able to completely control what his clients said publicly, while he shielded them from questions he wanted to avoid.

A Brand New Technique

This is a relatively new technique.

Isn't this just like the old written press release that editors feel uneasy using? Well, sorta.

If the videotape is good stuff, however, they'll use it every time. They'll probably warn the audience that they didn't shoot it. Make clear where it came from. But they'll use it.

You don't have to own expensive video equipment. TV news is using more amateur video all the time. The quality of home video cameras is extremely good today. If you're in the right place at the right time, the news media will quickly buy your pictures.

The Zapruder Film

The assassination of President John F. Kennedy, captured on 8-mm film by Dallas dressmaker Abraham Zapruder is the most fa-mous example of amateur photography broadcast and published worldwide. Now in the National Archives, the government in 1999 was ordered to pay the Zapruder family $16 million for the film.

Rodney King Video

Amateur news video really came into its own shortly after midnight on March 3, 1991, when George Holliday heard a commotion outside his apartment in Los Angeles.

He had a new video camera in his hand as he stepped onto his balcony. Down below and across the street, Rodney King had just emerged from his car after a high-speed police chase.

The novice photographer turned on his camera and videotaped the entire incident as police shot King with an electric stun gun, then beat and kicked him repeatedly.

Powerful Pictures

It made King's name a household word; led to the indictment and trial of the officers involved; the resignation of the police chief; and was instrumental in focusing the anger of the black community. That anger would explode in massive, deadly riots when the officers were later acquitted.

The King tape was shot at night, under very poor lighting conditions, but dramatically demonstrated what amateur cameras can do.

A striking recent example of amateur video in the news was the Concorde airliner as it took off in Paris in July, 2000. Shot from a moving truck, the 15-second videotape shows the plane billowing smoke and fire just before it crashed.

The most memorable photograph after the Oklahoma City bombing was shot by an amateur. It shows a firefighter carrying the limp, bloody body of a small child.

Security camera video of robberies is frequently in the news. The last pictures of Princess Diana were taken by a security camera as she left a Paris hotel.

Radio Actualities

Local radio news is becoming a rarity as station owners discover the profits to be made in completely automated stations. Those that still have local news staffs are cutting back to be competitive. Most radio news is now bought from a national service.

So they're often hungry for anything that can make their news seem more enterprising. This provides marvelous opportunities for taped interview quotes when you're trying to get coverage for your issue. Fed by telephone, this is the audio tape version of a broadcast news release. Call a radio station you think might be interested in receiving actualities. They'll tell you how to record and feed the sound bites.

Charts and Graphs

For television and print, charts and graphs that make numbers meaningful are critical if you expect the public to understand your operation, your problems, or your solutions.

You can create multi-colored graphics with virtually any Windows-based word processing program. Big-city newspapers won't run the copy from your written news release. But they'll run your charts and graphs.

Use Your Computer

The setup at some newspapers requires that graphics be in slide form. To do this, create your graphs and charts with your computer program. Open the file and have it on the monitor screen in a dark room. Shoot the screen with a 35-millimeter camera.

With a high-resolution computer monitor, you'll get excellent results. The darkened room is necessary to avoid reflections on the monitor screen. The slides can be printed at a photo lab if you need both slide and print versions. Sometimes newspapers will take the undeveloped slide film and process it themselves.

Higher Quality Graphics

In most cities there are graphics designers who will work with you to create computerized graphics and then copy them electronically for slides or prints. The equipment they use will give you higher quality than shooting off a monitor.

But the price of half a dozen graphics created this way will buy a sophisticated camera if you want to do it yourself.

Always include copies of your graphics in the media handout package when you hold a news conference, make an important speech, or testify at a public hearing. (See **SKILLS/News Conferences** and **Speeches**)

SKILLS

Off-the-Record

Guerrilla Tactics for Leaking So Plumbers Can't Find the Source

A crucial skill for the media game is knowing how to successfully leak information. It happens every day in politics, government, and the corporate world.

Suppose your competitor has a major skeleton in the closet. If the media wrote about the skeleton, the competitor would be embarrassed or eliminated. But the media will never know about it unless somebody tips them off.

Tips Have Many Uses

Confidential leaks have other uses:

- To brief reporters in advance, so they can produce better stories
- To negotiate for the delay of a story
- To correct a wrong when the system seems powerless or disinterested
- To bring reporters into an investigation, so they'll feel more personally invested and put more effort into their coverage
- To bring an outsider in as an observer when you feel vulnerable and overpowered

When I begin to talk about off-the-record skills, occasionally an officer in one of my law enforcement seminars frowns at that idea.

"I'd never do that," the officer says. "I'm not a snitch."

Cops consider informers a necessary evil. They don't respect them. That's because informers are usually the kind of people who should be in jail. But to catch bigger fish, you have to give the informer a "walk." Like hit-man "Sammy the Bull," who was given immunity for testifying against mob boss John Gotti.

Snitch = Traitor

Many in law enforcement think of informers as traitors who turn against people who trusted them. They'll sell their mothers if the price is right.

Information from an informer is always suspect. It is being sold — bartered — and the informer frequently enlarges the truth to improve the bargaining position.

Media Sources Different

Confidential sources who leak to reporters, however, are usually very different kinds of people, with very different motives.

As an investigative reporter, I made off-the-record agreements with dope smugglers, gamblers, con men, bagmen, prostitutes and murderers. But they were the exception.

My most frequent sources of confidential information were whistle-blowers. Conscientious cops, doctors, lawyers or government officials who became completely frustrated with injustice or incompetence and the system's failure to cope with it.

Setting the Agenda

They went outside the system, and their leak of information to me often led to stories that brought about sudden changes in the system. Prosecutors who had been blind to certain types of activity suddenly began personal crusades.

One of my most successful series involved the Original Sleazy Lawyer, who had lied, cheated and bilked his clients in two states for 40 years. Officials at several levels had tried to put him out of business. They failed. He had an uncanny ability to weasel out of it — or a corrupt connection somewhere in the system.

So one of those frustrated officials quietly came to me with a confidential file — the transcript of four days of secret, federal testimony. Using that as my springboard, I found the lawyer's victims. I interviewed them on camera, and gathered the documents that supported their accusations.

Amazing Things Happen

Once the story was on the air, amazing things began to happen. A federal agency that had seemed impotent announced a hearing on The Original Sleazy Lawyer's qualifications to practice. A federal prosecutor charged him with coaching a client to commit perjury. The lawyer was convicted, and went to prison.

Interestingly, all of the details about the client who had lied under oath were in the original information leaked to me. It was available to the prosecution all along. But nobody did anything about it until my stories turned up the heat, and moved the case to the top of the agenda within the Justice Department.

Tobacco's Whistle-Blower

The tobacco industry had never lost a lawsuit until an insider leaked key documents to *60 Minutes* and *The Wall Street Journal*. Shortly after, there was a sea change in the campaign to curb tobacco sales and advertising.

Tobacco executives who had sworn before a Congressional committee they did not believe tobacco was addictive resigned or were fired within months. The leaked documents proved the industry had been aware for years of tobacco's addictive qualities.

States began to sue tobacco companies for medical costs they'd paid for patients with tobacco-caused illnesses. After several large settlements, tobacco threw in the towel and negotiated a national settlement.

In Florida, a civil court levied the highest punitive damages in history against the tobacco industry. All of this happened as a chain reaction to those original leaks to the media.

Honest Insiders Leak

In working stories on law enforcement corruption and medical malpractice, my usual confidential sources were other officers or doctors anxious to clean up their own profession. I have met people in unusual places at all hours of the day and night, with signals that would tip us to each other's presence and all sorts of maneuvers to make sure neither of us was followed or bugged.

I have been brought into law enforcement investigations, to do my own work, because the officers knew that in a corrupt system, once their investigation surfaced, they would become the targets — of a dishonest prosecutor leading a grand jury, or a legislative committee that wanted to keep the status quo.

Outsiders Keep it Honest

They brought me in as an outside, objective observer, who would know the truth from the inside when the case finally surfaced. I have accepted information in confidence from people who would be killed if certain people knew they had talked to me.

But most leaks are not nearly so cloak-and-daggerish. The most frequent reason to leak to the media is to give them advance notice, so they can gather better information and produce a better story, when the time comes.

Sometimes, in the real world, you will leak to the media to counter your opposition's leaks. A well-timed leak can mean millions of dollars in corporate America. It can decoy attention away from what you need to do quietly. It can change the course of a political campaign, or a corporate takeover. Without "Deep Throat," the Watergate cover-up might never have been proven.

Plumbers Stop Leaks

In many cases, there is risk for the source who leaks. Government agencies — as the Nixon White House did during Watergate — appoint groups of "plumbers" to stop leaks — to fire and prosecute those who are leaking.

In 2000, one of Special Prosecutor Kenneth Starr's aides was arrested for leaking information on the Monica Lewinski case to the media. I cannot give you guidelines for your conscience. But if you decide to become a confidential source, I can help you do it successfully, with minimum risk.

What is Off the Record?

You can no longer be sure what "off-the-record" means. The Washington press corps has created half a dozen gradations for talking to the news media secretly. They accept information for "background only." Or "deep background." Or quotes for "non-attribution."

Few people outside the Washington bureaucracy know what those terms mean. Even insiders are sometimes confused.

Before you tell something to a reporter in confidence, be sure you both understand the terms on which you give — and the reporter receives — the information.

A Clear Contract

There should be a clear verbal contract before you stick your neck out. That contract is terribly important. If it's broken, you could lose your job, your reputation, or your life. The reporter's career could be destroyed.

Talking to a reporter, and then adding, "Now, that's off the record" won't work. The contract must be made *before* the information is given. You can't spill the beans and then ask a reporter not to tell.

Most good reporters won't accept information if they have to pledge they'll never use it. Their job is to gather, publish and broadcast information, not store it in their heads. They may already know what you're about to tell them. Promising you they will never write it would prevent them from using it.

"In Confidence"

I recommend that you abandon the term off-the-record, and say instead, "I'd like to tell you something in confidence." The reporter will usually say, "What do you mean by that?" Then you begin to negotiate the terms on which you will release the information, and what the reporter can do with it. Go over, step-by-step, your joint agreement on exactly what you expect of each other.

Variations of the contract:

1. **You may use the information I'm about to give you** in any way you choose, so long as you are very careful not to quote me directly, or to even hint where it came from. This kind of information is often attributed to a "confidential source" or a "highly reliable source."

2. **You can indicate my organization or group.** The story's credibility is increased if the source is less vague. "A confidential source in the police department." Or "a highly-placed executive in a major oil company."

3. **You must agree to hold the story until a later time.** "I want you to be aware of this," you say, "Because I know you'll need to do some advance work." Lengthy police investigations are often leaked in advance to the media on this basis. Television, particularly, needs extra time to create visuals.

4. **You may use this information if you can confirm** it with another source. This involves a lot of trust on your part. It is usually used if you think very few people know, and the story would immediately point the finger at you as the source. The information may be more widespread then you realize.

5. **Backgrounding.** "I want you to be aware of some things that are happening. In the next few days or weeks, a story will break, and then you'll understand the importance of what I'm about to tell you. You cannot disclose I briefed you."

6. **No quotes.** "You may use everything I'm about to tell you, and use my name, so long as you don't quote me directly. You must paraphrase what I say." This is a protection for the source, in case there is bad public reaction to a trial balloon. "That's not exactly what I said. Let me clarify."

7. **You may never attribute anything to me** unless I specifically give you permission. This is a time-saving device if you have a continuing confidential relationship with a reporter. There is an ongoing contract every time you talk.

Caution the Reporter

If the information is leaked for later use, be sure to discuss with the reporter the care that must be taken in gathering background material. Stories like the retirement of a key executive; the introduction of a new model or product; the filing of a lawsuit; a revolutionary medical technique. If questions are asked, there is always a risk the competition may find out, and break the story.

Competitive Risks

In some contracts, the reporter agrees to hold your information until the agreed time *unless the competition is about to break the story*. If that is imminent, then the reporter may go with the story. This will involve your being able to trust the reporter to be honest with you about any competitive threat.

A good reporter will also insist that you agree, under this kind of contract, to tip the reporter if a competitor approaches you, asking questions about the story.

I once negotiated with a law enforcement agency that was willing to let us put a camera into their sting operation and videotape thieves selling stolen property to undercover police officers posing as fences. I had to agree to hold the story until arrests were made. So much stolen property had been purchased in the operation, it would take six months or more to process the arrest warrants. It seemed like a simple contract, at first. But we kept running into "What ifs?" Eventually, after two hours of negotiation, we came to an agreement that was satisfactory to both sides.

Confidentiality Guidelines

Here are five broad rules that you should review when you make a confidential source agreement with a reporter:

- **You must know and trust the reporter**
- **Does the reporter have authority to make the deal?**
- **How many others will know the information or the source?**
- **How far will the reporter go to protect you?**
- **The exact words to be used in referring to the source**

Let's go over each rule.

Know the Reporter

I call this a contract, but it is a contract you probably cannot legally enforce. If you are a secret source, and want to remain invisible, how can you publicly accuse the reporter of violating a section of the contract?

Some reporters can be trusted more than others. All those who call themselves reporters do not live up to the generally recognized ethics of journalism. (See **STRATEGY/Ethics**)

As a general rule, reporters for major publications and broadcast outlets will be more reliable to deal with in confidential relationships. The ethical standards at *The New York Times* should be higher than the *Podunk Tattler*. But not always. Older, established reporters may be more reliable in this kind of agreement.

Older May Be Better

Younger reporters' primary motive is *getting the story to prove they can*. Older reporters, with an established reputation for getting the story, will let a story die rather than taint their reputation for integrity in dealing with sources.

If you don't know the reporter, call friends in your field and ask what they know. Your call, however, can be a tip to those friends. Once the story breaks, they'll realize you were the leak.

Undercover References

When I left my job as Washington correspondent for *The Miami Herald*, I moved under deep cover to investigate political and law enforcement corruption for WHAS-TV in Louisville, Kentucky. I knew nobody in law enforcement there. I would be working alone. To protect my cover, only the station owner, manager, and news director were aware of my assignment.

To succeed, I needed confidential sources.

So I called law enforcement officers with whom I had worked closely all over the country. I asked them if they knew anyone in the Louisville area that might be helpful. Several did. They called ahead. You will be approached by a reporter named Clarence Jones, they said. He is a reporter you can trust. With those kinds of recommendations, I immediately began confidential relationships with honest officers who were willing to help.

Complaining

If you feel a reporter has violated a confidence with you, in most cases the immediate superior will know you are the confidential source. You should yell loudly to that superior. And perhaps to the entire world. Violating a confidence is one of the most serious sins a reporter can commit. (See **STRATEGY/Ethics**)

Do You Have Authority?

Does the reporter have authority to promise you confidence? In some news organizations, only an editor or news director can give that pledge.

There are atrocity stories of reporters who pledge sources confidence, then run to tell their editor what they've learned. "Hell of a story," the editor says. "We'll lead the front page with it tomorrow morning."

"Wait a minute, boss," the reporter says, in panic. "I told my source we'd hold this until next Friday."

"You did, but I didn't," the editor says, with a smirk. He shafts both the source and his own reporter.

If you have any question about the reporter's ability to pledge confidence, bring the editor into the negotiation before you make your agreement.

Who Else Will Know?

How many others in the news operation will be aware that you are the source?

Secrecy is often broken by accident, not intentionally. The more who know, the greater the chance of a leak.

When Janet Cooke wrote her famous "Jimmy's World" feature story about an eight-year-old heroin addict, she refused to tell her editors at *The Washington Post* how she found the boy, or where he lived. She said she was doing it to protect the confidential agreement that led her to the family of junkies.

In April, 1981, *The Post* published the story, graphically illustrated with an artist's drawing of "Jimmy" with his fist extended toward the reader, as if he were shooting up.

She won the Pulitzer Prize before the story was unmasked as fiction. Embarrassed, the newspaper had to admit the hoax and return the prize. Because of that danger, most newsrooms now require a cross-check by editors or attorneys who know the identity of sources for stories that hinge on confidential information.

How Far Will You Go?

You should ask how far the reporter is willing to go to protect your confidence. Would the reporter go to jail rather than disclose you as the source?

Some states have shield laws that give reporters legal protection for confidential information. The law shields them from subpoenas so they cannot be forced to disclose their confidential sources.

Most states shield ministers, lawyers and accountants from being forced to disclose information given them in confidence. There was an assumption that reporters had that same kind of shield under the First Amendment until the 1970s, when the U.S. Supreme Court ruled otherwise.

If a state wants to give reporters that protection, it may, the Supreme Court said. But if the state does not, then a judge may decide whether the public good is more important than the reporter's claim of First Amendment rights. The judge can order the reporter to disclose the source. Refusal can become contempt of court, that carries a jail term until the court order is obeyed.

The Exact Words

One risk you might not think about is the way in which the reporter will refer to the source. This part of the contract may be especially critical. Confidential sources often ignore it, leaving it to the reporter to disguise the source.

The problem here is that the reporter can unintentionally identify you. "A veteran executive in the power company's research and planning division" may tell everybody in the company you are the source, since nobody else in the division has been there more than two years.

Your leak will be a lot safer if you discuss with the reporter *the exact words* to be used in referring to the source.

Confidentiality and Libel

Confidential sources raise major problems in libel litigation. To win libel suits, the facts published or broadcast by the media must be accurate. In the case of a public person or public official, the media must *believe* the story is true when it is published or broadcast. (See **INSIDE THE MEDIA/Libel** and **Privacy**)

If the story is based entirely on confidential sources, reporters cannot prove truth without disclosing the source. In some states, their refusal to answer questions during pre-trial discovery will result in an automatic judgment against them.

Affidavits & Escape Clauses

One way to cover that possibility is to give the reporter a sworn affidavit, with a written agreement that your identity will be kept confidential unless it is needed to defend a lawsuit.

This technique is invaluable if the story is extremely sensitive.

I worked as producer and editor for a series of investigative reports after a group of doctors at a major hospital became concerned about several staff members. They said heart specialists were performing experimental, unnecessary surgery on elderly patients so they could publish their findings in medical journals. The death rate in those procedures was very high.

The Doctor Was Not In

Some anesthesiologists at the same hospital were not even present during major surgery, their colleagues told us. They substituted interns, but the patient was billed as though the more experienced anesthesiologist had been there the entire time.

A number of more ethical doctors on the staff were alarmed about what they knew, but were reluctant to go public with their accusations.

If we produce this story, we told our sources, we will almost certainly be sued. We can't do it unless we know we can defend such a lawsuit.

So they leaked internal hospital records to us, and gave us sworn affidavits about what they had seen and heard in the operating room. On the back of each affidavit, we gave the doctors a written agreement never to disclose the doctor's identity unless the statement was needed to defend ourselves in court.

In our script, we said, "We have sworn affidavits from a dozen doctors who say they have seen ..." There was never even a suggestion of a lawsuit from either the doctors or the hospital. They knew we had the evidence that would convince a jury.

Anonymous Calls

An anonymous telephone call to a reporter is sometimes all it takes to get the story started.

When I was working in Louisville, a caller one afternoon told me half the traffic tickets written by city police were "fixed." I didn't believe him. So he began reading me specific percentages of cases that were nolle prossed (dismissed by the prosecutor). My ears picked up. "Sounds like you have some kind of computer analysis," I said. "You're right," he said, "And if you're a good reporter, you'll get a copy."

Fixing Traffic Tickets

Then he hung up. Within a week, I had found a source who had a copy of the court analysis. I learned that political precinct captains had the power to fix tickets. So many were brought in, the court clerk had to work overtime to mark the cases as dismissed before each court session. That was the first story.

Based on my experience, I knew the dismissal of drunk driving arrests is a major money-maker in a corrupt system. So I hired a group of law students to help me collect all the data on several years of drunk driving arrests. We learned that not a single drunk driver had ever been sentenced to jail. That was the second story.

Missing Students

Most drunk drivers who were found guilty were sent to traffic school. So I went to the traffic school records and discovered that half the drivers sentenced to attend class never showed up, and nobody did anything about it. That was the third story.

In the process of investigating all these court cases, I learned that one particular bail bondsman was a key player in arranging for charges to be dismissed. That led to a documentary on corruption within the bail bond system.

As a result, the Kentucky Legislature outlawed bail bondsmen. Until recently, Kentucky was the only state in the Union where the state acts as the bondsman.

All that from one anonymous call.

Beware Caller ID

But be careful. With caller ID, your identity can be easily discovered. Use a pay phone.

Another way to get information to reporters is to mail it in a plain envelope. The reporter is protected in that way, too. If the source ever becomes the focus of a lawsuit, a grand jury or legislative investigation, the reporter can honestly say, "I don't know who sent those papers to me."

Still another technique is to write a detailed memo and circulate it widely inside your organization.

A copy will probably wind up in a reporter's hands. It could have been leaked by lots of people.

Partial Shield Laws

Some states have partial shield laws. The reporter cannot be forced to reveal the source, but any physical evidence provided by a confidential source can be obtained through a court process.

This happened to me once in Kentucky, which had a partial shield law. I had broadcast a tape recording of a police official carefully explaining the payoff system to a man who wanted to open an illegal gambling joint.

The tape had been made as the officer drove the ambitious gambler around in his squad car. You could hear the police radio in the background.

How Was the Tape Made?

I was hauled into court and asked how I obtained the tape. I refused to say, and the judge upheld my right to remain silent. But the prosecutor was able to obtain the audio cassette. It was put through extensive laboratory testing. The police wanted to know how the tape was made, and how I got it. There might have been other microphones in other cars. They wanted to know where the leak was. They never found out.

Fingerprints & Copy Machines

Another caution: wipe fingerprints from anything you mail a reporter anonymously. Use rubber gloves in handling the documents and the envelope you mail them in. If you're sending copies of restricted documents, make the copies at a public copying machine, or one that is used by dozens of people. With microscopic analysis, sometimes copies can be traced back to the machine that made them.

Leave it on Your Desk

Another favorite trick is to simply leave it out on your desk, as the prosecutor did in the movie, *Absence of Malice*. One of the first skills young reporters develop is reading upside down.

When a corruption investigation surfaced in Miami, I tried to obtain the list of people who were being notified that their conversations with a court fixer had been intercepted through a police wiretap. The list contained dozens of public officials.

Disclosure a Federal Crime

But it was a federal crime to disclose the list. I checked my mailbox each day, looking for the Plain Brown Wrapper. No luck.

One afternoon, I received a call from someone I knew. "Can you come over to the boss's office right away?" he asked. "He needs to talk to you about something important."

I dropped what I was doing and ran over. When I arrived, the man who had called me was sitting in the outer office, alone. The receptionist was gone. The boss' office was empty.

I Must Look Stupid

"The boss is down in the men's room," my contact told me. "Go on into his office. He'll be back in a minute."

I thought it was strange to be ushered into the inner sanctum with the boss absent. Then it became stranger. My contact left me in the office alone, and closed the door.

On a table in plain sight was the list of people intercepted on the wiretap. Beside it was a blank legal pad.

I know I look dumb, but that day I must have looked truly stupid. My contact in the outer office rolled a pencil under the door.

SKILLS

Speeches

Waking Up the Photographers

It is a major speech. You know the media will be there. You *want* them to be there. The audience you need to reach is the entire community, far beyond the civic club or union hall. So you spend a lot of time writing the speech. Polishing phrases. Trying them out on your co-workers.

The big day comes. Sure enough, three television cameras are there, legs spread wide, standing directly in front of the platform. The bright lights come on as you're introduced, and you begin, with all the cameras rolling.

But the beginning is jokes and fluff. By the time you reach the heart of the speech, the lights are dark and the cameras dead. The photographers are back at their seats, eating their pie. Not even paying attention.

Where's the Good Stuff?

Speeches are like white water rafting. Hard to tell where the exciting stuff is. You coast on smooth water, so quiet you can hear birds in overhanging trees. Then, quite suddenly, there is a rush of sound ahead. You come around the bend into rapids and the roar of white water.

When you get to that point in your speech, the reporters will nudge the photographers. Wake up! Get the camera rolling! But by the time the cameras are going, you may be back in calm water. The photographers shrug their shoulders and go back to their pie.

You may interrupt dessert several times. The real message may never reach the television audience.

Don't let it happen next time. Here's how to make sure the photographers will be alert and rolling at the critical moment:

Release Advance Copies

Give copies of the speech in advance to every reporter there. This gives them an opportunity to read through and pick the sections they want to videotape.

Since they will only have air time to report your major thrust — perhaps one side issue — they will mark those sections, and tell the photographer to shoot them.

Back at the station, this saves editing time. They know exactly what they have on tape. It doesn't have to be logged, and they don't have to roll back and forth through long sections of dull tape, searching for a usable bite.

Print & Radio Like It

Radio will usually record the entire speech. A transcript helps them, too, find what they want on the audio tape. If you're in a room where the speaker system is feeding into a source for the news media, radio reporters can save tape and editing time by only recording what they've marked in the script.

Print reporters won't have to take notes. They will follow along, marking the spots where you deviated from the prepared text. You'll find the quotes on tomorrow's front page are much more accurate this way.

Leak Part of It

Leak portions of the speech to the morning newspaper the day before. This will work only if what you're saying is truly newsworthy. If it is, the morning paper will have a story:

> *In a speech prepared for delivery at today's meeting of the Chum and Chowder Society, Power Company President Mike Megawatt says electric bills will rise much higher if his company is not allowed to burn coal in its Smoky Hollow plant. Environmental groups are expected to oppose any shift from natural gas.*

The advance story in the newspaper convinces radio and television assignment editors they should have reporters there to cover it. In most communities, a local radio newscaster will read the newspaper story on the air, word for word.

The newspaper will be there to see what else happens. You might say something in the question-and-answer session following the speech. Or the audience might lynch you.

Two for One

Leaking the speech gives you two newspaper stories for one speech; radio coverage with no effort on your part; the newspaper and radio stories alert readers to watch for the story on TV tonight; it convinces the television assignment editor the speech is worth covering, and the advance stories in both print and radio will probably turn out a bigger, more responsive audience.

IMPORTANT: Don't leak everything to the newspaper in advance. Save the best quotes. That way, your audience won't feel like they're hearing a secondhand speech. There will also be fresh material for radio this afternoon and TV tonight.

Signals for the Good Stuff

Many of the best, most newsworthy speeches are not written in advance. They're spontaneous and unrehearsed. So you need to develop signals that tell TV photographers and radio reporters you're approaching something worth taping.

You're moving along, and you know the exciting stuff is just around the corner. You look over. The cameras are idle. To wake up the photographers, give them a warning. Something like:

Listen Up, Now

- "Now, if you don't hear anything else I say today, I want you to hear this. This is important." Or —

- "What I'm about to say is going to make a lot of people angry. It's going to cause a lot of hard feelings." (They're rushing now to turn on the cameras and tape recorders) Or —

- "Before I came here today, I gave a lot of thought to what I'm about to say. Nobody else has been willing to say this in public. I think it's time we talked about it."

Winning with the News Media

That kind of tease not only wakes up the photographer, it also whets the appetite of your live audience.

Tell 'em What You Told 'em

Remember to tell them what you just told them, but make it shorter. You'll discover that the summary is the perfect form for the time limitations of broadcasting. After every important section of a speech, either prepared or off-the-cuff, **summarize**. The summary will often be the bite broadcasters use in their stories.

You should never again make a speech without drawings, pictures, charts, videotape, slides, overheads — something visual.

Show While You Tell

You must show me something while you're telling me something. Otherwise, I won't remember. Television has conditioned an entire generation of Americans who listen, learn and remember only if the message is both sound and pictures.

Often the pictures will be the stronger element in their memory, and the more powerful motivator. You can do it with a wide variety of techniques that range from poster boards and flip charts to LCD projectors that project onto a wall-size screen the text and presentation graphics from a laptop computer and/or a videotape recorder. (See **SKILLS/News Conferences**)

Try Not to Read It

Try not to read your speech. A speech read to a live audience is never as good as one that seems spontaneous. Conversational. Impassioned. Unless you're an accomplished reader and actor, reading a speech puts the TV and radio audience to sleep.

Virtually every word processing program can generate very large type that's easy to read at a glance. Rather than print the entire speech, have a simple outline. Bullets in 72-point type.

Then you talk extemporaneously about each point.

Speech TelePrompTers

If the speech is especially sensitive and you can't trust yourself to deliver it extemporaneously, you can rent a TelePrompTer® that works just like those the anchors use in TV studios.

You may have noticed little panes of glass on each side of the podium at political conventions or presidential speeches. Years ago, when I first spotted them on TV, I wondered if they were bulletproof glass to protect the speaker. Awfully small, though.

They're actually glass reflectors for a small computer monitor. The monitor is lower, where you can't see it. On the monitor screen, the speech scrolls by. The glass reflects the words and the speaker reads them. The speed of the scrolling is controlled by an operator who keeps pace with the speaker. (See more on how TelePrompters® work in **INSIDE THE MEDIA/Newscast**)

Presidential Speeches

All recent presidents have used TelePrompTers® for important speeches. Because they don't do it every day, they're not as skillful as TV anchors. Watch the next presidential speech closely on TV. The President will read a sentence or two from the prompter to his left, then switch to the prompter at his right. It looks like he's simply making eye contact with the entire audience.

If you didn't know how major speeches are choreographed, you wouldn't be aware he was reading. Occasionally, though, he'll give it away by lapsing into a steady rhythm, swinging back and forth between prompters. One sentence to the left, turn; one sentence to the right, turn; one sentence to the left, turn again.

The Contact Lens Trick

Suppose you wear contact lenses, but need reading glasses. Some people who work hard at their speech technique have a contact lens for one eye with a reading prescription; a lens for the other eye with a distance prescription.

If they're reading from a prepared text, they read with one eye. When they look up and make eye contact with people in the audience, they use the other eye. It takes concentration, practice, and a strong stomach. Looking at the audience with the reading lens can make some people instantly seasick.

Wireless Microphones

One of the neatest gadgets to free you from the podium and let you be more animated is a wireless microphone. They're widely available now in electronics stores for less than $100. A professional-quality system that will do a better job in very large auditoriums or hotel ballrooms will run $350 to $500. I highly recommend them.

Podium Paralysis

Behind a podium, many people grab hold and can't let go. The podium inhibits their normal gestures. We can't see the speaker's body English. They get podium paralysis.

Coaching clients for a major speech, I often suggest that they come out to the side of the podium. Perhaps lean on it, to give the impression of a more intimate, off-the-cuff conversation. But you'll need a wireless mike to do that. Otherwise, the audience can't hear you.

The tiny microphone is clipped to your tie or lapel. A wire runs to a transmitter clipped to your belt. The transmitter is battery-powered, about the size of a pager.

The mike transmits to a small radio receiver, which plugs into the room's loudspeaker system. The wireless lets you wander from poster board or laptop to point at what you're projecting on the screen.

Freedom to Wander

When you finish speaking and take questions from the audience, the wireless mike will allow you to walk into the crowd and have a close-up conversation with those who ask questions. The mike picks up their voices, as well as yours, and amplifies them through the speaker system. The people who ask questions feel they get a much more personal response this way.

During breaks, remember to turn the mike off. Otherwise, everything you say in the hall or restroom will be amplified through the speaker system.

When the speech is over, don't leave too soon. Stay long enough to let reporters covering the speech talk to you. In this way, they can make their stories unique. They'll get better play if they're not a carbon copy of the competition's.

SKILLS

Talk Shows

Learning to Be Acceptably Rude

There are two kinds of talk shows.

The first are the syndicated shows that have replaced the old-time, freak show at the carnival. New, miniature replicas of the Inquisition, where exhibitionists confess the most intimate details of their lives and lusts while the voyeuristic crowd, aroused and loving it, plays holier-than-thou, clucking their tongues, pointing their fingers, screaming their condemnation of the vile guests in the pit.

In 1998, a new element was introduced. Jerry Springer's ratings leaped past the competition when fistfights between bizarre guests, and sometimes the audience, became a regular event.

This is About the Other Kind

This chapter is about the other kind of talk show, where guests philosophize, discuss current events and sometimes engage in cerebral, witty exchanges with sophisticated hosts like Tim Russert, Ted Koppel or Larry King.

If you're a guest for one of those shows, the studio will seem like a huge, dark cavern. The ceiling will be a jungle of black, oddly-shaped stalactites, wires, booms, catwalks and stage lights.

Over in one corner, there may be a cozy little set designed to create an illusion. Perhaps a cardboard bookcase, a fireplace, or a mural of the city skyline. Sometimes a potted palm and two chairs, where you and the moderator will chat as though you were at the beach without your sunglasses.

Or it may be a panel show, where you sit at a desk facing a group of reporters who fire questions at you. Other guests may be there to attack your point of view. Some of your adversaries may be in another city thousands of miles away, connected by satellite.

It's Cold in There

The air conditioning is set low in television studios to counteract the heat of the lights. If it weren't that cold before the show, you'd sweat and be uncomfortable before it was over. The thermostat is usually set for men who wear coats and ties. Women wearing thin, short-sleeved dresses sometimes turn blue and have to fight to keep from shivering. Long sleeves will help you cope with the cold.

If the audience remembers what you wore, you wore the wrong thing. Wear clothes and jewelry that won't distract us. Unless you're trying to tell us something about clothes or jewelry. (See **SKILLS/Interviews-Broadcast**)

Arrive Early

It's a good idea to arrive about a half hour before the show is scheduled. Producers have nightmares about guests arriving late, or missing the show entirely. Being on time is just as critical for a taped show as a live one. At most stations and networks, the studio and crew are scheduled solidly for months in advance. If you miss today's taping time, there may not be another opening. Getting there early gives you time to get acquainted with the place, the moderator and the other guests.

Time for Makeup

You'll need some extra time to apply makeup. For field interviews, women should wear the same makeup they'd wear to work. But in a TV studio, the light will be much brighter and harsher. You'll need heavier makeup. You may look better if your eye shadow and cheek blush are a tone darker than usual.

Outside the studio, men don't normally use makeup. In the studio, to look normal, you need to wipe pancake makeup across your beard area and the shiny places. The floor crew will have makeup and a communal sponge. You may want to bring your own. It's available in most drug stores, in different shades to match skin tone. To apply, wet a small sponge, rub it on the hard cake of makeup, and then wipe it on your face.

It doesn't smell, and will wash off easily when the show is over. Receding hairlines and noses are particularly shiny in bright studio lights. And even if they shave just before they go to the TV station, some men with very dark beards look like they came in from skid row.

Apply just enough makeup to look normal through a studio camera. If it's done right, you can walk out of the studio and nobody will know you're wearing it.

The Choice Place to Sit

By arriving early, you can get a better idea of the ground the moderator intends to cover. If there are more than two people on the show — and you have a choice — take an end seat, rather than the middle. From the end, you can look at the other guests without moving your head back and forth. In the middle, it's like a tennis match as the conversation bounces back and forth.

Hiding the Mike Cord

Clip your mike so we won't see the cord. This may take some effort, but it's worth it. If the mike is clipped to a tie, run the cord inside a buttoned shirt to the waist band, then inside the waist band to one side. The only cord we'll see will be at the mike.

Clipped to a coat lapel, the cord can run from the lapel under the coat to your waistband at the side.

Women's clothes can make this a lot tougher. With a pullover top, you may have to run the cord inside your blouse, then out at the neck. Another route tapes the wire up the center of your back, then under a collar to the front where it's clipped.

You Can Take More Control

In some ways, in-studio interviews are very different from field interviews. Most of these shows will not be edited. They're broadcast live, or videotaped and broadcast later just as they were shot. You have more control over subject matter.

Through your answers, you may be able to lead the discussion from one area to another. Your answers can be a little longer. But if you begin to ramble, a good moderator will cut you off, try to force you to answer the question, or move on to the next subject before you make your point.

In a taped field interview, you can make your point repeatedly. They'll edit and use just one. You must be much more clever on a talk show. To repeat the same thought, you have to state it very differently. Otherwise we think you're getting forgetful, and can't remember that you said that before. Or that you've been programmed by a speech writer and can't hold a conversation without a script.

Late in the 1988 presidential campaign, Michael Dukakis appeared on ABC's *Nightline* with Ted Koppel. No matter what Koppel asked, Dukakis reverted to his canned campaign material, repeating it several times. He had been trained to do that in taped interviews. On a live show, he looked like a wind-up toy.

Quick and Snappy

When the moderator asks a question, the best answer is usually a concise, one-sentence statement of your feeling or opinion, followed by your explanation of why. If you begin to talk too long, and get cut off, you'll still make your point.

Compared to other forms of radio and television, talk shows are boring. They normally feature "talking heads." No visuals for TV, no natural sound for radio. No interviews to insert, and change the pace. Just talk.

Talk shows work best when there is quick, snappy dialogue between guest and moderator. The quicker the exchanges, the more interesting the conversation seems to listeners and viewers.

Yell and I'll Believe You

The person who is loudest and most aggressive is usually the most believable. Particularly if the obnoxious person goes unchallenged. That's why so many talk show hosts are so aggressive and insulting. It also keeps the audience awake.

A talk show on radio or TV will often have more than one guest. Sometimes they have very different points of view. There's only so much time. And there are no rules to give each guest an equal share of that time. The assertive guest will get more time than the others.

So you have to learn how to be what I call "acceptably rude."

Learn to Be Acceptably Rude

For television and radio, you'll find that you're much too polite. You wait until others have finished their thought. You're patient while they ramble, trying to find their point.

When they make a mistake, or say something that is obviously untrue, you've been conditioned to sit quietly until it's your turn.

DON'T DO THAT.

As soon as the moderator or another guest says something that's inaccurate, interrupt. "Wait a minute!" you say loudly. "That's not true, and you know it's not true. Why would you say something so obviously phony?"

Not Challenged, It Must Be True

If you don't interrupt, the thought or statistic will be lodged as truth in the minds of viewers and listeners. It's much harder to dislodge it several minutes later. Interrupting also gives you an opportunity to take center stage.

If the guest or moderator you've interrupted comes right back, then the show becomes more interesting.

I remember hosting a talk show on capital punishment. The proponent was the state attorney general. The opponent was an American Civil Liberties Union lawyer. Both had done this before. They knew how to mix it up to make it interesting.

All I had to do as moderator was introduce them and then separate them for commercial breaks. The half-hour went by in a flash. As I passed through the control room on my way back to the newsroom, a technician who'd watched the taping said, "Boy, that was good television. I'd watch that!"

Conflict Makes Us Listen

Sharp conflict is a major element for intellectual debate and spectator sports. We like contests where the two opponents are evenly matched and eager to do battle. Team sports with lopsided scores — boxing matches where the fighters only dance and clinch — make us go to the bedroom, the bathroom, the kitchen, or another channel.

Knowing how far you can go without being obnoxious or rude is very difficult unless you've seen or heard yourself on tape. In my media training for the talk show format, I push people to be more rude and assertive.

I goad them until they feel they're out of bounds. Then they look at the tape. In playback, they're not nearly as rude or assertive as they thought they were. Audio and videotape tend to tone down the conflict. It takes some practice to position yourself with just the right amount of assertiveness.

If you overdo it, you'll be shrill. You turn us off. Or you can overpower another guest and make us feel like you're a bully. We will side with the underdog.

Take Along Your Visuals

If you have visuals (videotape, film, still pictures or slides) that will help tell your story, let the producer of the TV talk show know several days in advance. The producer needs to look at them and decide whether to use them.

Your visuals may have to be converted to fit the station's technical format. You and the producer work out in advance how you'll cue the pictures. You can do it like a sportscaster — "OK, let's go to the videotape." This accomplishes several things for you:

- By pre-planning the use of the visuals, you have much more control over the content of the show

- Switching the camera from talking head to the visuals makes it possible for you to continue much longer than the usual 10 or 15 seconds; if the video is good and captures our attention, you can talk as long as the video runs

- If you're in a debate format, your pictures will be much more compelling to sell your side of the issue; and they may also enable you to have more time than your opponent

Bring the Book or Product

If you're there to talk about a book or a product, bring it along so the studio cameras can show it while you're discussing it.

If you're dealing with a very technical subject, or one that involves a lot of numbers, the producer may want to sit down with you well in advance. This way, the station's artists can sketch or diagram what you're talking about to make it more understandable.

Avoid the Monitor

In the TV studio, there will be monitors that show what the audience is seeing. After the show begins, avoid the powerful temptation to watch the monitors. It's very difficult not to sneak a look at yourself on TV, but the camera may catch you. Very amateurish.

Pay attention to what other people are saying. Look at them. Remember, the director will be constantly switching to cutaway shots to make the video more interesting. Don't get caught on camera picking your nose or yawning when someone else is talking.

Bring an Assistant

In **SKILLS/Interviews-General**, I suggest having a staff member present for an interview, to help you retrieve information you can't remember.

When you participate in TV or radio talk shows, the assistant is even more vital. The assistant should bring a briefcase with pertinent documents, a legal pad and a Magic Marker®. The aide sits in the TV studio, where you can see the cues, but the camera can't. If you forget a point or a number, the staffer writes it on the legal pad and holds it up like a cue card.

During radio talk shows, the assistant can sit across the desk, in plain view.

Between Rounds

If you're in a debate format, the assistant can run over during commercial breaks to whisper in your ear, or hand you a document to use during the next block.

Just like the assistants who help boxers between rounds, your staffer can patch up your cuts, tell you what seems to be working, and which strategy to abandon. The aide will probably have a better feel for how well you're doing than you will.

Pace Yourself for Time

Once the show begins, you need to pace yourself, and be aware of time. If the conversation is lively, 30 minutes goes very quickly. When it's over, you may realize that you never got to the main point you wanted to make. If it looks like the moderator is not going to reach that area, look for some way to take the conversation there yourself. Something like —

"You know, we've danced around this entire subject without getting to what I believe should be our main concern." Then tell us what it is.

Time Signals

There are some strategies that can be played with time segments of the broadcast, particularly if you're debating with another guest. A 30-minute show usually has two or three commercial breaks. The floor crew holds up signs that tell the moderator when to break for a commercial. A big "2" means two minutes. A "30," thirty seconds before the break.

The signal that tells the moderator to hurry is both hands rolling — the same signal a football referee uses to restart the clock. In television, that means speed it up. If they need to slow down and fill time, the floor manager gives a signal that looks like stretching taffy — "Stretch it out." Waving at the moderator means, "End the show. Tell everybody goodbye." And a finger drawn across the throat means, "Cut it NOW. RIGHT NOW."

If you're aware of those signals, it helps you form an answer that will fit before a break. The moderator won't have to interrupt you in mid-thought.

Time Strategy

If you want to drop your big bomb so the camera can catch your opponent's surprise and fluster, make sure there's enough time before a break. You'll lose the effect if you drop the bomb and the moderator says, "We'll be right back to get the other side's response." That will also give your opponent about two minutes to hide the shock and come up with a good alibi.

Surprise!

There are few surprise witnesses or shocking new evidence in criminal trials these days. Unlike the Perry Mason show, most rules of court procedure now give each side an opportunity before the trial to take depositions from every witness who will testify. They get to examine every shred of evidence long before the trial begins.

One of the attractions of live television debates is the chance that we'll see the gladiators use a surprise attack. We want to see them speared to the wall, writhing in mortal agony. There's no better place to drop new documentary evidence than in front of a live television camera.

The Zap! Scenario

The scenario can go something like this:

SENATOR BACKWATER: Nobody has a better voting record than I do when it comes to civil rights issues. I have spent my entire life fighting for justice and equality, regardless of race, creed or color.

CHALLENGER UPSTART: (reaching into a briefcase) Funny you would say that, Senator. I just happen to have a picture here of you, at age 21, leading a Ku Klux Klan parade down the main street of the little town where you went to college. I'll hold it up so the cameras can see it.

SENATOR BACKWATER: (flustered) That's a damned lie. Whatever trash you have there is a phony, cheap counterfeit.

CHALLENGER UPSTART: I thought you might say something like that, Senator, so I did some more research and came up with this column which you wrote for the college newspaper. Let me refresh your memory. In it, you say that blacks — I guess I should quote you directly — you say "niggers" are genetically inferior and should never be allowed to enter the campus because they would not be able to understand abstract thought or civilized behavior. And I have here a sworn affidavit from the editor of that newspaper, certifying that you are the same Phineas Backwater who led Ku Klux Klan rallies and wrote this essay. I'll make all of this material available to the reporters here in the studio just as soon as this debate is over.

ZAP!

Be Sure It's True

No other forum can match the impact of live, juicy exposure on television. But you must be sure the information is absolutely true. If it's not, you'll be accused of dirty tricks. If you hit below the belt, or take cheap shots, you'll look shady and sleazy. In the end, you'll be damaged more than your opponent.

Evasion Is Amplified

If you're on the receiving end of a tough question, radio and television make an evasive answer much more obvious. Pauses and stumbling for the right word are amplified. It's probably best to answer the question as directly as you can, put your position in its best light, and move on. Use the question that points to your weakness as a springboard to reach your strength. Like:

OTTO MAKER: Yes, we fought the recall of that model because there has not been a single critical injury as the result of a failure of that part. Not one. On the other hand, we voluntarily recalled the 1994 model when we realized we had a problem with a bolt in the rear suspension system. Nobody had to force us to spend 80 million dollars for that recall. We did it voluntarily, once we were able to confirm there was a problem. And while we're talking about accidents, let's look at the difference in fatal accident frequency for domestic cars versus imports. I just happen to have the latest study here with me, charted so the camera can pick it up.

Take the Tough Ones First

For best overall effect, get the troublesome questions out of the way early. Then you have the rest of the show to counter with a brighter side. TV producers format their news shows that way. Put all the bad news at the beginning of the newscast. Close the show with a light, funny feature story — a "kicker" that leaves the audience smiling or feeling maybe everything's not so bad after all.

Radio Talk Shows

Some radio talk show hosts are so insulting you have to be a masochist to be their guest. You'll feel flattered when the producer calls you. But it may not be in your best interest to accept.

On the show, you'll get some wacko calls. Laughter is sometimes the best defense for stupid or insulting questions. The callers to these shows tend to be at the far ends of the opinion spectrum.

You're not going to change their minds. State your point, and if the host doesn't cut them off, move on with something like a chuckle and "It's very clear to me that I'm not going to change your mind and you're not going to change mine. But I respect your right to that opinion."

Section Three

INSIDE THE MEDIA

INSIDE THE MEDIA

Editing

Did I Really Say That?

Editing is an art form. Your interview can be edited so skillfully, you can't tell what they took out, or stitched together. You can't see the scar where a good plastic surgeon makes the incision. Or — when they've finished editing what you said, you may think the editor used a chain saw.

Once you've given an interview, you're at the mercy of the reporter and the editor. A tiny fraction of what you say in the interview will ever be published or broadcast. Maybe none of it. You may wind up on the cutting room floor. Simply a notation in the print reporter's shorthand pad.

Broadcast Interviews

The usual hallway interview, on the run, as you go in or out of a meeting, will last about five minutes.

A sit-down session for radio or TV may go 10 to 20 minutes. Out of that, a maximum of 20 to 30 seconds will be used — and that much, only if they use several of your sound bites, separated by reporter narration or bites from interviews with other people. For one sound bite, they'll normally use only about 10 seconds of what you said.

Newspaper reporters may spend an hour or two with you for a daily story; a day or two for a lengthy profile. Magazine writers may live with you for a week.

FACE Formula for Print

An interesting phenomenon is taking place. Print reporters are choosing the same kind of formularized quotes for their stories that radio and TV use. They simply use more of them. The FACE Formula applies for all media. (See **SKILLS/Interviews-Broadcast**) The editing for television is more complicated, because it must deal simultaneously with both words and pictures.

People who work in broadcasting change the way they listen to conversation. Even when they're not working, they find themselves involuntarily scanning what you're saying, marking off usable sound bites. It is like panning for gold. Somewhere in that muddy dialogue, there must be a few bright, memorable nuggets.

TV News Editing

Let's watch the TV editing process.

At a city council meeting, Councilman Luther "Red" Light proposes that the city revoke its current prostitution ordinances. He wants to make prostitution legal in a specially-zoned area near the downtown convention center. A local television crew catches up with him in a hallway after the meeting. He is persuaded to come back to his desk in the council chamber for an on-camera interview. This is a transcript:

1 REPORTER: Councilman, you
2 proposed tonight that the city le-
3 galize prostitution. Why?
4 LIGHT: It seems to me that
5 we've wasted enough time and
6 money and law enforcement
7 resources chasing them from one
8 street corner to the next. Have
9 you ever tried to figure what it's
10 costing this town to bring a
11 hooker to court, so she can laugh
12 at the law, pay her $50 fine, and
13 get back on the street in time to
14 catch the lunch-hour customers?
15 It's ridiculous. An absolute waste
16 of time and resources. It's time

17 we had police officers chasing
18 murderers and rapists and robbers
19 who terrorize and kill and maim,
20 instead of a few women trying
21 to make a living, supplying a
22 service for which there seems to
23 be a great demand.
24 REPORTER: You say a few
25 women. It's hard for a man to
26 walk from City Hall to the police
27 station without being propositioned.
28 Aren't you just —
29 LIGHT: Exactly. The present
30 law doesn't work. The vice squad
31 made 84 arrests for prostitution
32 last month. You know how many
33 of those arrested spent any time
34 in jail? I'll tell you. None. Not a
35 single one. I've done my home-
36 work on this. The vice squad consists
37 of eight detectives, a lieutenant
38 and a captain. Ten altogether,
39 who draw total salaries of $37,280
40 per month. Add cars, medical
41 insurance, other fringe benefits,
42 and the price to the taxpayers is
43 roughly $50,000 per month —
44 $600,000 per year. Now, they
45 arrested 84 prostitutes last month —
46 alleged prostitutes. Thirty-two
47 of those arrests were thrown out
48 by the prosecutor's office and
49 never got to court. That leaves
50 52. Twenty-one of those were
51 dismissed by the judge. That leaves
52 31. Every one of them pleaded
53 guilty and paid a $50 fine. A total
54 of $1,550 for the city coffers.
55 Why, that won't even pay for the
56 gasoline to run the cars for the

57 vice squad, much less their salaries,
58 and the salaries of the clerks,
59 the prosecutors, the judges and
60 secretaries and bailiffs. It's not
61 cost-productive. Never has been.
62 And it doesn't stop prostitution.
63 The world's oldest profession is
64 here to stay. I say zone it into an
65 area where we can control it.
66 Properly done, it might even draw
67 more people to the city. Might
68 as well make some money from it
69 instead of wasting more than half a
70 million dollars a year, trying to
71 enforce stupid, hypocritical laws
72 that don't work.
73 REPORTER: You realize the
74 preachers will organize to fight
75 your proposal?
76 LIGHT: Sure, I do. But every
77 single preacher knows, down
78 deep in his heart, I'm right.
79 They've got their job to do, I've
80 got mine. But hellfire, this is the
81 20th century. Sex isn't going to go
82 away. It's time we quit pretending
83 it will. I know the preachers
84 will come after me. But in their
85 hearts, they know I'm right.
86 REPORTER: The opponents of
87 legalized prostitution say it increases
88 violent crime.
89 LIGHT: What do you think ten
90 officers fighting crime, instead
91 of chasing little girls down the
92 sidewalk, would accomplish?
93 That's a lot of crap. Put those ten
94 officers to work catching robbers,
95 rapists, killers and thieves, and
96 you'll see the crime rate in this

97 town go down, not up.
98 REPORTER: Thank you, Councilman.

This is what the finished script looks like:

(V/O is Voice-Over videotape. SOT is Sound-On-Tape)

Lead-in

ANCHOR LIVE   CITY POLICE SHOULD QUIT CHASING
                           PROSTITUTES AND CONCENTRATE ON
                           VIOLENT CRIME. THAT'S WHAT CITY
                           COUNCILMAN "RED" LIGHT PROPOSED
                           AT TONIGHT'S COUNCIL MEETING.
                           NEWSWATCH REPORTER SUSAN SCOOP
                           SAYS THE COUNCILMAN WANTS TO
                           CREATE A ZONE FOR LEGALIZED
                           PROSTITUTION NEAR THE DOWNTOWN
                           CONVENTION CENTER.

Videotape begins

SCOOP V/O   THIS IS GOODTIME STREET, JUST TWO
(wide street shot)   BLOCKS FROM THE POLICE STATION.
                           A PRIME AREA FOR PROSTITUTION.
V/O (Hookers waving)   IT COSTS ABOUT $600,000 A YEAR TO
                           OPERATE THE CITY VICE SQUAD.
V/O (Light)   COUNCILMAN RED LIGHT SAYS THE
                           EXPENSE IS A WASTE OF TIME AND
                           MONEY.

SOT LIGHT
(Line 80)   This is the 20th century. Sex isn't going to go
                           away ...
(Line 29)   The present law doesn't work ...
(Line 15)   It's ridiculous. An absolute waste of time
                           and resources. It's time we had police
                           officers chasing murderers and rapists and
                           robbers.

SCOOP V/O   LIGHT SAYS THE VICE SQUAD MADE 84
(File tape of vice   ARRESTS LAST MONTH. MOST OF THE
squad raid)   CASES WERE DISMISSED BEFORE THEY
                           WENT TO TRIAL. THIRTY-ONE
                           PLEADED GUILTY AND PAID FIFTY
                           DOLLAR FINES. NOBODY WENT TO JAIL.

SOT LIGHT
(Line 55)   That won't even pay for the gasoline to run
                             the cars for the vice squad . . .
(Line 63)   The world's oldest profession is here to stay.
                             I say zone it into an area where we can
                             control it.

SOT SCOOP   LIGHT SAYS THE CITY'S RELIGIOUS
(standup)   LEADERS WILL ATTACK HIM AND HIS
                             PROPOSAL — BUT IN THEIR HEARTS,
                             THEY KNOW HE'S RIGHT. I'M SUSAN
                             SCOOP, ON THE NIGHT BEAT FOR
                             NEWSWATCH ELEVEN

Building the Edited Tape

Audio phrases can be shuffled and spliced together, and you can't hear the edit. But editing the video requires some finesse. You will not even be aware of where the edits were made, unless you understand the process. Here's how they do it:

The reporter first reviews the interview tape and decides which sound bites she'll use. The story will be built around the interview.

She may have recorded the interview separately on a small audio recorder. She can listen to it in the car, on the way back to the television station, and save valuable time if she's close to deadline.

When the script is written and approved, the reporter and editor work together in the editing booth. At most stations, the photographer who shoots the tape also edits it.

Networks and stations in large cities are more specialized. Photographers shoot, and editors edit.

The Editing Console

The editing console is in a soundproof booth. It has two large videocassette recorders (VCRs), each with its own TV monitor. There is a microphone and a sound mixer in the booth. The voice-over sound for the story is recorded here.

The videocassette recorders are wired together so that what is played on the LEFT VCR can be copied over to the RIGHT VCR.

The editor puts a blank videocassette in the RIGHT VCR. The story in its final, broadcast form will be assembled on this cassette.

Reporter's Voice, No Video

The script begins with reporter voice-over. Scoop reads the first section of script into the microphone. Her voice is recorded on the blank cassette in the RIGHT VCR. There is no picture to go with the voice. That comes later.

The RIGHT VCR can record audio, or video, or both at the same time.

Sound Bite Voice & Video

The first sound bite from Councilman Light comes next. The editor puts the interview tape, recorded at City Hall, into the LEFT VCR. He rolls to the section Scoop has selected.

Scoop gives him the "in-cue" — the words at the beginning of the sound bite — and the "out-cue."

In-cue: "This is the ..."
Out-cue: "... going to go away."

In- and Out-Cues

Leaving a half-second pause after the reporter's voice, the editor copies from LEFT VCR to RIGHT VCR Councilman Light saying, "This is the 20th century. Sex isn't going to go away." Both audio and video are copied at the same time. Then they search for the next phrase in the script and connect it to the first one — "The present law doesn't work." And then a third one — "It's ridiculous. An absolute waste of time and resources."

Scoop records more voice-over onto the tape in the RIGHT VCR, then another section of edited interview, and finally, Scoop's videotaped standup in the council chamber closes the story.

Standups

When we see a reporter talking on camera, it is called a standup. Whether she's sitting, walking, riding or standing, it's still a standup. Reporters want to be seen as much as possible in their stories. So most "packaged" stories include a standup.

If we looked at the tape in the RIGHT VCR now, we would see blank screen while reporter Scoop talks; Councilman Light talking; blank screen while Scoop talks; Councilman Light talking; Scoop doing her standup.

Covering Video Holes

They will go back now, to "cover" the video holes in the story. As the crew left the council meeting, they took time to shoot streetwalkers waving at cars near City Hall. They now edit this video under Scoop's voice, mixing in some of the natural sound from the street. The same process puts file tape video of a police raid to cover the second section of reporter voice-over. Now for the sleight-of-hand that will hide the interview edits

Jump Cuts

The edits are clearly visible. Dramatically visible. You can't miss them. They're called "jump cuts." The interview subject will always jump where the cut and splice was made.

At the beginning of the interview, Light was leaning forward, elbows on his desk. Then he lit a cigar. At one point, he shifted back in his swivel chair and put his hands behind his head.

In the first phrase they edited, Light is puffing on his cigar. The next phrase, butted against it, shows his hands, but no cigar. On arm is on the desk. In the third sound bite, he is leaning back with his hands behind his head.

As you watch the edited tape, it looks like the councilman suffers from a strange nerve disorder that makes him suddenly jerk from elbows-on-table to hands-behind-head. He also seems to do magic tricks that make cigars appear and disappear.

Cosmetic Cutaways

In the early days of television news, they decided jump cuts were too distracting. They developed the "cutaway" technique to hide them.

The cutaway shot is edited onto the story cassette for only a second or two. It replaces the picture of the councilman, so that your eyes cut away to something else. The sound is not changed. As soon as the jump cut passes, you see Councilman Light again.

In that brief cutaway second or two, you forget that he was smoking a cigar before you looked away. Your mind assumes that in the cutaway moment, he put out his cigar, or leaned back in his chair. If you diagram the finished videocassette as it will play on the air, it will look like the next page —

AUDIO TRACK	EDITED TAPE (combines audio & video)	VIDEO TRACK
Reporter script voice/over mixed with natural sound	Reporter narrates while we see streetwalkers	Streetwalkers
Councilman Light's voice	Interview line 80 — (Edit point) — Interview line 29 — (Edit point) — Interview line 15	Councilman — listener cutaway — Councilman — listener cutaway — Councilman
Reporter voice/over mixed with natural sound	Reporter narrates while we see file tape of recent vice squad raid	File tape of police raid
Councilman Light's voice	Interview line 55 — (Edit point) — Interview line 63	Councilman — two-shot cutaway — Councilman
Reporter sound-on-tape shot at City Hall	Reporter closes story with standup in Council chamber	Reporter standing in Council chamber

Favorite Cutaways

The two most frequently used cutaways are:

- **Two-Shot** - A wide-angle shot that shows both the reporter and the subject of the interview. The interviewee is talking, but the camera is too far away for us to tell whether the movement of the lips matches the words we're hearing.

- **Listener** - The reporter listening, or the reporter making notes. It is sometimes shot from behind, and over the shoulder, of the person being interviewed. Many reporters have a bad habit of nodding during listener cutaways, like those little toy dogs that sat in the rear windows of automobiles in the 1980s.

Print Also Edits

Print journalism interviews are heavily edited, too. Unless the full transcript is printed, a newspaper story takes a phrase here, a phrase there, often out of sequence.

But if the words are direct quotes, the ethics of print require an ellipsis (. . .) to tell readers where the edit points are.

That's the difference. People who work in television understand that a cutaway means an edit point, but most viewers don't know that. Complaints about TV news accuracy and quotes used out of context have been raised since the inception of television in this country.

Did He Really Say That?

The Selling of the Pentagon, a CBS documentary, caused a major furor — eventually a Congressional investigation — in the early 1970s. The criticism was based largely on editing of the interviews. "I said those words, but not in that order," the military spokesman argued. "When you string the phrases together in a different order, it changes the meaning of what I said."

Broadcasting Needs a Signal

If broadcasting would create some signal to tell viewers where an interview is edited, much of that kind of criticism could be avoided. During the cutaway, for instance, an audio beep could be inserted to tell the audience an edit took place. If the beep were standardized, it could become broadcasting's equivalent of the ellipsis.

In both broadcasting and print, an ethical reporter is very careful to make sure the edited version of an interview does not change the meaning or intent of what was said.

Jump-Cut Commercials

In the 1960s, the "hidden camera" was a favorite technique for television commercials. A woman, supposedly unaware of the camera, was asked to compare her laundry before and after it was washed in Brand X. An old man described his headache in great detail (like two billy-goats butting heads) and then told about his miraculous relief after taking two of the new pain killers.

Those interviews were heavily edited. Somewhere along the line, somebody said they were misleading if the edit points were hidden with cutaways. So commercials began letting the jump cuts show. As a result, we have become much more accustomed to jump cuts. Some news organizations, concerned they will be accused of distortion, let jump cuts show now in sensitive interviews.

Reverse Questions

Another editing device for broadcasting uses the "reverse question" between answers. After the interview, everyone is told to stay in position. The photographer shoots cutaways. The reporter is shot re-asking the same questions asked during the interview. The camera is reversed, shooting in the opposite direction, over the shoulder of the interview subject. The reverse-shot question can then be used as a bridge to get from one answer to another.

Instead of a cutaway at the edit point, we see and hear the reporter asking a question. Then we jump to an answer that may be five minutes away from the last answer. The effect is a continuously flowing conversation.

Listen Carefully

The danger in the reverse question technique is that the question may not be phrased exactly as it was when you answered it the first time. A slightly different question, spliced to the old answer, can be misleading.

When a broadcast reporter completes your interview, listen carefully as reverse questions are taped. If they're not restated exactly as they were when you were answering the question, politely point that out to the reporter.

If you have some reason to suspect the reporter's integrity, have a staff member make a shorthand transcript of the reporter's questions during the interview. The staffer can then compare the shorthand notes with the reverse questions that are taped.

Make Your Own Tape

If you have any reason to doubt the reporter's competence or integrity, make an audio or videotape of the entire interview. Make sure the reporter knows you're recording the interview, to avoid legal problems. The tape is the only proof you'll have if you complain that editing of the story was unfair or out of context. (See **SKILLS/Interviews** and **Defending Yourself**)

Double-Shooting

On a major TV network documentary — particularly a sensitive, controversial subject — interviews will be "double-shot." The entire interview is recorded by two cameras — one camera shooting the interview subject, the other taping the reporter.

In that way, reporter's questions and reactions are recorded exactly the way the interview subject saw and heard them. There can be no reverse question distortion. But few local stations or network field crews are given the resources to double-shoot interviews.

Sloppy Shorthand for Print

The big problem for print interviews is reporters whose shorthand is sloppy. They scribble furiously, and you think they're capturing your every word. Actually, most of them are only getting key phrases. So when it's time to write their story, they reconstruct the quote as best they remember it.

Sometimes the quote is distorted. Sometimes it's improved. Or it can be changed in such a way that it has no resemblance to what you really said.

Print Uses Tape, Too

Many print reporters now use audio recorders. The spread of the technique was prompted partly by readers' ability to compare quotes in newspapers with the same quotes on radio or TV.

But the problem for print reporters is that going back to review audio tape is a slow, tedious process. Even though there is an audio tape, the print reporter will usually make extensive notes. It's a lot easier to use the notes and ignore the tape. The tape becomes a backup.

One of your goals should be learning how to craft a quote so the reporter — whether print or broadcast — will use it exactly as you spoke it, without editing or taking it out of context. (See **STRATEGY/Accuracy** & **SKILLS/Interviews** chapters)

Editing by Headline

A perennial complaint about newspapers is the inaccuracy of headlines. That, too, is a form of editing. When the headline distorts the story, you should complain. (See **STRATEGY/Accuracy** and **STRATEGY/Fighting Back**)

Headline writers are true specialists. They must condense the thrust of the story into five or six words. And the words must fit the column, very much like a crossword puzzle.

On deadline, the headline writers sometimes write the headline after reading only three or four paragraphs of the story. If they had read a little further, they would have a very different perspective, and a more accurate headline.

Editing by Committee

Newspaper and magazine stories go through the hands of a series of editors. At each stage, the story may be changed to suit the whim of the latest editor. That process can gradually distort the story and make it inaccurate or misleading.

Most of the news stories in magazines like *Time* and *Newsweek* are written by writers in New York, based on information sent in by correspondents all over the world. That can also lead to distortions.

The traditional newspaper story formula made it easy to shorten stories with little distortion. It was called the inverted pyramid. The main point of the story up top. The who, what, where, when, why and how in the first paragraph or two. Then the importance of the information dwindling until pure trivia in the last paragraphs.

The inverted pyramid has largely been replaced by the Sony Sandwich story formula. It is harder to shorten during the editing process without shifting the original accuracy. (See **Interviews** chapters in **SKILLS** section)

Soft Leads

Soft leads are very popular in today's newspapers. In some of these stories, the real news is delayed until the middle of the story. Sometimes until after the jump to another page.

Because electronic news outlets usually have the story first, print reporters use news magazine writing style. Readers already have the basic facts, so the newspaper journalist attempts to give us something the broadcasters did not. The story becomes an artistic production, beginning like a novel, with a "soft" lead, like this one:

David Dentz got out of bed, stretched, yawned, and brushed his teeth. He wondered why he hadn't heard his three-year-old son, who usually got up before his parents.

Dentz checked his son's room. He wasn't there. The TV was dark. Then Dentz looked out the patio door and stark terror gripped him. There, on the patio, was a huge Bengal tiger, licking his chops.

The tiger had devoured David Jr.

Sports writers, competing against live coverage of the ball game, go all-out to give us a feature slant on yesterday's game. So much so, they sometimes forget to tell us the final score.

Stories with soft leads are much harder to edit. The editing takes extra time and skill. So do the headlines. With deadline pressure, these stories are sometimes chopped from the bottom to make them fit. This can badly distort them.

When it does, you need to complain. (See **STRATEGY/ Fighting Back**)

INSIDE THE MEDIA

Fairness & Equal Time

Should Nobody Get Equal Time?

Congress shall make no law respecting an establishment of religion, or prohibiting the free exercise thereof; or abridging the freedom of speech or of the press; or the right of the people peaceably to assemble, and to petition the government for a redress of grievances.

Take another look. Nowhere does the First Amendment to the U.S. Constitution say the news media in America shall be fair.

Early History

The early journalists in this country were revolutionary philosophers — zealots who used their printing presses to spread their personal opinions — especially about politics and religion.

The American Revolution was conceived and sustained by writers like Thomas Jefferson and Tom Paine. They believed with religious intensity that ideas — and the freedom to express those ideas — were sacred. So they preserved that belief in the Constitution.

It was a novel idea. A noble experiment. The press was the only business given Constitutional protection. Early American newspaper stories were grossly distorted to make the editor's friends appear saintly, his enemies grotesque. Editorial cartoonists who disagreed with Abraham Lincoln drew the President in caricature as a gorilla. Until early in the 20th Century, most newspapers announced their political bias on their front pages or mastheads. You didn't need to look at the declaration of their political point of view. You knew, from reading them, they were Whigs or Tories, Republicans or Populists. Many of these early, personalized publications were not concerned with making money.

Advertising's Influence

Economic pressure forced newspapers to be more fair. As advertising became an accepted part of daily and weekly newspapers, the stories were toned down. It was important not to alienate advertisers, or the readers those advertisers were paying to reach.

Still, the mass circulation dailies in the early 1900s were not exactly fair. Sensational stories fueled the circulation wars. They mangled both truth and the small group of people they wrote about — people unfortunate enough to be caught in the crossfire.

The American news media just before Watergate (early 1970s) were probably more fair than at any time in our history. The pendulum is now swinging the other way.

No Holds Barred

Today's audience has developed a new appetite for bloody combat and sensational stories. They tune in and buy the most outrageous examples of sensational, unfair coverage.

People say, in public opinion polls, that they detest political attack ads and candidates who savage their opponents. But those tactics often work. Just as people publicly condemn the brutality of a new, more violent form of wrestling on TV. Yet those shows have some of the highest ratings on cable television.

Government Control

U.S. Supreme Court decisions have made it very clear that government cannot interfere in any way with the content of the *printed* press. For a long time, government *has* regulated broadcast content. But that is about to fade away. More about that later.

There are some laws making it a crime to publish national defense secrets. The courts have said government can punish the publisher, but cannot prevent the publishing. To do so is called prior restraint.

Civil suits can be filed against the media after they damage you or invade your privacy. (See **INSIDE THE MEDIA/Libel** and **Privacy**) But you cannot prevent them from doing the damage.

Broadcasting Different

Despite the First Amendment guarantee of free speech and free press, for more than half the 20th Century, Congress passed laws, and created agencies to tell broadcasters what they could — and could not — say on the air.

Government can still take away the license of a broadcaster who breaks the rules. But that is rarely done. There is a major movement now to do away entirely with the FCC as a regulator of broadcast content — particularly as an arbitrator of fairness.

The Fairness Doctrine

For many years, the broadest exercise of governmental control was through a regulation called the Fairness Doctrine.

Because radio and TV were a new form of distributing information, Congress, the FCC and the courts ruled broadcasting was not "the press" given special freedom by the founding fathers.

How did they get to that conclusion?

Early Radio

As AM radio spread across the world in the 1920s, radio signals began to override each other, much like the spread of CB radio in the 1970s. As the number of stations grew, finding a clear channel became more and more difficult. Even if you found one, there was no guarantee it would stay clear very long.

Broadcasters went to Washington to solve the problem. Their lawyers came up with a theory that would get around the First Amendment and allow Congress to regulate the new medium.

It goes something like this: Radio waves cross state lines. Therefore, broadcasting is interstate commerce. The Constitution gives Congress the right to regulate interstate commerce.

Of course, newspapers cross state lines, too.

So a second argument was devised. Broadcasters do not own the medium that carries their signal — the sky. Radio waves must go through the sky.

The sky belongs to the public. Therefore, government acting for the public has a right to regulate how the sky is used.

1927 Federal Radio Commission

Congress created the Federal Radio Commission in 1927 to give order and decency to the airwaves. Anybody using the public sky had to get a license. The commission decided who was fit to hold a license. Shortly after it was created, the Radio Commission began to regulate not only radio signals and equipment, but what broadcasters *said* over the air. And how they allocated air time.

1934 — the FCC

In 1934, Congress rewrote the Radio Act and created today's Federal Communications Commission. There was no question that Congress, through the FCC, restricted freedom of both speech and the press. Most people accepted it as a practical, though unconstitutional solution. Without it, radio simply wouldn't work.

Radio created an immediate political problem. During a campaign, the owner could use a radio station to help one side, and hurt — or ignore — the other. Equal Time was conceived to prevent radio from meddling in politics.

Many people confuse fairness and Equal Time. If a broadcaster criticizes them or their business, they demand equal time to reply.

Equal Time for Politicians Only

But Equal Time applied only to candidates for political office. Congress and the FCC made it that way. That changed dramatically in 2000. More on that later.

To carry out the pretense of press freedom, the FCC's Equal Time Rule had a clause exempting news coverage. The same kind of clever maneuvering that enabled Congress to waltz around the First Amendment could also take Equal Time for a spin.

Presidential Debates

In 1960, after Richard Nixon and John F. Kennedy agreed to a series of nationally televised debates, Congress ordered a temporary suspension of Equal Time requirements for that year's presidential campaign so every candidate wouldn't have to be included.

The question came up again in 1976, when the networks planned a series of debates between challenger Jimmy Carter and incumbent Gerald Ford. Then-Cong. Shirley Chisolm, also a candidate for the presidency, demanded that she be included.

Carter vs. Ford vs. Chisolm

The Equal Time Rule seemed to be on her side. Other, more obscure candidates would also have to be invited to the debate.

So a plot was hatched. The networks canceled the debate. Then the League of Women Voters announced it would sponsor a debate between Carter and Ford. Aha! the networks said. If you sponsor a debate between the two major candidates, it will be a news event, and we'll cover it. Equal Time won't apply.

Chisolm and the National Organization for Women (NOW) ran to the FCC. The FCC announced it had been misinterpreting Congress' intent by requiring equal time for all candidates if any debate was broadcast. Equal Time did not apply to the League event.

Chisolm v. FCC

538 F.2d 349 [D.C. Circ.] (1976)

Chisolm and NOW took the FCC decision to court. A panel of U.S. Circuit judges agreed with the FCC's decision. Government can't make news judgments for broadcasters, the court ruled.

The U.S. Supreme Court refused to hear an appeal, in effect endorsing the lower court opinion. The League-sponsored debate was televised, with only Carter and Ford on the platform.

Compare broadcasting's Equal Time requirement to an almost exact parallel in the print media.

Equal Newspaper Space

In 1913, the Florida Legislature passed a law protecting the election process from unfair newspaper influence. It was introduced by a lawmaker who was a newspaperman and signed by a governor who was a newspaper publisher.

It said that candidates had the right to reply to newspaper attacks or endorsements during a political campaign. The newspaper had to give equal space to the other side, and print it in the same general section of the newspaper.

Until 1972, the Florida Equal Space Law had never been seriously challenged. That year, Pat Tornillo, leader of the teachers' union in Miami, ran for the Florida Legislature. *Miami Herald* editorials attacked Tornillo. *The Herald* denied him equal space.

Miami Herald Publishing Co. v. Tornillo

418 U.S. 241, 94 S.Ct. 2831, 41 L.Ed.2d. 730 (1974)

(Full text available at www.findlaw.com)

Tornillo went to court. After he had lost his political race, the Florida Supreme Court sided with Tornillo. The state justices said the Equal Space Law was not a violation of the First Amendment. In their ruling, they emphasized the similarity to the federal Equal Time concept for broadcasters. *The Herald* appealed.

This time, Tornillo and Florida's Equal Space Law lost. Writing the opinion for a unanimous court in June, 1974, U.S. Supreme Court Chief Justice Warren Burger said:

> *The choice of material to go into a newspaper ... whether fair or unfair ... constitutes exercise of editorial control and judgment. It has yet to be demonstrated how governmental regulation of this crucial process can be exercised consistent with First Amendment guarantees of a free press.*

In his opinion striking down all equal space laws for print, the Chief Justice did not mention the court's very different attitude about Equal Time and the regulation of broadcast material.

The Rules are Changing

But the rules are changing. As this book goes to press, the federal appellate court in the District of Columbia has thrown out the FCC's Personal Attack and Editorial Reply rules.

They were an outgrowth of the FCC's old Fairness Doctrine, and very similar to the Equal Time requirements for political campaigns. Both the National Assn. of Broadcasters and the Radio-Television News Directors Assn. argued in court against the FCC's Equal Time, Personal Attack and Editorial Reply rules.

Rather than enhance broadcast news, they said the rules actually discouraged radio and television from assuming their Constitutional responsibilities as part of the American "press." Coping with the right-to-reply and Equal Time requirements was so difficult, they said, most stations simply avoided editorial endorsements of candidates, as well as serious political and investigative reporting.

FCC Chairman William Kennard and the other two Democratic appointees on the five-person commission said they might vote to appeal the court decision. And perhaps even restore the Fairness Doctrine — a plank in the 2000 Democratic Party Platform.

The outcome of the November, 2000, election in both the White House and Congress will affect the future of Equal Time and fairness requirements.

The Old Fairness Doctrine

The old Fairness Doctrine was a much broader concept which evolved over a period of years as the FCC heard complaints about broadcasters abusing their licenses to use the public airwaves.

The Fairness Doctrine said broadcasters must be fair in covering "controversial issues of public importance." Because broadcast outlets were limited, the FCC said stations had an *obligation* to inform the public by carrying all points of view on those issues.

Supreme Court Endorsement

The Fairness Doctrine was not approved by the U.S. Supreme Court until 1969. The justices ruled in *Red Lion Broadcasting Co. v. FCC* that the scarcity of broadcast channels required a different kind of Constitutional treatment for broadcasters. The court said TV and radio — because of their special license and privilege to use the public sky — had to be fair.

Government Deregulation

As part of its philosophical belief in deregulation, the FCC conducted a series of hearings on the Fairness Doctrine and issued a 1985 report. It concluded that the explosion of new technology had made the old argument about scarcity of channels obsolete:

> *The public has access to a multitude of viewpoints without the need or danger of regulatory intervention. ... In stark contravention of its purpose, [the doctrine] operates as a pervasive and significant impediment to the broadcasting of controversial issues of public importance.*

In that 1985 report, the FCC said the Fairness Doctrine had actually reduced public discussion, not broadened it. In practice, stations had avoided controversial issues, rather than go through the hassle of airing opposing points of view.

The 1985 report said the FCC believed the Fairness Doctrine was unconstitutional. But the Commission refused to repeal it, saying it would leave that decision up to Congress or the courts.

Congress disagreed with the FCC, and in early 1987 wrote the Fairness Doctrine into law. President Ronald Reagan vetoed it. Congress could not muster enough votes to override. In August, 1987, the FCC finally repealed the Fairness Doctrine.

Public Affairs Programs

The FCC once required a certain amount of news, public affairs programming, and public service announcements at all stations. No longer.

Public affairs programming at local stations was often a weekly talk show, where guests discussed a current issue. The Personal Attack Rule tended to keep them dull. They're almost extinct.

The Future for the FCC

Some in Congress have proposed doing away with the FCC altogether. Let the free marketplace and competition decide how broadcasting will be conducted, this point of view says.

The FCC may evolve into an agency which simply regulates the technology of broadcasting, with no control whatever over its content. Technology (especially the Internet) has opened up virtually unlimited channels for journalists to express their views.

The original concept that created the Radio Commission and then the FCC was based on a limited number of broadcast outlets. That argument no longer applies. Other forces at work that could end restrictions on station ownership, as well as broadcast content:

- Present attitudes in both major political parties that private industry should have as little government regulation as possible.

- The decline of print as the predominant news medium. Future courts are more likely to look at broadcasting, cable and the Internet as forms of free expression the framers of the First Amendment would have protected, if they had been able to predict the evolution of communication technology.

INSIDE THE MEDIA

The Internet

Future Delivery System
For Every News Format

I read a newspaper cover-to-cover at breakfast every day.

Always have. But I ask myself these days — is the newspaper providing anything that's not on the Internet — available at any hour, updated to the moment I connect?

Yes. I can't get local newspaper display ads on the web. But that's about all. The hometown newspaper I read is on the web. When I travel, I read it wherever I am. Along with the full content of any major newspaper I choose. All of it free.

Unlike my local newspaper, some of those other papers now include their display advertisers. I can also flip back through archived stories, indexed for the last 10 to 15 years. Research into recent history is a click away. Wow!

Television News, Too

I also have a DSL high-speed (784 kb) Internet connection. When the Concorde crashed in Paris in July, 2000, I was able to view the *NBC Nightly News* story — full sound and video — on the MSNBC website three hours before NBC broadcast it.

One of my local TV stations has its weather radar constantly on the Internet. With a high-speed connection, you can watch the storms moving across the map, just as they show them on TV.

Everything about the delivery of news and information is in turmoil. The entire financial structure is being reexamined and rebuilt. Some news outlets will die. The survivors will be those who figure out how to use the new medium. Eventually, I believe, virtually all forms of communication will use this single delivery system. (See **Preface** at the front of this book and **INSIDE THE MEDIA** chapters on **Newspapers** and **Networks**)

News Pushed to You

"Push" technology was pioneered by Pointcast.com. By pioneer, I mean *truly ancient* cyberspace history — 1996. But the technique evolved so rapidly, the original company withered and went broke.

With pushed news, you can set up your computer to bring you from the Internet the kind of news you want, when you want it. From a virtually unlimited choice of sources.

Political news can come from *The Washington Post*; international news from *The New York Times*; news bulletins from *CNN*; computer news from *ZDNet*; business news from *The Wall Street Journal*; news about your state from your favorite local paper.

How Often Do You Want It?

Once you've made your choices, you then tell the software how often you'd like your news updated. You can do it every 30 minutes, if you like. Or just before your alarm goes off every morning. That way, up-to-the minute news will be ready about the same time the coffee's perked. You can connect manually whenever you need a news fix, whatever the automatic setting.

As this book goes to press, the latest incarnation of this idea is being worked into the "portal" websites browsers go to each time they connect to the Internet. Most portals now offer a wide range of up-to-the-minute news sources, by category.

You choose categories such as national or international news, business, technology, science, sports, health. The portal page shows you headlines, with links to the full story. If you go to the full story, you can read the news on-screen, with pictures, or print it and read it as you would a magazine or newspaper.

There are all kinds of bells and whistles. Some portals offer a miniature stock ticker with your investments and the latest trading price crawling across the screen. Or weather, or sports scores. Whatever you like. And it's all free.

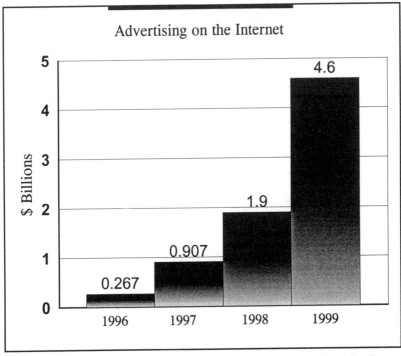

Source: Internet Advertising Bureau

Internet Advertising

Advertising foots the bill, just as it does for virtually all other media. No other advertising medium has ever grown so fast.

The Internet Advertising Bureau says Internet ads grew 240 per cent between 1996 and 1997; 112 per cent the next year; 141 per cent between 1998 and 1999.

If the 2000 figures show the same growth rate, spending for Internet advertising will surpass cable television and match total advertising in magazines. (See how advertising dollars are split in **INSIDE THE MEDIA/Newspapers**)

Bill Gates' Goal

Even Microsoft Founder Bill Gates — computer trailblazer, world's richest entrepreneur — did not grasp the importance of the Internet early on. In the first printing of his book *The Road Ahead* (late 1995) very little was said about the Internet.

Shortly after it was published, he realized how badly he had miscalculated. Gates told his staff to drop everything else until Microsoft caught up with the emerging Internet technology. The entire company went into overdrive.

A December, 1996, a Microsoft memo quoted by the *Columbia Journalism Review* said:

> *We are challenging old and established businesses like newspapers, travel agencies, automobile dealers, entertainment guides, travel guides, Yellow Page directories, magazines. ... We must devise ways of working with them or winning away their customers and revenue streams. ... We must be aggressive.*

Classified Ads

About 40 per cent of gross revenue for the average American newspaper comes from classified ads. Take classifieds away, and the newspaper dies.

Gates spoke to the Newspaper Association of America convention in April, 1997. Not to worry, he said. It will be at least 10 years before most classified ads shift to the Internet. A shiver went through the audience.

On the Internet, classifieds are automatically sorted to make it easier to find what you're looking for.

Suppose you're trying to find a 1997 Toyota Camry, silver, four-door, with a CD player and less than 35,000 miles on the speedometer.

In an instant, Internet classifieds will sort and highlight every car fitting that description. In your city, your state, or the entire nation. Many large Internet classified services are still free to advertisers. Once the service is firmly established, they'll probably start charging. Banner ads within the classifieds also make money.

Newspapers Respond

By mid-2000, some major newspapers were responding to the threat. They banded together to launch regional classified Internet listings that duplicate the classifieds in their newspapers. People who buy classifieds in most of these initial offerings pay a small surcharge to have their copy included in the Internet listing as well as the print version. Almost all of them elect to pay the surcharge.

Success Can Be Fatal

Newspapers were dominant so long, they lost their competitive edge. In my seminars, I chart fatal accident rates for commercial airline pilots. Young pilots have a relatively high rate. But then accidents drop to almost zero until pilots have a lot of experience.

Then the crash rate increases. Not because they're old. Because they're successful. They've become complacent. Careless. Too sure of themselves.

By 2000, only 18 cities in America had local competing newspapers that were separate and apart. (See **INSIDE THE MEDIA/Newspapers**) Because they had not competed with other, local papers for more than a generation, they lost their edge and did not realize the Internet's power to destroy their revenue stream.

Threat to Television

The Internet threatens television, too. But television was not as slow to recognize what was happening. Perhaps because TV has been so much more competitive than newspapers. Television stations and networks battle each other every day. TV news may be the most competitive business in America.

The networks saw the future and got into the Internet game early. Particularly NBC. With cable channels CNBC (cable NBC) and MSNBC (a partnership with Microsoft), NBC has the ability to cross-plug, expand and rework its stories for every conceivable audience.

The broadcast stories remind you that you can find more detail on their Internet website. Broadcast stories are repeated on the cable channels, which also cross-plug the network and its websites.

As more people get fast Internet connections, more websites are featuring full-blown audio and video. Soon, they will all be able to distribute their TV programming simultaneously on the Internet, just as many radio stations do.

"The Newspaper of Record"

At one time, the dominant newspaper in most communities considered itself "the newspaper of record." It kept the minutes — the history — of local society. Virtually everything that happened at the courthouse, city hall and the state Legislature was faithfully recorded in those newspapers. Births, deaths, marriages, arrests, trials, property sales, election results, legislative action.

As production costs increased and profits fell, newspapers decided they could no longer provide that service. They became much thinner. The news hole shrank. Full transcripts are very rare in newspapers these days.

Complete Transcripts

The Internet has taken over that function.

Want to read every word spoken at the O. J. Simpson criminal trial? The complete transcript is on the Internet.

You can find federal and state laws. Postal rates and regulations, courthouse files, IRS forms, current stock prices, weather, sports scores, telephone directories, maps, every U.S. patent back to the 1700s. The full text of every U.S. Supreme Court decision cited in this book is available on the Internet. New decisions are posted immediately. (See page xvi)

Serious researchers who once haunted public libraries and government record depositories now find everything they need on the Internet. It is a worldwide bulletin board, posting just about every document, speech, graduate thesis and government proceeding.

And a lot of junk.

The Web Garbage Dump

The Worldwide Web today is very much like the American newspaper of the late 1700s. Only more so. In those early days, anybody with access to a printing press thought the world wanted to read his thoughts, fears, political rhetoric and religious ranting.

It is much easier today to publish on the Internet than it was to print in Colonial America. People who fear new things are wringing their hands about the amount of trash and misinformation on the Net. A lot of garbage was published in Benjamin Franklin's day, too.

Democracy at Work

I see it in a different light. The Internet is true democracy at work. If you believe in democracy, you believe humans should be free to express themselves. That they have the intelligence to weed out misinformation, judge for themselves, and make their own decisions.

If *The New York Times* and *The National Enquirer* have contradictory versions of the same story, which do you believe?

It will take a little time, but we are already beginning to recognize Internet publishers who have as much integrity, talent and respect as *The New York Times* or *The Washington Post*. Perhaps more.

No Waiting for News

And we don't have to wait until tomorrow morning to read it. When a major story breaks, I turn on CNN and go to the Internet at the same time.

Within a few hours, key Internet sites will have complete resource documents. Unedited transcripts for those who really want to dig for themselves. Like going back into the stacks at a University library to read the original stuff — not somebody else's translation of it.

Random Knowledge

There is one major problem if most people get their news from a customized Internet service where they've tailored the delivery of categories they're interested in.

When I read a newspaper, I often come across headlines that capture me, and I read the story. It would not have ordered that story. It is not on my usual list of personal interests.

So I learn something new. I acquire random knowledge. The same thing happens when you read through a magazine or newsletter. You are not as likely to pick up extraneous information when you special-order your news from the Web.

Instant Alerts

But the Internet and e-mail have a huge advantage in alerting you to stories you're concerned about. Like Jakob Nielsen's essays, published every other week on the Internet.

Nielsen knows more about what makes websites work than anyone in the world. Back in ancient times (early 1990s) Sun Microsystems gave Nielsen the time and resources to do nothing but think about, and research, the Internet.

How it could be used. Its future. Designs that make it effective. He had earlier worked for IBM. Nielsen is now an independent consultant and author of nine books.

He publishes a new essay at his website about every two weeks. When a new essay is posted, I get an e-mail telling me it's ready, at http://www.useit.com. Just about everything he's written and researched is archived there. Great stuff.

New Deadline Pressure

The Internet has created new, competitive deadline pressure for conventional news media. The Monica Lewinsky story first broke on the Internet's *Drudge Report* — a gossip column whose author admits to a high degree of error and inaccuracy.

Newsweek had been working the story for months, but held back, trying to get more solid proof. Once it was on the Internet, *Newsweek* published what it had on its own Internet website — in effect, scooping itself.

Competition is pushing the news media to post their news stories on the Internet as soon as they're written, rather than wait for their regular publication/broadcast times.

Newspapers now regularly post tomorrow morning's stories on their websites, so they can brag they had it first.

The Internet is into the bulletin business, along with radio and television. In some situations, rumors are thrown into cyberspace without even a cursory check for truth or accuracy.

Until the Internet gains some maturity and responsibility, we may be in for a rough ride. (See **STRATEGY/Accuracy** and **Ethics**)

INSIDE THE MEDIA

Jargon

Strange Things
Media People Say

A-B Roll

An old term from the days of film in television news, where the director in the control room could switch video from the "A" roll of film to the "B" roll while audio continued on the "A" roll. See Cutaway for one of the most common uses of A-B roll technique.

ABC

The Audit Bureau of Circulations, which audits and certifies the circulation of print media to make sure advertisers reach the audience they pay for.

Actuality

Radio term for recorded sound from the scene of the story, in contrast to sound originating in the studio. Can be natural sound captured during an event, or a taped interview.

Ambush Interview

A sudden confrontation with a TV news crew, in which the interview subject is physically ambushed, caught by surprise, and frequently appears guilty or furtive.

Anchor

The person who introduces and reads news stories in the radio or TV studio during a newscast. The job gets its name from a ship anchor, which is supposed to hold the ship firm, no matter which way the wind blows. In TV news, most formats revolve around the anchor or anchor team, as the focal point giving the newscast its style and direction.

Arbitron

One of the rating services which measures broadcast audiences. Arbitron is the leading service for radio. The company no longer provides national TV ratings.

Ascertainment Interviews

Before deregulation, the FCC required broadcast stations to interview local people, ascertaining from them the community's problems and how to solve them. The station was required to show how its programming met those community needs and problems. No longer required, but some stations continue similar programs as a public relations technique.

Assignment Editor

The person in a radio or TV newsroom who decides how the station's reporters and photographers will be used. Expected to know what is happening, and dispatch the station's resources to best cover the news. The person to notify when you think you have a story for broadcast media.

Audio

The sound you hear during a radio or TV newscast, as distinguished from video — what you see.

Below the Fold

Anything in the lower half of the front page of a newspaper section. More important stories are above the fold.

Bird

TV slang for a satellite in space. As in, "I'll send it to you by the bird this afternoon. We've got time on the bird at 2:30."

Bite

Short for sound bite. A small portion of a taped interview which is edited into the reporter's story. Usually less than 15 seconds. In network news stories, frequently less than 10 seconds. One bite is sometimes edited to another in a way that makes it appear both sentences or phrases were spoken together, in sequence.

Black

A blank TV screen. Can happen if the station loses its transmitter. The visual fade-out between sequences, called "going to black."

Block

A block of uninterrupted news stories. Those between the opening of the newscast and the first commercial are the "first block."

Break

In broadcasting, the interruption in the newscast for commercials. In newspapers, the place where a story is cut on the first page and continued on an inside page. In print, also called the "jump."

Bright

A short, funny news story.

Broadband

The electronic "pipe" for very fast, high-volume data transmission. DSL and cable modems are broadband devices which can give Internet service many times faster than a standard telephone modem, which is limited to 56,000 (56k) bits of data per second.

Bug

A very small radio transmitter, used to secretly intercept conversations. Without a court order, always illegal if *nobody* in that intercepted conversation is aware of the electronic eavesdropping. In some states, illegal even if one party to the conversation is aware.

Bulldog Edition

The first edition of a newspaper.

Bullets

The dark circles, squares or other symbols used to highlight major points in a print story.

Call Letters

A broadcast station's unique identifying letters. Some early stations have only three letters. Most of those east of the Mississippi River begin with W. Those west of the Mississippi begin with K.

Canned Story

A story that is finished and ready for publication or broadcast. The story is "in the can." Sometimes used to distinguish a wire or network story with no time factor, rather than a fresh local story.

Chroma-Key

An electronic device used by a TV station to insert graphics or video in the broadcast picture. Often used to insert a generic graphic over the shoulder of the anchor.

City Room

Old newspaper term for the newsroom.

Color Bars

The row of rainbow-colored bars transmitted when TV stations are off the air. Can be used to check and adjust the receiving television set. Also used internally to check the accuracy of the color being transmitted.

Control Room

The nerve center of the television studio, where a director, sitting at a huge board of lights, switches and television monitors, controls what goes out over the air. The buttons and switches can control devices in other parts of the building — cameras, microphones, TelePrompTers®, videotape players, slide projectors, audio volume, supers, video inserts, etc.

Copy Boy

Quaint old newspaper term for boys who carried reporters' copy to the editor's desk, tore wire service stories off the teletype machines and delivered them to the proper editors. No longer needed in electronic newsrooms.

Copy Desk

Before computers, the desk where editors and headline writers reviewed reporters' copy before it was set in type.

Copy Story

A news story read by the anchor in which there is no reporter and no videotape. Sometimes called a "reader."

Correspondent

The proper title for network reporters, probably because they're always on the road. They were given this title in the early days of radio and TV news, in the same way that newspapers have traditionally called their out-of-town reporters correspondents.

Countdown

A countdown similar to that marking the moment of ignition and liftoff during a rocket launch. Used to help editors find the exact spot where a quote begins on audio or videotape. A correspondent calls to dictate a story. Once he knows the recorder is rolling, he says, "Three — Two — One — This is Dave Doomsday reporting from Armageddon. The world ended today at exactly 2:17 p.m."

Crawl

Information, usually words and numbers, that "crawl" across the bottom of a TV screen while the regular programming continues. Often used to give weather bulletins, stock prices, sports scores or election results without interrupting the regular program.

Cross-Cutting

See intercut.

Cutaway

An editing shot, used to cover a TV edit point, or "jump cut." The most frequently used cutaways show the reporter listening or taking notes; the crowd during a meeting or a speech; or a "two-shot," in which we see both the reporter and the interview subject from far enough away that we can't tell whether the movement of the interview subject's lips matches the words we're hearing.

Cutline

The text describing the contents of a photograph.

Dateline

In newspapers and magazines, the first words used to indicate the story was not produced locally. Frequently at the beginning of wire service copy, as in NEW YORK (AP) —. Before correspondents' stories could be transmitted and printed the same day they were written, the dateline included the date the story was written. Most papers have now dropped the date, but the city where the story originated is still called the dateline.

DBS

Direct broadcast satellite. A system that broadcasts television signals from a satellite in orbit straight to the viewer, rather than to a cable or broadcast company which then relays it to the viewer.

Demos

Demographics. The profile of a broadcast audience or newspaper readership. Advertisers want good demos — younger, upscale people who spend a lot of money.

Digital TV

Higher quality TV signals that are converted to computer code before broadcast. The receiver must also be digital to decode. Dubs of stories are exact copies, with no degeneration in quality. The FCC and Congress are pushing to force all TV stations into digital broadcasting. Set-top boxes that decode the signal can also be designed to handle many other tasks, such as pay-per-view programs, inter-active shopping, advertising, e-mail and the Internet.

Dish

A parabolic antenna to receive satellite signals.

Display Advertising

Large blocks of advertising in newspapers, to distinguish them from classified ads with small print and no drawings or pictures.

Dissolve

The fading out of one picture while another fades in. Frequently used to make the transition from one place to another less jarring.

Double-Truck

Two facing pages of newspaper advertising or copy.

DSL

Digital Subscriber Line. Technology that permits Internet data transmission over a telephone line many times faster than a regular modem. Speed is limited by the distance to the phone company central office. Can carry voice transmission at the same time.

Dub

A copy of an audio or videotape. The sound and picture are dubbed from one cassette onto another.

Dummy

A schematic drawing of a newspaper or magazine page, showing where the ads, headlines and stories will be placed.

Ear

The small box in the upper corner of a newspaper front page on either side of the newspaper's name. Often carries weather information, the newspaper's slogan, etc.

ENG

Shorthand for electronic news gathering, rather than film.

Equal Time

An old FCC rule law that required broadcast licensees who gave time to a political candidate to give equal time to opponents. Only politicians during election campaigns got equal time. Abolished in 1987. In late 2000, a federal appellate court ruled unconstitutional the FCC's similar Personal Attack and Editorial Attack rules.

Exclusive

Used correctly if no other news outlet has the story. Sometimes used fudgingly if the newspaper, magazine or broadcast outlet has a portion of the story that nobody else has.

Fairness Doctrine

An old FCC rule that required broadcasters to present all sides of controversial issues of public importance. Repealed in 1987.

FCC

The Federal Communications Commission, appointed by the President and confirmed by the Senate, to regulate all electronic transmissions in the U.S. Includes radio, TV, cell phones, etc.

Feed

To transmit audio or video via radio or wires. Each afternoon, network TV crews use satellites to feed their stories to New York. Can also be a noun. As in "When are we going to get the feed?"

Field Interview

An interview taped in the field — away from a radio or TV station.

Field Producer

A radio or TV producer assigned to work with a reporter or camera crew in the field, as distinguished from the producer who acts as editor and production manager for a specific newscast.

Flack

Derogatory term for a public relations person. Can also be a verb, as in "He's flacking for the mayor."

FOI

Freedom of Information Act. A federal law which makes certain records public. To gain access to many of them, however, a formal FOI request must be filed.

Freeze Frame

In effect, a still picture taken from movie film or videotape. Sometimes used when the picture is so fleeting most viewers would not be able to see what the camera recorded.

GM

Short for General Manager of a radio or television station.

Graphic

A picture, drawing or graph used to help illustrate a TV story.

Grip

Another name for the camera assistant who works with a TV news crew. Grips usually double as sound technicians. Becoming more rare as size and weight of equipment gets smaller.

Hot

Broadcast term for sound that is too loud, or a light that is too bright. Or an open microphone that can pick up conversation not intended for broadcast. As in, "Be careful, that mike's hot."

HUT

Households Using Television. The HUT-level is the same as Share in TV ratings lingo. A HUT-level of 30 means 30 per cent of the households watching TV were watching your show.

In-Cue

The first words of a sound bite. Sometimes written into the script to identify the bite the reporter wants inserted at that point.

Intercut

An editing technique, where two interviews are cut so the video-tape switches back and forth between interviews without interruption by the reporter. Used to heighten conflict between opposing points of view. Also called cross-cutting.

IVDS

Interactive video delivery system. An electronic device through which the viewer can send programming requests to, or buy items from, the program provider. In the future, viewers will be able to have news or other programming on demand, rather than wait for a scheduled broadcast. (See Digital TV)

Internet

The worldwide network which allows anyone with a computer and a modem to connect and communicate through telephone lines, cable TV lines, or by satellite. It has had explosive growth since 1995, and may be the future conduit for virtually all printed, radio and TV news. Originally created in the late 1960s to help military and university researchers communicate with each other.

JOA

Joint Operating Agreement between two newspapers who use the same printing and circulation facilities to produce two separate papers. Most are created to prevent the death of the afternoon paper.

Jump

The place at which a front-page story jumps to an inside page. The continuation of the story carries a "jump head," and that part of the story is called the "jump." As in, "I read the beginning of the story, but didn't go to the jump."

Jump Cut

The point at which a TV interview videotape is edited. Gets its name because the interview subject appears to suddenly jump to another position. Jump cuts are usually covered by a cutaway shot for esthetic reasons. The print ethic requires three dots — an ellipsis — to tell the reader the quoted words have been edited.

Key

Short for Chroma-Key. The picture inserted, or "keyed" into a small section of the television screen.

Kicker

The last story in the newscast. Almost always a feature or human interest story that is upbeat, to wash away the bad feelings viewers get from stories involving death, destruction and pain.

Lead-In

The introduction to a TV news story read by the anchor. Usually less than 15 seconds. A headline, designed to tell you what the story is about and alert you to pay attention.

Leak

A covert release of information to the news media. Usually done by a confidential source who does not want to be identified. A standard technique, widely used by both government and corporate executives with political, competitive or revenge motives. Also used as a last resort by frustrated whistle-blowers.

Listener

A type of cutaway shot in television, used for editing purposes, in which we see the reporter listening to the interviewee.

Live Shot

A reporter standup or interview relayed back to the TV station for immediate, live broadcast during a newscast.

Make-Good

A commercial offered free or at a discounted price to an advertiser when a broadcast fails to draw the expected audience. The station or network "makes good" its promise to deliver a certain number of people per dollar spent on advertising in the show.

Makeover

Changing a newspaper page, usually to get late-breaking stories into this edition, or to update stories. Also called a "replate."

Market

The area served by a radio or television station. Usually about 50 to 75 miles in all directions for FM radio and TV, depending on the nearest competing stations or topography that blocks the signal.

Masthead

The box that shows the newspaper name, owner, and editors. Usually on the editorial page.

Meters

An electronic device wired to a TV set to collect constant data on whether the set is turned on, and which channel it is tuned to. Used extensively to determine TV ratings. Updated in 1987 with People Meters, which also record *who* is watching.

Microwave

One type of radio frequency used to transmit audio and video back to a television station. Converted to the TV band for broadcast.

Mixer

An electronic device which allows an editor to mix two sounds. In both radio and TV, the reporter's voice is sometimes mixed in the studio with natural sound recorded at the scene of the story.

Modem

The electronic device used by a computer to communicate with other computers by telephone, TV cable or satellite. It can also send faxes and dial or answer telephone calls.

Morgue

The library that keeps newspaper clippings and tape of previous stories. Reporters go to the morgue to get background and history on a story or person they are covering.

MSO

Multiple system operator. A company which delivers TV programming by more than one system. The same company can own and operate broadcast stations, as well as cable and satellite delivery systems.

Natural Sound

Sometimes called "wild sound." Background noise. Adds realism to audio or videotape. A reporter will sometimes use natural sound, full volume, at the beginning of the story to set the scene. You will hear the noise of a gun battle or the crackle of a fire as the reporter narrates, "voice-over."

Network

An organization providing radio or TV programs to stations or cable systems. Local stations affiliated with a network agree to carry the network's programming, but are not owned or controlled by that network. Each major network owns and operates some stations. The four largest are ABC, CBS, Fox and NBC.

News Director

The person in charge of everything in a local radio or TV station's news department. The person who hires and fires news staff. The news director answers to the station's general manager.

News Hole

The space in a newspaper for news stories. On days when there is more advertising, the news hole is larger. On slow advertising days, the news hole shrinks.

News Peg

A local story pegged to a national or international news event.

Nielsen

Nielsen Media Research, the national rating service which measures TV audiences. Formerly A. C. Nielsen.

O and O

One of the local stations owned and operated by a network. The 1996 Telecommunications Act increased the number of broadcast stations which can be owned by one company.

Op-Ed

The page opposite the editorial page in a newspaper. Often used for columns and letters to the editor.

Out-Cue

The last phrase in a sound bite. Sometimes written into the script, along with the in-cue, to help an editor find the bite the reporter wants edited into the story at that point.

Out-Takes

Photographs, audio or videotape which was not published or broadcast. Often the center of conflict between law enforcement, government and news organizations. Some journalists, as a matter of principle, refuse to give up out-takes, even if subpoenaed.

Package

The term used at some stations for a reporter's story, complete within itself, "packaged" on an audio or videocassette. Will usually include one or more interviews. Sometimes called a "wrap."

Peanut

TV term for a small microphone, originally about the size of a peanut, that clips to your tie or collar. Current designs are much smaller than a peanut, but the old term is still used.

People Meters

An electronic measuring device to determine how many people are watching TV, and the demographics of the audience, at any given time. First used for national network ratings in the fall of 1987. Differs from older, passive meter systems in that household members must "log in" through remote control devices when the set is turned on, or when the channel is changed.

PIO

Short for public information officer. The person designated to act as spokesperson and to help reporters find people and information within the organization. In some government and military agencies, called **PAO** for public affairs officer.

Plug

Mentioning an item or service in a news story that will promote that item or service. In effect, free advertising. Highly unethical for journalists to accept anything of value for a plug.

Plumbers

Staffers assigned to find and stop leaks of information to the news media from inside an organization. The term was coined by the Nixon White House staff during the Watergate investigation.

Pool

An agreement by a group of reporters and photographers by which one or more of them will cover a story and provide information and/or pictures to other members of the pool.

Pot

Broadcast term for volume control. Sound is "potted up" or "potted down."

Producer

The person who decides how a radio or TV newscast will be organized; the structure and length of news stories. Roughly the equivalent of a page editor or section editor at a newspaper.

Promo

Short for promotion. A commercial touting a television or radio show on the same station is called a "promo."

Public File

A public record required by the FCC to be available at each broadcast licensee's office, giving ownership information about the station, its application for licensing, and certain publications explaining how the FCC regulates broadcasters.

Pyramid Story Formula

Another name for the who-what-when-where-why formula for newspaper stories. All main facts are at the top of the story. Additional information that is less important follows, so that information at the bottom is trivia. With this formula, editors can easily chop from the bottom to make a story fit a hole in the page.

Rating

The percentage of households in a market area listening to, or watching, a certain program at any given time. A rating point is one percent of the entire *potential* audience. Ratings are usually stated rating/share. Share is the percentage of all those who were *watching or listening at a given time.*

Reader

A story read by an anchor without visuals or reporter involvement. Also called a "copy story."

Release

The written agreement giving permission for the media to use your likeness, name or voice for commercial purposes. Not needed for news coverage. Also called a "model release."

Reverses

Videotape of a reporter asking an interview subject questions. The camera direction is reversed to shoot over the shoulder of the interview subject after the interview is finished. The question can then be edited to an answer already videotaped. Can distort a TV story if the question is not worded and spoken exactly as it was when the answer was given. Another way to avoid a jump cut.

Rim

The outer edge of a horseshoe-shaped desk used in old-time newspaper newsrooms to process copy and write headlines. The copyreaders and headline writers sat around the rim while the editor who supervised their work sat in the "slot."

Scoop

An exclusive. A story that nobody else has. Also called a "beat."

Second-Day Story

A follow-up story.

Second Generation

An audio or videotape copy, made from the original. If that tape is dubbed again, the new copy would be "third generation." With each generation, audio and video quality decrease. Digital technology introduced in 1995 in TV news provides exact copies with no loss of quality, in the same way computer files are copied.

Share

A share is that program's share of all those who are listening to radio or watching TV at a specific time. A show's rating is the percentage of the *potential* audience in the entire market area. Unless *everybody* in the market is listening or watching, your share will always be higher than your rating. If half the people in the market are watching TV, but all of them are tuned to the same station, that program will have a 50 rating, 100 share.

Shield Law

A state law shielding reporters from court or governmental subpoenas that might force them to identity confidential sources. The U.S. Supreme Court has ruled reporters have no Constitutional right to protect sources, but states can enact shield laws for journalists.

Shotgun Mike

An elongated, directional microphone which can be pointed at a person to pick up conversation at a greater distance than the ordinary mike. Often used by broadcast crews in a large crowd when they're not able to get close to the person talking.

Sidebar

A secondary story involving some element of a major story. Usually placed in a newspaper beside the primary story. Often a profile of a major character in the main story, or a feature-type treatment of some factor in the primary story.

Sig Out

The close of a broadcast reporter's story in which the reporter signs out. As in: "I'm Earl Egotist, Channel 14 Action News."

Slow News Day

A day in which very little of interest is happening. A good day to sell your story to an editor.

Soft Lead

The beginning of a print story that uses a feature approach to make the story seem more interesting. Often used by sportswriters because the basics of yesterday's game — score, most valuable player, etc. are already old news.

Sony Sandwich

TV term for a reporter "package" or "wrap." At some stations, Sony Sandwich is used to denote only live shots, in which the reporter speaks, then interviews someone, then closes the story. The interview in the middle of a story is the meat in the Sony Sandwich. The reporter's introduction and close are the bread.

SOT

Short for Sound-on-Tape. Used in a script to tell the editor both the audio and video are on the same section of videotape.

Sound Bite

A short portion of a taped interview which is edited into the reporter's story. The broadcast equivalent of a print "quote." Frequently shortened in broadcast jargon to "bite."

Squeeze Zoom

An electronic device that enables the director to insert a videotape or live picture in a small area of the TV screen, then zoom out to fill the entire screen, or vice versa.

Staging

Creating an event or encouraging people to do something for TV, which viewers believe is spontaneous and unrehearsed. A serious violation of FCC guidelines, and media ethics. Dramatizations and re-enactments not clearly labeled can be a form of staging.

Standup

A TV reporter's narration where we hear and see the reporter talking. Whether the reporter is standing, sitting, talking, driving or lying down, it's still a standup.

Sticks

A camera tripod — particularly in television.

Super

Writing which is superimposed over video during a television broadcast. The names of reporters or interview subjects are supered when we first see them, to tell us who they are. With a super, they don't have to be verbally introduced. The super is generated electronically as the broadcast is aired.

Sweeps

Four standard rating periods in which TV audiences are measured, and on which advertising rates are based. Traditionally, November, February, May and July.

Talent

TV talk for those staffers who are seen on camera. Reporters, anchors, sportscasters and weather forecasters are "talent."

Talking Head

Just what it says. Someone talking on camera with nothing to break the visual monotony.

Tap

Short for wiretap — physically tapping into a telephone or cable line to intercept conversations or data. Taps are always illegal, unless a court order grants permission for a tap by law enforcement.

TelePrompTer®

The electronic device which reflects a scrolling script on a pane of glass in front of a studio camera, allowing TV anchors to read the script while they look directly into the camera lens.

The Get

The person news outlets are trying to get for an interview. If absolute proof turned up that Elvis Presley is alive, reporters everywhere would be hunting him. He'd be "the get" of the century.

Think Piece

An analysis of a complicated story or event. Often an essay about an ongoing news story.

-30-

Traditional end of a newspaper story. Shorthand for "the end."

Tight Shot

A close-up or telephoto shot, where the scene or person appears to be very close to the camera. A tight shot of a person might fill the TV screen with just the face. A wide shot will show half the room from the same camera position.

Tombstone

Two newspaper headlines of similar size and width side-by-side, so readers might read the first line of the right headline as a continuation of the left headline. To be avoided.

Two-Shot

A picture that includes two people, usually the reporter and the interview subject. Also used when two people are on camera at the same time in a TV studio.

Typo

Short for typographical error.

UHF

Ultra High Frequency TV band. Channels 14 and higher.

VDT

Video dialtone. Television delivered by telephone line.

VHF

Very High Frequency TV band. Channels 2 through 13.

Video

The picture you see on TV, as distinguished from audio — what you hear. Video and audio are carried on separate tracks of the videotape. During the editing process, the audio that originally was recorded when the tape was shot can be replaced with other audio, or mixed with it.

Voice-Over

This can be done live, or edited onto audio or videotape. We hear the voice of the reporter or anchor narrating over the sound recorded in the field, when the event occurred.

Voting

The process where viewers in a ratings sample cheat and log a favorite program in their daily diaries, even if they didn't watch it. Viewers in rating samples also are inclined to vote for cultural or educational programs when they were actually watching wrestling or sit-com reruns.

Wallpapered Story

In TV, a news story with lots of visuals. The story is wallpapered, beginning to end, with pictures while the reporter's voice narrates. The pictures can have so much impact, however, the content of what the reporter is saying can be lost on the average viewer.

Wide Shot

A wide-angle camera shot, showing a broad area. A wide shot in an office would show half the room. A tight shot would fill the screen with the face of the person being interviewed.

Wild Sound

See Natural Sound.

Wireless

Short for wireless microphone. This is a small microphone and radio transmitter frequently used to pick up a reporter's voice or natural sound. Referees in sporting events wear wireless mikes so the audience can hear their calls. Reporters on the floor of a political convention use wireless mikes. The wireless enables them to talk to the camera across the convention hall. A wireless is legal under federal law so long as one person in range of the microphone is aware of it. In some states, it is illegal if all persons whose voices are transmitted by the wireless are not aware. A hidden wireless, secretly transmitting, can become an illegal "bug."

Wiretap

See Tap. A tap is not a bug. Bugs are secret wireless microphones.

Wrap

TV term for a reporter's story that includes a videotaped interview. The interview is wrapped inside the reporter's introduction at the beginning of the story, and the reporter's conclusion after the interview. The same story formula is sometimes called a "package" or a "Sony Sandwich." Also used in movie-making and TV to indicate a successful "take" of a scene. The movie director, TV producer or photographer says, "That's a wrap."

INSIDE THE MEDIA

Libel

Can They Do That and Get Away With It?

It depends on who you are, as well as what they show and tell. No matter how powerful the media seem to be, there are ways to get even if a story damages you unjustly. Sue. For libel, or invasion of privacy.

The lawsuit might make you a millionaire. But before you rush to the courthouse, you should know what you're getting into. Collecting damages may take years. You'll need a very good lawyer, because libel law is extremely complicated. It's constantly evolving.

A Long, Painful Process

Your lawsuit will be a very long, expensive, painful process. The station, network, newspaper or magazine will have on its side some of the best legal counsel available. Because they carry insurance to protect them against this kind of attack, they can spend an enormous amount of money defending themselves in court.

Appearing on a panel at an American Bar Association conference in 1998, lawyer George Vradenberg told how much money was spent defending two major libel suits. This was a very rare disclosure. Vradenberg was on the legal team representing CBS in the lawsuit filed by Vietnam War General William Westmoreland.

CBS spent $8 million before the Westmoreland suit was finally settled in 1985, Vradenberg said. He estimated *Time* spent twice that much defending another libel suit the same year.

If your suit has no merit, the judge might issue a summary judgment and make you pay attorneys' fees for the other side.

Currently, about four out of five libel suits never get to a jury. They are found to be without merit by the judge, and dismissed.

If your case has merit, don't expect a quick settlement. Settlements tend to encourage other suits. In the long run, it's sometimes cheaper for the media to fight to the bitter end — and lose — than to put up with the hassle of a new lawsuit every week.

Your Life An Open Book

Once you file suit, you bare your entire life. If there is anything in your past that could be embarrassing or painful, it will almost surely be found, placed in the public record, and reported. One of the best defenses the news media launch in a civil suit is a good offense.

Your suit will give the defendant subpoena power to get records, and drag in witnesses who must testify under oath. They will explore everything about your finances, your family, your medical history, your professional career, your education and your sex life.

Still want to sue? OK. You should also look at **INSIDE THE MEDIA/Privacy**. Invasion of privacy by the media can also be attacked in a civil suit. Some of the rules and tactics for the two kinds of litigation are similar. But some aspects are also very different.

In matters of governmental regulation, the courts have had different standards for print and broadcasting. (See **INSIDE THE MEDIA/Fairness & Equal Time**) In libel and privacy, the courts make few distinctions between the media.

Defamation Becomes Libel

You have been defamed if a publication or broadcast damages your reputation. It becomes libel if there is no legal immunity or justification for the defamation.

If your friends, your family, the people at work or the club think less of you after they see or hear the story, you have evidence of your being damaged. The people who see the report don't have to know you for the story to damage your reputation.

The story can hurt you financially, by decreasing your future income, or your ability to borrow money. It can damage you emotionally, by causing embarrassment, anguish and ridicule.

News stories defame thousands of people every day in America, yet relatively few suits are filed. The law provides protection for the media, based on the Constitution's First Amendment guaranteeing freedom of press and speech. To win a libel suit, you must prove more than the fact that you were defamed.

Issue #1 - Truth

The law says they can defame you and get away with it if the story is true. Truth is an almost perfect defense in a libel suit.

How do you prove something is true? How many witnesses does it take, what kind of evidence? There are no rigid rules.

Truth is what a jury will believe.

A half-dozen burglars and robbers testify they met you at your jewelry store every Sunday morning at 11 o'clock to fence what they'd stolen. Your priest says you never missed 11 o'clock Mass on Sunday morning. The jury will probably believe the priest, even though the witness score is 6-1.

Relaying the Defamation

A journalist does not have to initiate the libel. If the media pass on something someone else says about you, the media outlet generally must take responsibility for the truth of that statement.

Suppose you fire one of your employees. The employee then holds a news conference and says you are a drug user who regularly encourages teenage employees to use cocaine. You supply them with the drug. A reporter covers the news conference and reports what the disgruntled employee says about you.

It's True You're Accused

It is true that the accusation was made. But that alone will not protect the media outlet which publishes or broadcasts what the employee says. If the media act as a relay for the employee's accusations, they must be prepared to prove to a jury that you are, indeed, a drug dealer who encourages teenage employees to use cocaine and supplies them with the drug.

If the media convince a jury that you do those things, you cannot win a libel suit, no matter how much damage has been done to your reputation.

Issue #2 - Privilege

If the damaging information comes from a part of the governmental process, the news media have very limited responsibility for the truth of that information. This is called privilege.

The legal theory says government officials should be able to do their jobs freely, without worrying about libel suits. A Supreme Court justice once said freedom of speech does not give you the right to yell "Fire!" in a crowded theater when there is no fire.

But a senator can run up and down the aisles of the Senate Chamber yelling "Fire!" — or anything else — without fear of reprisal. And the media can report with impunity what the senator said. The courts have said the public needs to know — through the news media — what public officials are doing and saying.

Suppose that during a debate in the Senate Chamber, a U.S. Senator announces that you are a war criminal who murdered hundreds of innocent civilians in Vietnam. The story is widely reported. As a result, you lose your job. An angry crowd sets fire to your house. Your children are beaten on their way to school.

What the senator said was absolutely false. But you cannot win a slander suit against the senator, or a libel suit against the media. What the senator said is privileged, unless he said it in a private conversation, completely outside the governmental process.

Judicial Process Privileged

If you are charged with a crime, or sued, almost everything in the judicial proceeding (part of the governmental process) is privileged. The civil or criminal complaint, records or testimony, the contents of a governmental audit, what a policeman says during the investigation of a crime — all will almost always be privileged.

Notice as we go through this chapter how often I hedge with qualifiers like probably — almost always — generally — usually — virtually. The law is constantly changing. The rules can be bent — and often are — by judges and juries who feel they should cure an injustice.

The rules are different in state and federal courts. Most courts would probably extend privilege to what is said in political advertising and debates, or presidential press conferences, even though they technically are not part of the governmental process.

Issue #3 - Absence of Malice

In the early 1960s Martin Luther King, Jr. was waging war against racial segregation in Alabama. He moved from city to city, encouraging black followers to break the law. Use segregated rest rooms, he told them. Sit in segregated sections of the bus. Demand service in restaurants and hotels that — by law — bar blacks.

King reasoned that if the law was bad, the only way it would be changed was to get media coverage of public officials enforcing bad law. The civil rights movement became a major national story. The police who enforced the law became the villains in that story as they used clubs, fire hoses, attack dogs and tear gas to rout and arrest the demonstrators.

Martin Luther King v. Alabama

King became a master at using the media in his campaign. On the front pages of the world's newspapers — night after night on television — the confrontation between the police and King's followers was the top story.

A committee went to *The New York Times* and paid $4,800 for a full-page ad pleading for public support to continue the campaign in Alabama. *The Times* published the ad without checking its accuracy. In the advertisement, the police and other unnamed public officials were portrayed as the evil force trying to stop King and racial justice. The demonstrators, the ad said:

... are being met by an unprecedented reign of terror.

... In Montgomery, Alabama, after students sang "My Country, 'Tis of Thee" on the State Capitol steps, their leaders were expelled from school, and truckloads of police armed with shotguns and tear-gas ringed the Alabama State College Campus. When the entire student body protested to state authorities by refusing to reregister, their dining hall was padlocked in an attempt to starve them into submission.

... Again and again, the Southern violators have answered Dr. King's peaceful protests with intimidation and violence. They have bombed his home, almost killing his wife and child. They have assaulted his person. They have arrested him seven times — for "speeding," "loitering"

and similar "offenses." And now they have charged him with "perjury" — a felony under which they could imprison him for ten years.

Montgomery Police Commissioner L. B. Sullivan and a group of fellow public officials sued *The Times* for libel.

Although they were not named in the ad, they said they were defamed because the ad blamed law enforcement, state and local government for the "reign of terror." They said it suggested the police were somehow involved in bombing King's home.

Times Ad Not Entirely True

The New York Times could not use the truth privilege, because some of the statements in the ad were false:

- The students on the State Capitol steps did not sing "My Country, 'Tis of Thee" — they sang the National Anthem

- Nine students were expelled for demanding service at a segregated lunch counter, not for the Capitol steps demonstration

- Students protested the expulsion by boycotting a single day of classes, not by refusing to reregister

- The dining hall was never padlocked

- King had been arrested four times, not seven

In Montgomery, a state court jury found *The Times* had, indeed, libeled those local public officials and should pay them the maximum in damages allowed by Alabama law — $500,000. The Alabama Supreme Court upheld the verdict. By the time the U.S. Supreme Court got the case, a second half-million dollar verdict had been returned. More cases were pending.

New York Times Co. v. Sullivan

376 U.S. 254, 84 S.Ct. 710, 11 L.Ed.2d 686 (1964)

(Full text available at www.findlaw.com)

In 1964, *New York Times Co. v. Sullivan* made new libel law for the nation, and changed the rules for publishing truthfully.

Before the U.S. Supreme Court's *Sullivan* decision, the media had to prove their stories were true in a libel case.

With this ruling, the burden of proof shifted to the victim of the libel, who must prove the story is false.

The press cannot be held responsible for an untrue story about a public official, the Supreme Court said, unless the libel is published with **malice**. The plaintiff must prove the journalist or news outlet had a grudge against the libel victim; knew the information was false, or had reason to doubt the truth of what it published.

The Supreme Court decision in the *Times* case coined a new phrase to define malice. The media must be found guilty of *reckless disregard for truth* before a public official can collect for libel.

If You Can't Take the Heat

In their decision, the justices acknowledged that many public officials would be damaged by untrue stories as the new ruling was applied. But the court said the democratic process demands full and free debate — a continuous open season on public officials.

The public must be able to hear every accusation thrown at those in public office, and decide whether they deserve a position of public trust. If you can't take the political heat, the court warned, stay out of the kitchen.

Justice William Brennan, writing the Sullivan decision for the court, said:

> ... *The general proposition that freedom of expression upon public questions is secured by the First Amendment has long been settled by our decisions. ... The maintenance of the opportunity for free political discussion to the end that government may be responsive to the will of the people and that changes may be obtained by lawful means, an opportunity essential to the security of the Republic, is a fundamental principle of our constitutional system.*

What Is Reckless Disregard?

How far must the news media go to check out damaging information about a public official to meet the absence of malice test? That's up to a judge or jury.

In the *Times* case, the Supreme Court felt the newspaper had no warning it needed to check the accuracy of the ad. The committee which submitted the ad included some very prominent people.

A hypothetical: Suppose the mayor has been waging war against local chemical companies that have polluted the river and neighborhoods near the firms. The mayor has a reputation as Mr.

Environment. His campaign has persuaded city departments and many local companies to stop buying from the polluters. They have switched to suppliers in other cities.

Anonymous Calls

An anonymous caller tells a reporter the real motive for the mayor's crusade: Mr. Environment has a hidden interest in a Chicago company whose business is booming as a result of the mayor's crusade. The company in which the mayor is involved is a horrible environmental villain in its Chicago neighborhood.

To be fair, the reporter asks the mayor if the charge is true. The reporter gets an angry denial, and then writes a story that says: "Our sources tell us the real reason for the mayor's crusade. He holds a financial interest in a Chicago chemical firm that signed a contract with the city after the mayor's environmental campaign put three local firms out of business. The mayor denies it."

Anonymous = Reckless

Reckless disregard for truth? Almost certainly. If the only evidence is an anonymous tip, most juries will say the reporter and the newspaper or broadcast station were reckless with the truth. If the mayor proves they were wrong, the jury will punish them by ordering them to pay damages to the mayor.

But suppose the reporter pursues the tip, drives to Chicago, and finds two employees at the chemical company who say the mayor is in the main office of the plant a lot. They say the mayor has also been talking to employees at the plant, asking them for suggestions to improve the company.

Even if the mayor proves to the jury he has no ownership interest, the jury will probably decide the reporter was not reckless with the truth. That the media outlet, with strong evidence, published the accusation *believing it was true*.

Who is a Public Official?

The court in the *New York Times* case did not clearly define who is a public official.

All of the plaintiffs in that case were elected or appointed government officials. Other cases since then have drawn some guidelines.

You can probably assume you are a public official, and that reckless disregard for truth is the level of proof you will need to win a libel suit if you are:

- An elected or appointed public official
- A candidate for public office
- A law enforcement officer
- A public school teacher or administrator
- A public health nurse, social worker or administrator of a government-owned medical facility
- A private citizen or company hired to manage a government facility
- A private auditor hired to monitor government spending

Case Law Guidelines

The cases seem to say public officials covered by the *Times* decision are those government employees who have the most contact with the public; and those who have major roles in developing and carrying out governmental policy.

Where a school teacher or administrator would be seen as a public official, a maintenance worker at a public school or police department would probably not be. The cases so far say public officials are especially those employees whose responsibilities are government spending, public health or public safety.

Issue #3A - Public Figures

Back to the 1960s. As integration spread across the South under court edicts and the muzzles of army rifles, a federal court ordered the University of Mississippi to admit James Meredith, its first black student. To insure his safety, he was escorted to the campus by a squad of U.S. marshals.

That night, the marshals and a small army of reporters were driven into the university administration building by an angry mob. As the night wore on, a full-fledged riot developed. The mob began to shoot at the marshals and the building.

Small groups charged, carrying Confederate flags, trying to break in. A reporter was killed. The federal government was once again in a shooting war with the rebellious South.

Who's Leading the Charge

In the heat of the battle, an Associated Press reporter called the AP's Atlanta bureau to report a famous man — retired U. S. Army General Edwin Walker — was giving technical advice on tear gas to the rebels. The general, he said, was leading and encouraging the charges at the Old Miss administration building. A bulletin was quickly teletyped. The story was published all over the world.

Gen. Walker had been in command of the federal troops dispatched to keep peace during the school segregation confrontation in Little Rock, Arkansas, in 1957. A career soldier, he believed strongly the Communist Party was a huge threat to America.

As commander of U.S. forces in Europe, he had recommended that his troops read the John Birch Society's *Blue Book*, which accused former President Dwight D. Eisenhower and other national leaders of being communist dupes.

Walker was relieved of his European command. He retired and went on the lecture circuit. The wire services transmitted a picture of the general, flying an American flag upside down outside his home as a distress signal that the country was in trouble.

Oswald Missed

Someone took a shot at Walker. Evidence before the Warren Commission indicates the unsuccessful assassin was Lee Harvey Oswald. Oswald narrowly missed Walker, then went on to Dallas.

So the AP reported the famous general was leading the charge against the U.S. marshals. Walker denied it. The AP story had run all over the country. Walker chose to file his libel suit in Texas.

He testified he *was* on the Old Miss campus that night, but had counseled the mob to use restraint. Walker categorically denied leading any charge against the marshals. The state court jury awarded Walker $800,000. The trial judge reduced it to $500,000.

Associated Press v. Walker

388 U.S. 130, 87 S.Ct. 1975, 18 L.Ed.2d 1094 (1967)

(Full text available at www.findlaw.com)

The AP appealed, and again the U.S. Supreme Court reversed. In 1967, the court extended the *New York Times Co. v. Sullivan* guidelines to "public figures." Public figures, like public officials, cannot win a libel judgment, the court ruled, unless the media show *reckless disregard for truth*. In the chaos of the riot — under deadline pressure — the court decided the AP was not guilty of "reckless disregard" and should not be penalized.

The Walker decision was sandwiched into another "public figure" case, in which the justices used the same legal standards, with a different result.

Curtis Publishing Co. v. Butts

388 U.S. 130, 1 Media L. Rep. 1568 (1967)
(Full text available at www.findlaw.com)

The Saturday Evening Post published a story that said University of Georgia Athletic Director Wally Butts had called University of Alabama Coach "Bear" Bryant on the telephone to "fix" a game between the two teams in late 1962.

The sole evidence came from Atlanta insurance salesman George Burnett, who claimed one of his telephone calls was accidentally patched into one between the two coaches. Burnett said he listened as Butts gave Bryant the Georgia team's offensive plays and how they planned to defend against Alabama. Burnett said he made notes as he eavesdropped on the conversation.

Investigative Reporting Standards

Butts filed a libel suit in federal court contending the story was untrue, and that the magazine failed to follow accepted standards of investigative reporting.

Editors at the magazine had not looked at Burnett's notes of the call; had not talked to another man supposedly with Burnett at the time of the phone call; and had not reviewed films of the game to see if Alabama changed its tactics.

The magazine was not under deadline pressure and had time to do a better job of checking out the story.

A jury awarded Butts $60,000 in general damages and $3 million in punitive damages. The trial judge reduced the punitive damages to $400,000.

The U.S. Supreme Court approved the outcome in the lower court. Butts was a public figure, the justices decided; the *Sullivan* case guidelines should be extended to public figures; but the magazine had been guilty of reckless disregard for truth.

Rosenbloom v. Metromedia, Inc.

403 U.S. 29, Media L. Rep. 1597 (1971)
(Full text available at www.findlaw.com)

In 1971, the Supreme Court loosened the truth standard even more. George Rosenbloom was a distributor of nudist magazines in Philadelphia. The police arrested him in 1963 and seized his entire inventory. Newscasts on radio station WIP said the magazines were obscene and referred to Rosenbloom as a "girliebook peddler" in the "smut racket."

Rosenbloom was tried and found not guilty of distributing criminal obscenity. He then went to federal court and sued the radio station owner for libel. Rosenbloom was not a celebrity. None of the jurors at the start of the trial had even known who he was. A jury awarded Rosenbloom $750,000. The trial judge reduced the judgment to $275,000.

When the case reached the U.S. Supreme Court, the justices overturned the verdict and extended the *Sullivan* standard even further. People caught up in "issues of public concern" could not win a libel suit, the court said, unless they proved reckless disregard for truth.

The Court Pulls Back

The Rosenbloom decision shows how confused the issue had become. The court was badly split. There are five separate opinions, using different legal reasoning. The bundle of opinions runs 32 pages, single-spaced.

In 1974, through *Gertz v. Robert Welch, Inc.* a more conservative Supreme Court pulled back. Chicago police officer Richard Nuccio had been convicted of second-degree murder in the shooting of a teenager. Attorney Elmer Gertz was hired by the shooting victim's family to file a civil suit against the officer.

Communists vs. Police

American Opinion was a monthly magazine published by Robert Welch, Inc. — parent corporation for the ultra-conservative John Birch Society.

The magazine had been running a series of stories about a communist plot to discredit local police agencies. There was a

INSIDE THE MEDIA

Networks

Scattered Nightly Audience
Batters the Money Machine

Once upon a time, in a media land far, far away, there were three very large broadcast television networks. They were incredibly profitable. Gold mines. Each night in homes across the land, 75 per cent of the natives huddled before the tube, warmed by the glow of the prime time network shows.

The tribe has scattered now, drawn to other sources of news and entertainment. As this book goes to press, there are about 275 broadcast, cable and satellite networks. The originals have evolved into different animals. ABC, CBS and NBC make more money owning TV stations than they do from network operations.

And Then There Were Four

There are now four major TV broadcast networks. Out of nowhere, in a dozen years, Fox is head-to-head with the original Big Three. PN (the former UPN) and WB are growing.

The prime time (eight to 11 p.m.) broadcast audience has drifted away from broadcast programming. To other shows on cable TV; to television programs delivered by satellite; to video games; to movies on videotape or DVD, and to the Internet.

To understand this next section, you need to be clear on the industry terminology. A **broadcast network** delivers its programs by *broadcasting* through the air, using a network of local stations to transmit those shows. Satellite systems also transmit programs through the air, but the industry doesn't call them broadcasters.

Cable Must-Carry

Programming provided by a broadcast network can also be delivered by cable, satellite, telephone lines, or the Internet. Cable and satellite network programming (like A&E or The History Channel) are not broadcast by local stations. The quality of broadcast signals for most homes is always inferior to the picture delivered by cable or satellite.

So to keep broadcasters competitive, Congress and the FCC dictated that their signals must also be transmitted by cable systems in their local communities. It is called "must-carry."

There is a hot, continuing battle in Washington between the powerful broadcast and cable lobbies over which local stations must be carried. In 2000, satellite companies were also allowed to carry local stations so they could better compete with cable.

Most cable systems now have at least 50 to 75 channels. Many have hundreds of channels. From the time they were launched, satellite systems had that capability.

Original Model Destroyed

With so many choices, there will never again be the huge, nationwide audience on which the original network economic model was based. (See prime time audience chart, next page)

The entire television delivery system and financial structure are going through a revolutionary reformation. Nobody can say for sure what they will look like 10 years from now.

When it overhauled telecommunications law in 1996, Congress also gave telephone companies the right to deliver TV programs through telephone wires. The court decision that broke the AT&T monopoly on long distance service had barred telephone companies from the TV business. By late 2000, more than half a million homes received multi-channel TV by non-Internet telephone lines.

Long Distance & TV via Internet

Everything is changing. Within a very short time, high-quality long distance calls and full-featured, digital television will be delivered through the Internet. Print and radio are already there. Cable companies are offering long-distance phone service. Consumers can access the Internet by telephone lines, cable, or satellite.

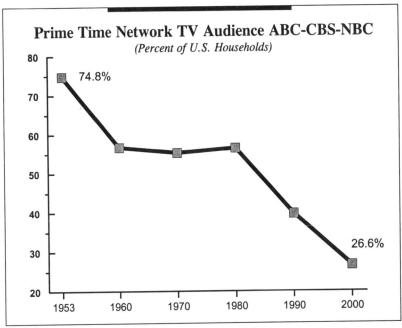

Source: Nielsen Media Research

The Prime Time Audience

In 1953, three out of every four homes in America were watching one of the Big Three networks in prime time (between 8 and 11 p.m.). Television was new. America was enthralled. By 1960, there was a steep decline, but more than half the homes were still tuned in to the three networks in the evening.

How things have changed.

In the 1999-2000 season, only about a quarter of the homes were watching the original TV networks. Network newcomers Fox, PN and WB captured another 11.2 per cent.

Evening Network News Down

The audience for the network news shows earlier in the evening on ABC, CBS and NBC has also shown a steady decline (see chart, next page).

As this book goes to press, Fox — the closest network contender — does not yet have a national evening newscast. Newspaper circulation continues to drop.

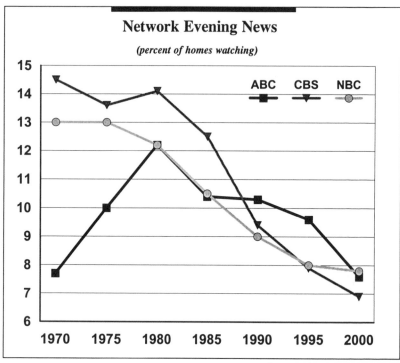

Source: Nielsen Media Research

Where'd the News Audience Go?

So where did that news audience go? To round-the-clock national newscasts and specialty channels on cable and satellite like CNN, ESPN, CNBC, Bloomberg and FNN. To *local* 24-hour TV newscasts. To the Internet.

The appetite for news has actually grown, not diminished. But there are now hundreds of specialized TV sources. Like business news, sports, weather, home and garden channels.

We are watching the same kind of audience shift that killed national, general-interest magazines like *The Saturday Evening Post* and *Colliers* while the number of specialty magazines grew.

This is also a factor in diminishing daily newspaper circulation. Some people buy a newspaper only to read about sports. So why not get much more of that news from a source that only covers your narrow interest. For the same reason, local TV news sportscasters and meteorologists may also be endangered species.

Network TV Affiliates

In the beginning (late 1940s, early 1950s) virtually all local TV stations were affiliated with either ABC, CBS or NBC. Without their network feeds, they would have had very little to broadcast.

In those pioneer days, local stations produced very few shows of their own. Few stations were on the air 24 hours a day.

The entire news staff at many stations was an anchorman (at first, there were no anchorwomen) who was also news director, reporter and photographer. These were primitive times. News programming was really radio, but you could *see* the announcer.

Some early stations didn't even own a movie camera. Polaroid photographs were shot by the anchor/news director/reporter/photographer. At six o'clock, he sat at a desk, read the news, and held the Polaroids before a studio camera.

The network affiliates were almost all VHF (Very High Frequency) stations on Channels 2-13.

Low-Rent Independents

Once a community had three TV stations, a new station had no network to affiliate with. New stations were called "independents." They were low-rent, low-prestige operations, with very few employees, and no news.

Mostly, they ran old movies. And they were usually UHF (Ultra High Frequency) stations on channels above 13. UHF signals were inferior, both in signal quality and in reach.

Cable in those early days could deliver a high-quality picture for a UHF station, but very few homes had cable. There was little incentive to produce original programming for cable. Too few viewers were connected.

Growth of Cable Systems

Cable finally conquered its major obstacle in the late 1980s when — for the first time — a majority of American homes were connected to a cable system.

Once most homes were subscribers, commercials for cable programming also grew, raising the money to stimulate more channels and new cable programs. Cable systems provided a better picture and many more channels than broadcasters.

By 2000, 68 per cent of American households subscribed to cable and another 11 per cent to satellite systems. Only 3.4 per cent of the nation's homes did not have cable service as an option. Satellite-delivered programs could reach every part of the country.

Original News Monopoly

The networks originally had a monopoly on the delivery of national and international news. They built their own coaxial cable system, connecting their affiliate stations, in virtually every part of the country.

Satellites changed all that.

More and more communications satellites were launched. By the late 1980s, most local television news operations had their own satellite capability.

They could send reporters anywhere in the world and beam stories back, live, with a local angle. Once they could do that, network coverage sometimes seemed second-rate to the audience.

What Should Network News Do?

If the networks' monopoly on a national audience AND the ability to report live from anywhere in the world no longer exist, what should network news be doing that will be profitable?

The people who run the networks are trying to figure that out.

Proliferating magazine shows are one answer. Some analysts predict magazine shows, with longer stories, will become the early evening TV network news. Shorter news stories will be available on the 24-hour, continuous news channels.

The FCC definition of a broadcast network is a central source offering at least 15 hours a week of programming.

Fox, through broadcast stations that were previously independents, met that definition in late 1990, and by early 1993 provided programs every night.

The Affiliate Relationship

The relationship between the networks and their local affiliates is often misunderstood.

It became even more so in 1997, when the networks asked their affiliates to start identifying themselves as "Channel 8 - NBC" or "Channel 10 - ABC."

They wanted to build more loyalty to network programs on those stations after the news. It also helps the confusion among viewers after ownership shuffles in which stations switch networks.

The tie between a network and its affiliates does not involve ownership. Networks and local stations have contracts to supply services to each other.

Network-Local Station Contract

When advertisers buy network time, they want to reach the largest possible audience. So the network contracts with local stations to broadcast network programming.

In return for that service, the network has traditionally paid the local station a fee, based on market size. It was historically only about what it cost to operate the local station for the time allotted to network shows. As network profits dwindle, the old network-local station relationship is changing.

Local Station's Percentage

The real money for the affiliate comes from local advertising slots that are built into network programs. Each hour of a network show carries about 10 minutes of commercials. About three minutes of that 10 minutes is set aside for local commercials.

Watch a network show. Most of the advertising will be national — cars, detergents, aspirin, beer or office machines. But some of the commercial breaks will advertise Aunt Millie's Delicatessen or a local car wash. That's the local station's cut.

New Network Deals

Broadcast network executives are now telling their affiliates their financial relationship will have to be completely reworked.

Some are even telling their local affiliates they'll have to *pay the network* if they want to carry the most popular and expensive network programs (like sports). Station owners cannot even imagine such a thing. The battle is on.

Cable systems have traditionally paid cable content providers like A&E, CNN or The Discovery Channel who provided them programming. In order to get an immediate audience, Rupert Murdoch in 1997 paid cable operators $10 per home to include his startup Fox News Channel in their systems. A truly radical idea.

Conflicts and Hybrids

The networks and their affiliates need each other. But the changing technology and increasing competition from other delivery systems are creating enormous conflicts, and new hybrids.

When a television news provider has a website, the video shot for broadcast or cable can also be used on the Internet. Links to other, related sites and additional, full-text resource material can be included in the Internet version.

NBC is ahead of the other Big Four in preparing for the time when TV programming with high-quality sound and digital video will be accessible through the Internet, cable, satellites, or the old-fashioned broadcast signal. Take your pick.

Network News Cooperation

There is usually a cooperative working relationship between network news organizations and the local affiliates. Suppose a tornado touches down in your area. There's no network correspondent available to cover the story. The network will call the local station and ask for a copy of its tornado videotape.

Sometimes, the network will ask for a complete "package" from a reporter at the local affiliate. When the reporter "sigs out" at the end of the story, you can tell whether he's network or local.

If he's local, he says, "In Topeka, I'm William Windy, *for* ABC News." If the story is done *for* the network, the reporter is telling you he's not a network correspondent.

A network correspondent would close his piece, "In Topeka, I'm William Windy, ABC News." When a network uses videotape shot by an affiliate, it usually pays the reporter and camera crew a fee. They're moonlighting for the network.

If the network sends a crew to a town where it has no bureau, the crew will usually use the local affiliate's newsroom, telephones, satellite and editing facilities.

News Appetite Increases

Until the middle 1970s, news was rarely a moneymaker for local stations or networks. It was considered a prestige item. Local news on stations affiliated with the three networks distinguished them from the independents, who did not have news.

Watergate whetted America's appetite for news. CBS' *60 Minutes* grew to be one of the most-watched shows on the air in the early 1980s, and still ranks regularly in the top ten.

Ted Turner & CNN

When Ted Turner started CNN in 1980, few people believed the country could absorb that kind of news saturation. Many thought Turner was on an ego binge that would drive him to bankruptcy. In 1997, Turner donated a billion dollars to charity and thumbed his nose at those who had doubted his success.

CNN was so popular, a number of round-the-clock news channels were created. Regional, 24-hour news channels are proliferating — some operated by local newspapers. Everybody's scrambling to have constant, ready-when-you-are news on the Internet.

Network-owned TV Stations

A growing number of local TV stations are owned and operated by one of the national networks. They're called "O and O's."

Until 1985, the FCC limited the number of TV outlets owned by one company to five VHF and two UHF stations. The rule was enacted to prevent monopolies that could narrow the control of TV content. So for many years, each network had five O and O's.

Station Ownership Expanded

In 1985, the rules were rewritten, allowing one company to own as many as 12 stations, so long as that owner's stations reached no more than 25 per cent of the national audience.

The 1996 Telecommunications Act expanded it even more, permitting one company to own an *unlimited* number of TV stations, so long as the total audience reached by all its stations was no more than 35 per cent of the nation.

Radio Consolidation

The 1996 law also eliminated national ownership limits for radio stations and allowed companies to own (based on a ratings formula) up to about 20 per cent of the radio stations in the same city.

As a result, there was a rapid consolidation of radio station ownership. At the end of 2000, Clear Channel Communications,

Inc. owned 1,018 of the nation's 10,549 radio stations. The stations' total annual revenue was just over $3 billion.

The Number Two radio conglomerate — measured in annual revenue — was Infinity Broadcasting Corp., Inc. with 187 radio stations and a little over $2 billion in revenue. Viacom, Inc. owns both Infinity and the CBS television network.

Number Three at the end of 2000 was ABC Radio, Inc., with 52 radio stations and $406 million in revenue. Walt Disney Co. owns both ABC Radio and the ABC television network.

As a result of large corporate owners whose primary goal is profit, local radio reporters who gather, write and read the news are almost extinct. Stations that carry news (many don't) either read it off the wire, or simply relay stories written and voiced by a national news service.

Lights Are On, But Nobody's Home

With today's technology, it is possible to own and operate a radio station with no local staff.

All programming can be sent to the station by satellite. Halfway across the country, a company monitors and adjusts the control room dials by satellite. If the telemetry indicates something needs fixing, they call a local technician to do the work.

Mega-Merger Shuffle

As this book goes to press, there is a great deal of confusion on who will be allowed to own what. In a series of mega-mergers, communications giants like Viacom, Time-Warner and News Corp. have acquired large blocks of local television stations.

Some of the newly merged companies are in violation of the FCC ownership limitation. They can reach more than 35 per cent of the national audience through their local stations.

The conglomerates are challenging those government restrictions by filing lawsuits and lobbying Congress. The ownership caps might very well be removed. It has become politically correct in both political parties to favor the deregulation of private industry.

When the three original networks were primarily concerned with broadcasting, their news operations were major, prestigious arms of the companies. They took their obligations as journalists seriously — though not as seriously as most newspaper owners.

Most of the early network anchors, correspondents and top news executives had begun their careers in newspapers. They understood the responsibility that Constitutional protection implied.

New Owners, New Goals

By the late 1990s, with the major network audience split and profits down, the networks were gobbled up by corporations with a different kind of heritage. For the most part, the people who run these companies have no journalistic background. Their primary goal in life has always been to make money for the corporation and its stockholders.

They found new ways to make their broadcast and cable properties money machines. What is happening now is a reformation, where the corporations that own the major radio and TV networks will once again reach a very large national audience. But it will be split among the corporation's many outlets and subsidiaries.

The news segment of their operation is a tiny niche.

Newspapers, aware of their own dire financial positions, are forming alliances with the big communications conglomerates, just to stay in the game. "Convergence" is the term being used when one company provides news in many formats.

The following ownership interests are not complete and comprehensive. They're just samples, to give you an idea of the interconnected maze. The holdings are constantly shifting.

AOL Time Warner

Time-Warner, with its foundation in movie-making, national magazines (*Time, Fortune, Sports Illustrated*) and extensive cable systems, first bought Ted Turner's TV empire that included CNN.

Then AOL — by far the largest Internet service provider — announced it would merge with Time-Warner. As this book goes to press, many facets of the merger do not yet have government approval. The company will be called AOL Time Warner.

CNN has contracts with hundreds of local stations to provide packaged national and international news stories to them, even though they are affiliated with ABC, CBS, Fox or NBC.

Besides its magazines and movie production studios, Time Warner also owns HBO, Cinemax, Court TV, TBS, TNT, Turner Classic Movies, the Cartoon Network, book and music publishing companies, World Championship Wrestling, and three Atlanta sports teams.

Walt Disney and ABC

The ABC TV Network is owned by the Walt Disney Company. Disney also owns 10 TV stations, half a dozen newspapers, and about 50 radio stations.

Its cable TV interests include A&E, E!, ESPN, The History Channel, and Lifetime. It produces movies (Buena Vista, Miramax, Touchstone), recorded music, magazines and books. In addition to its theme parks, it also owns sports franchises.

Viacom and CBS

In 2000, Viacom bought the CBS TV Network. At the time the merger was announced, Viacom owned Paramount movie studios, more than 1,000 movie theaters, 18 TV stations, the United Paramount Network (UPN), Simon and Schuster, Scribners, six theme parks, plus Blockbuster Video and Music stores.

The new stations gave it a total of 32, reaching 41 per cent of the national audience. A violation of the federal rules. Its cable interests include MTV, VH1, Nickelodeon, the Sundance Channel, the Movie Channel, Showtime, FLIX and the All News Channel.

It also produces and sells TV shows like Frasier, JAG, Star Trek: Voyager, Sabrina the Teenage Witch, Moesha, Entertainment Tonight, Judge Judy, Leeza and Montel Williams.

News Corp. and Fox

The Fox Network is owned by News Corporation — the worldwide communications empire of Australian magnate Rupert Murdoch.

In 2000, News Corp. bought 10 TV stations owned by Chris Craft Industries, giving it a total of 33 stations in the U.S. Those 33 stations have the ability to reach 40.5 per cent of the national audience. More than the 35 per cent allowed by the FCC.

Fox has filed a lawsuit contending that the limitation on the number of stations a company can own (and the audience they serve) violates its First Amendment rights.

Fox's other interests in the United States include the *New York Post*, HarperCollins and Morrow/Avon book publishers, TV

Guide, Twentieth Century Fox movie studios and distribution, Madison Square Garden, four professional sports franchises, and the Staples Center in Los Angeles.

On cable TV, Fox has interests in National Geographic's cable channel, the Golf Channel and Outdoor Life. It owns Fox Sports, the Health Network, the Family Channel, MTM Entertainment and the Fox News Channel.

General Electric and NBC

In addition to its worldwide manufacturing and financial operations, GE owns NBC and 13 local TV stations. It has a joint venture with Microsoft in MSNBC on the Internet; owns part of A&E and the History Channel with Disney; and has an interest in Fox Sports and the National Geographic cable channel.

NBC was far ahead of its network competitors in realizing the future of the Internet. It was also one of the first broadcast owners to venture into cable television, partnering with Dow Jones (owner of *The Wall Street Journal*) to create CNBC.

GE has ownership interests in cable channels Bravo, American Movie Classics, the Independent Film Channel and Romance Classics.

The Insider & the Gatekeepers

Journalists in this culture have always been described as gatekeepers, choosing which stories they will allow the public to read, hear or view. The crucial issue now is how the new media owners will handle news that could help or harm the mother corporation.

The movie *The Insider* was based on real events. A tobacco insider leaked documents to *60 Minutes* that showed tobacco executives had known for years their product was addictive and deadly.

Great news story. All the top tobacco company CEOs had sworn before a Congressional Committee that they did not believe tobacco was addictive. A huge national lawsuit against the tobacco industry was pending.

But because the sale of CBS was being negotiated, corporate lawyers prevented *60 Minutes* from broadcasting the story. They felt the story would result in a major lawsuit, and they were afraid Viacom might back out of the deal. So the insider took his information to *The Wall Street Journal*. The *Journal* ran with it.

Disney's Hiring

In January, 1999, *Brills Content* reported that ABC's *20/20* — afraid of offending its parent corporation — suppressed a story that would have exposed hiring practices at Disney World. According to the magazine, background checks were so loose, convicted child molesters were able to obtain jobs there. The allegation surfaced again in late 2000 in the *New Yorker*. Disney denied it.

GE is a major manufacturer of aircraft engines worldwide. If one of their engines begins to have problems, will GE let NBC, MSNBC and CNBC report the story with no holds barred?

Congress' $70 Billion Gift

Part of the 1996 Telecommunications Act gave a huge chunk of unused airwaves to the owners of television stations, requiring that they use that new spectrum to upgrade their signals to high-definition television (HDTV).

At the end of 2000, that has still not happened. Based on other auctions of similar broadcast wavelengths, the gift was valued at $70 billion. Opposing the giveaway, Republican Senator John McCain predicted neither radio nor TV would report it.

In researching his book, *Megamedia*, author Dean Alger timed network TV news stories during the nine months the bill was debated. He counted a total of 19 minutes of news about the Telecommunications Act. According to Alger, none of those stories said anything about the spectrum giveaway.

The broadcasters said they needed the additional spectrum space to perform the *public service* of providing HDTV. But they bitterly fought — and defeated — a section of the bill that would have required the *public service* of free air time for candidates.

That part of the Congressional story was not reported fully by radio and television news, either.

Will hard-driving corporate raiders discourage their news departments from covering stories that might harm their stock prices or a corporate deal that's in the works?

When the movie critic for a morning show gushes about how good the new flick is, how do we know whether his network has an interest in the movie? Are the people interviewed on those shows just a crass cross-plug for other network financial interests?

These days, it's hard to tell.

INSIDE THE MEDIA

Newscast

For the End of the World, Two Minutes

Time dictates almost everything in radio and television news. Broadcast deadlines are absolute. The news begins at exactly six o'clock, or ten, or eleven. The lead story in broadcast news must be ready when the anchor says, "Good evening."

Sure, you could place that story later in the newscast. But if the audience is expecting today's big story and it's not ready at the top of the newscast, they'll switch to the competition.

A Precise Fit

Time restricts broadcast stories in another way. The producer who assembles the newscast must build a collection of taped stories, live material and commercials that will fit the time slot exactly. The time tolerance is so precise, listeners and viewers will notice if there is an awkward split-second of dead air. Producers live with stopwatches hanging around their necks.

A television newscast, in its entirety, will be 30 or 60 minutes long. The time slot is rigid, just as the "news hole" in a newspaper (the space set aside for news stories) can't be stretched. The newspaper news hole varies from day to day, depending on how much advertising has been sold. The newscast length remains the same.

Radio Even Shorter

A radio newscast producer will have only five or 10 minutes. Most radio news stories are 10 to 15 seconds long. In radio, 30 seconds is a *very* long story. Unless it's National Public Radio.

The 17-Minute Newscast

Time is absolute, and it is precious. After you subtract commercials, weather, sports, good evening and good-bye, a 30-minute local TV newscast is only about 17 minutes of news. Most stories will run 30 seconds, or less. A few will have the luxury of a full minute. For a major story — 90 seconds.

Half-hour network newscasts contain about 22 minutes of news. They don't have weather and sports segments.

There is an old joke producers scream when young reporters say they need more time for a story. "What do you think you're covering?" they yell. "This story isn't worth it. For the end of the world, you get two minutes. But only if you have good video."

TV Alters the Mind

Television has radically altered the way most Americans receive, retain, and react to information. Fifty years ago, first graders had an average attention span of 20 to 30 seconds. Today, that is beyond the limit for most adults. Television's ability to flick from one picture to another — sometimes several times per second — has conditioned us to *expect* frequent changes of scenery on the tube. When it doesn't happen, our attention drifts.

A new form of TV commercials evolved in the mid-1990s. Dubbed "MTV-style," they got their name from music videos. It had become trendy to edit videos with extremely rapid cuts. Some shots were so brief they were virtually subliminal.

Young People See the Cuts

Marketing researchers ran some tests to see how much of the information in these commercials could be retained by the audience. Commercial time is precious. No reason to increase production time and cost if the product doesn't work.

They found that young people who had grown up with television and video games could see all the cuts. Older people whose learning process as youngsters developed without television could not see some of the very quick cuts.

The theory from that research is that heavy doses of television at an early age sharpen the natural ability to see and retain visual information that flicks by in milliseconds.

For TV, the 90-Second Rule

The TV industry spends billions of dollars on market research. Consulting firms are constantly studying viewers to learn what turns them on, and what makes them switch to another channel.

It was those consulting firms that issued the Ninety Second Rule. Sure, the rule is broken. But unless it is exceptionally well done, any story longer than 90 seconds tends to make viewers go to the kitchen, to the bathroom, to the bedroom, to sleep in their chair, or — horrors — to another channel.

Those same studies led to another time guideline: Never let anybody talk on camera for more than about 10 seconds. The voice can continue, but you must constantly give viewers new video. If you want to retain or improve your audience ratings, change the picture as often as possible.

Channel Surfing

The short attention span was cut even shorter with the invention of the TV remote control.

If the program is not constantly stimulating, we surf to another channel. As a result, one theory says the public also has a very short attention span for government and politics. If elected officials do not make us happy within a few months, we get irritated and impatient. We are ready to zap them and sample someone else.

The Internet may shorten the attention span of Americans even more. Most people surfing the Net do not really read. They scan, looking for links to something they *might* want to read. They jump from one page to another every few seconds.

Under 10 Seconds

When you watch network news tonight, time the interviews. Virtually all of them will run less than ten seconds. Some will be only three or four seconds. The exception is Public Broadcasting, which believes its audience is more mature and better educated. That its viewers are able to concentrate longer than Joe Sixpack.

The same time limit is used for live talk shows which feature experts talking about current events.

The larger the television market (and the more vicious the competition), the more research will be done to attract and retain the audience. As a general rule, the bigger the market, the shorter the sound bites. In radio, most sound bites will be less than five seconds.

Surveys year after year show America's greatest fear is stage fright. The real fear is looking stupid or incompetent in front of a lot of people. How can you possibly say anything intelligent about a complicated, controversial subject in ten seconds or less?

That's what makes talking to television or radio reporters seem so terribly difficult and scary. (See **SKILLS/Interviews-Broadcast** and **Interviews-General**)

Transferring Skills

But once you learn how, you'll discover it works in many other places where you need to communicate — to sell ideas. The people in those audiences have also had their minds altered by TV.

You'll be much more effective if you use some of television's techniques for your next civic club speech — when you testify at a legislative hearing — when you're trying to convince your staff or board of directors.

You need to be brief. You need to communicate with visuals as much as with words.

The most common formula for a TV news story that involves a reporter is the Sony Sandwich. Some stations call it a "wrap" or a "package." Most television stories will follow this simple formula, or some variation. Radio uses a very similar sandwich form. And now newspapers have adopted it, too. (See the chapters on **Interviews** in the **SKILLS** Section)

TV Creates Tribal Unity

Walter Cronkite once said television provides a headline service. Newspaper people love that quote. For much of television coverage, Cronkite was right.

But there are other times when neither the written nor the spoken word can come close to the awesome impact of the television sound camera.

Television has unified us more than any other force in history. The storytellers in ancient tribes gave people their sense of time and place and identity. But each person crouched around the campfire came away with a very different mental picture of what the chief or medicine man was reciting.

Then books served that purpose for civilization. But still, no matter how well written, every reader had a different mental image.

Identical Memories

We now have identical memories of the major events in our lives and recent history. Those moments, captured on film and videotape, bind us together as a people. More powerful, more intimate, more emotional than books, they are engraved in our collective past. Computerized encyclopedias now include news clips with full sound and video. The same images and sounds will pass to future generations.

We sometimes have to think a minute — did I see it on television, or was I really there? Major news events like:

- Martin Luther King, Jr. speaking at the Lincoln Memorial
- Law enforcement officers using clubs, fire hoses and attack dogs on Civil Rights demonstrators
- The Vietnam War
- The first step onto the lunar surface
- Richard Nixon's resignation
- The shootings of John F. Kennedy, Lee Harvey Oswald, Robert Kennedy, and Ronald Reagan
- The explosion of the Challenger spacecraft
- The bombing of the Federal Building in Oklahoma City
- Princess Diana's death

For those stories, television forgets about time. When it does — and when luck and skill put a camera and microphone in just the right place — no other medium can match its impact.

Newscast Mechanics

As a first step for coping with broadcast news, you need to understand some of the mechanics of producing a newscast. TV news stories are short, but broadcasting them is very complicated.

Some of the things they do are very puzzling if you don't know about the gadgets, the formats, and how they dictate the production of stories — and the newscast itself.

Attention Span Dictates

Many of the story forms for television news are dictated by the audience's attention span. That's why the double or triple anchor format was invented.

If viewers begin to nod, the new face and voice bring them back to attention. Many local stations believe male-female anchor teams offer maximum appeal and attention-span advantages.

The Anchor Balancing Act

The anchors are usually attractive people, easy to look at and listen to. The shift back and forth between male and female voices offers constant attention fresheners.

If they're not listening closely, men in the audience enjoy looking at a beautiful woman. Female viewers like to watch a good-looking anchorman. And the chemistry between a man and a woman on camera makes ad-libs more interesting.

Television stations balance their anchor teams in the same way a political party tries to balance its ticket. A city with a large black population needs black anchors. Stations with significant ethnic communities search for anchors who may have lost their accents, but have identifiable ethnic names and *look* Spanish, or Italian, or Polish.

Voice Monotony

Television and radio amplify monotony. Five seconds of a blank screen, or dead silence on the radio, seems like forever. Listen carefully to good disk jockeys — the way they talk to keep your attention.

Broadcasters train themselves to read so their voices go up and down, now slower, then faster without a breath, then a long pause. Paul Harvey — one of radio's most successful commentators — is almost a caricature of this technique, but you can better understand it by listening closely to how he does it.

In putting together a newscast, the producer tries to pace the show the same way. A long TV story will be followed by several short ones. The plane crash report may be played just before a break. When they come back from the commercial, there will be a fluffy, breezy story to make us feel better.

Copy Stories

The simplest and briefest television story is called a "copy story" or "reader." The anchor reads the entire story, on camera, with no videotape. There may be some kind of still picture or graphic over the anchor's shoulder.

TelePrompTers

While we're talking about copy stories, you may wonder how anchors read the news without looking at the script in their hands — and why they bother to even have a script.

TelePrompTer® devices enable anchors to read stories while looking directly into the camera lens.

The pages in the anchor's hand are a printout of the script, which was typed into a computer.

How it Works

A computer monitor is mounted under the big studio camera. The script scrolls down the monitor. The monitor is reflected onto a plate of clear glass in front of the camera lens.

The angle of the glass is fixed so the anchor can see the reflection of the pages. But the camera shoots right through the glass.

At home, we can't tell the glass is even there. And because of the reflection in the glass, the anchor can't really see the camera lens.

You Don't See the Eyes Move

The script is printed in large type and very short lines — usually two or three words to the line — so it can be read without noticeable eye movement.

The speed at which the script rolls can be controlled by a technician, or by the anchors themselves. Each time a page goes by on the monitor, the anchor turns a page on the desk, in case something goes wrong with the TelePrompTer®.

Should that happen, the paper script is a backup. The anchor can continue by reading from the script on the desk — glancing down and looking up, a sentence at a time. When experienced anchors stumble, and suddenly start reading from the script in their hands, it's usually a clue that something has gone wrong.

In front of the camera lens, a computer monitor is reflected by an angled sheet of glass. The anchor can see the reflection of the monitor, but the audience can't.

Stumbling is a Clue

The pages in the TelePrompTer® may be out of sequence. Or the scrolling may have stopped. The script on screen for the anchor to read may not be the story that's on the air, which the anchors can see in a small monitor built into the desk. When the prompter's problem is fixed, the anchor goes back to looking at the camera.

The best anchors glance down at the script on the desk each time they turn a page. They give the illusion that they've read the entire page at a glance, memorized it, and then recite it to you.

If they don't look down occasionally, the viewers begin to wonder why the anchors never look at the pages they're holding. Maybe they're in Braille?

To make a copy story more visually interesting, a graphic of some kind is "keyed" over the anchor's shoulder.

Story Keys

The graphic is inserted electronically, in the control room. You know, of course, the drawing, or picture, is not actually there in the TV studio. If it's a story about a postal rate hike, there may be a postage stamp, or a mailbox in the key. A copy story about a murder may key a gun, or a knife.

This is part of television's constant effort to show you something while they talk. It helps you understand and pay attention. It doubles your retention. You should do the same thing when you talk to the Kiwanis Club or the County Commission.

Invisible Weather Maps

The same electronics that key a graphic over the anchor's shoulder can make a blank wall look like a weather map. This is one of TV's most interesting electronic illusions.

The meteorologist works in front of a wall that is painted muddy blue or bright green. At home, you see a map of the area, the state, or the nation on the wall. It's not really there.

How Weather Maps Work

The electronic device merges two sources of video. The camera shooting the weathercaster is tuned to be blind to the color on the wall. The picture it takes is a cutout of the forecaster. The picture is blank everywhere else.

Another video source is fed into the device. It can be a computer-generated map, videotape, slides, or a live radar scope. The device inserts into the map the camera cutout picture of the weathercaster.

Electronic Cookie Cutters

Imagine two sheets of cookie dough. A cookie cutter (the studio camera) stamps out the image of the forecaster. That becomes the cookie.

The rest of that sheet of dough is thrown away.

The same cookie cutter then stamps out the same image on the second sheet of cookie dough.

Winning with the News Media

This time, you throw away the cookie and keep the remaining dough. There is a hole in the sheet of dough that will exactly match the silhouette of the cookie.

Then the cutout from the first sheet (the weathercaster) is inserted into the second sheet of cookie dough (the weather map). It is done so seamlessly we think the weathercaster cutout and the map are all part of the same sheet of video.

Smoke and Mirrors

When the forecaster is pointing to a storm system over the Great Lakes, the Great Lakes are not there. On each side of the set, where viewers can't see them, are TV monitors showing what we're seeing at home. The forecaster appears to be looking at the map on the wall.

Instead, the forecaster is watching a monitor. If the forecaster's finger pointing to the Great Lakes is actually over Arkansas, the forecaster can see it on the monitor and make a correction.

Live Remotes Do It, Too

At some stations, the same device is used when anchors are talking to reporters doing live remotes from the field. The anchors talk to what looks like a TV monitor. The monitor is actually a screen painted the same blue or green used for the weather segment.

The studio camera shoots over the shoulder of the anchors, and the image of the reporter is inserted into the blank screen the anchors talk to. The anchors have a small monitor on the floor that viewers can't see. They can view the reporter in the field as they have their two-way conversation.

The blue color was originally chosen because it was the color most absent in human skin tones. Later equipment worked better with a shade of green. Occasionally, anchors will have something in their clothing that is too close to that color.

A Window in Your Chest

An anchor's tie or scarf with the same blue or green will make that part of the anchor invisible. We will see the weather map where the tie or scarf is. Just as though the anchor had a window in that part of the body.

This same equipment is often used in commercials. A pair of hands holding the product seem to be unattached, floating in air. They're actually at the end of a sleeve that is the blue or green color. The arm seems to disappear. We only see the hands and the product.

Voice-Over Story Formula

In a voice-over story, the anchor begins to read the story on camera. About 10 seconds into the copy, the director in the control room switches the picture from the anchor to videotape of what the anchor is talking about. The anchor continues to read, live, while we see videotape. The tape may have sound with it, played very low. This is called **natural sound.** The anchor voice is *over* the picture and any background sound on the tape.

As the anchor talks about last night's Academy Award winner, you see the actor accepting the statuette. If the tape is used with natural sound, you will hear, softly, in the background, the applause when his name is pulled from the envelope.

Voice-Over to Sound

In the voice-over-to-sound formula (V/O to SOT), the anchor begins the story on-camera, just as before. The story becomes V/O as you watch the actor accept the Oscar. Then the anchor stops reading. The sound on the tape is turned up, full volume. You see and hear the actor thanking his mother, his father, his mistress, his director, and his dog.

For this kind of story, everything must be timed precisely. After the copy is written, a producer with a stopwatch takes it to the anchor, who reads at a normal pace. They time from the point where the live voice-over begins, to where the actor in last night's ceremony will speak on videotape. The voice-over section of tape is edited to run exactly as many seconds as it takes for the anchor to read the copy.

The Countdown

When the anchor reads the copy during the newscast, the director in the control room punches a stopwatch as the voice-over tape begins to roll. The anchor must read for exactly 16 seconds.

Winning with the News Media

The director has the entire newscast timed to a split second. As the anchor reads, voice-over, the director calls out the countdown to the floor manager.

If the reading is too fast, there will be a hole of silence between the anchor's voice and the actor's.

Read too slowly, and the anchor will drown out the beginning of what the actor says.

The director works with a microphone in the control room. The anchors wear hidden earphones. The floor crew all have headsets.

By flipping a selector switch, the director can talk to anyone in the studio, or to all of them. As the anchor reads the voice-over section of the story, the director watches a stopwatch and begins a countdown to the floor manager. The floor manager, listening on a headset, drops a finger each second as the director counts.

The floor manager gives the anchor hand signals on how much time before the sound-on-tape will begin.

Watch My Fingers Count

When the countdown reaches five seconds, the anchor will hurry a little, or slow down, to finish the voice-over just as the sound-on-tape (SOT) begins. When the Oscar winner finishes thanking everybody, the anchor comes back on camera to begin another story.

Scripting the Story

There is a form for television news stories, just as there is a form for movie scripts. They're different.

The notations at the left side of the television script are instructions for the editor who will put the story together. It is a blueprint that shows how the story is built. The editor can build the story on tape while the reporter who wrote it does something else.

The control room needs the script if the story is read live. It tells when to roll tape, when to bring up supers, etc.

V/O - SOT - V/O

The voice-over to sound-on-tape to voice-over (V/O-SOT-V/O) is a variation of the same formula. The anchor begins with a copy story, on camera. On the following page is a typical script.

ANCHOR LIVE	THE CITY'S GARBAGE COLLECTORS SAY THEY'LL STRIKE AT MIDNIGHT UNLESS THE CITY COUNCIL GOES ALONG WITH THEIR DEMAND FOR A 15 PERCENT PAY INCREASE.
V/O (Videotape of meeting)	THE GARBAGE COLLECTORS' UNION MET AT TWO A.M. THIS MORNING, AND WOUND UP WITH A UNANI-MOUS VOTE, SETTING THE WALKOUT DEADLINE.
SOT (Union president) super name	"The Council says we don't care about our city. Well, I say they don't care about us. We're human beings. We have to eat, too."
V/O (Mayor entering City Hall)	THE MAYOR HAS CALLED AN EMERGENCY MEETING OF THE CITY COUNCIL TONIGHT IN A LAST-DITCH EFFORT TO STOP THE STRIKE.

If the story is more complicated — getting the mayor's point of view, for instance — it will usually be handled by a reporter, who will "package" the story in Sony Sandwich form.

The Lead-In

On the air, the Sony Sandwich is introduced by the anchor. The anchor copy is called the lead-in. It is a headline, designed to tell you generally what the story is about, grab your attention, and make you want to listen to what the reporter is about to say.

The reporter's entire story is on videotape, both sound and picture. That's why, once edited, it is very difficult to change the length. In the Sony Sandwich formula, the reporter begins by giving viewers the basic facts while we see videotape — V/O NAT SOUND.

This is the bottom bread of the sandwich. It is 10 to 15 seconds thick. The interview is in the middle, followed by the top of the sandwich — another 10 to 15 seconds of reporter narration. (See **SKILLS/Interviews-Broadcast** and **Interviews-General**)

A Sony Sandwich Script

In the story scripted below, the beginning natural sound will include sirens and the crackle of the fire under the reporter's voice.

ANCHOR LIVE (Key fire)	FIVE PEOPLE ARE DEAD, THREE OTHERS MISSING AS THE RESULT OF A FIRE THAT SWEPT THROUGH THE UPPER FLOORS OF A DOWN-TOWN ROOMING HOUSE LATE THIS AFTERNOON. REPORTER DEBBIE DARLING SAYS ARSON IS SUSPECTED.

Sony Sandwich begins

DARLING V/O NAT. SOUND (flames)	THE FLAMES RACED SO QUICKLY THROUGH THE THIRD FLOOR OF THE OLD WOODEN HOUSE, FIRE-FIGHTERS SAY EVERYONE ON THAT FLOOR DIED.
(man jumping)	ABOVE, FROM A FOURTH-FLOOR WINDOW, A TERRIFIED MAN JUMPED TO HIS DEATH BEFORE FIREFIGHTERS COULD RAISE THEIR LADDERS.
(carrying people out)	THERE WERE DRAMATIC RESCUES THAT KEPT THE DEATH TOLL FROM CLIMBING EVEN HIGHER.

(Now the meat of the Sony Sandwich)

SOT (woman in blanket) (super name)	"The smoke was so thick I couldn't see anything. I knew I was dead.
V/O (fireman carrying victim)	Then this fireman knocks the door down, and he throws me over his shoulder, and goes
SOT (woman in blanket)	running right through the flames. He saved my life. I hope I can find him to say thank you."

(And the bread to top it off)

DARLING	THE NAMES OF THE DEAD HAVE
V/O NAT. SO.	NOT BEEN RELEASED. FIRE
(Covered bodies)	INSPECTORS SAY THE SPEED AT
(More fire)	WHICH THE FLAMES SPREAD
	MAKES THEM BELIEVE IT WAS SET
	BY AN ARSONIST.

DARLING STANDUP	IF IT WAS ARSON, WHOEVER
SOT	SET THE FIRE COULD BE GUILTY
	OF FIRST DEGREE MURDER.
	WE'LL HAVE MORE IN A FULL
	REPORT TONIGHT AT ELEVEN.
	I'M DEBBIE DARLING,
	CHANNEL 28, EYEWITNESS NEWS.

INSIDE THE MEDIA

Newspapers

Will the Last One Here Please Turn Off the Press?

"Angst in the Newsroom" was the cover story on a national journalism magazine. "Will Bill Gates Crush Newspapers?" headlined another. Newspapers as we have known them are dying. The percentage of Americans who buy and/or read a daily newspaper is steadily dropping.

Back in 1970, they sold roughly one newspaper per household every day in America.

By 2000, the number of households had increased by 64.83 per cent, to 104.5 million. In that same period, daily newspaper circulation *dropped* 9.98 per cent, to 55.9 million. (See chart, next page)

"A Dangerous Decline"

The National Newspaper Association of America (NAA), which has historically painted a rosy picture of the industry, commissioned a study in 1997 which showed only 51 per cent of Americans read a weekday paper, what the study called "a dangerous decline."

The NAA survey asked which news medium people would miss most if it were no longer available. Those polled said they would miss their Sunday newspaper most. But on weekdays, newspapers were not as valued as TV and radio.

People say they don't have time to read the newspaper any more. In 1998, the Pew Research Center for The People and the Press conducted its biennial national survey to find the average

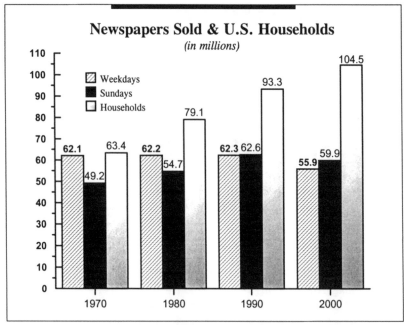

Newspapers Sold & U.S. Households
(in millions)

Source: *U.S. Census,* Editor & Publisher

American spending 31 minutes per day watching news on TV, 18 minutes reading a newspaper, and 17 minutes listening to radio news. A quarter of 18-to-24-year-olds get no news of any kind.

The competition of television is just part of the problem for newspapers. Other reasons for the drop in readership —

Illiteracy. A large segment of the population does not read well enough to tackle a newspaper. Publishers have made a nationwide effort to encourage programs that teach adults to read.

A mobile population, with few ties or personal identification with the local community. Newspapers in this country have traditionally been heavy on local news — particularly government. Other developed nations have national newspapers. The closest America has is *The New York Times*, *The Wall Street Journal*, and a newcomer — *USA Today*. In September, 2000, *USA Today* inched past the *WSJ* as the largest-circulation daily in the U.S.

Expanding options for using leisure time — particularly computers and the Internet. Much of the information that was once available only in newspapers is now accessible, 24 hours a day, with a home computer and a modem. Set-top devices that use a TV set as a monitor and provide basic Internet browsing were being heavily marketed at the end of 2000. E-mail and the Internet will soon become as common as television in American homes. Information on the Web is updated every few minutes. It's even more current than round-the-clock TV news shows. Customized news, stock market prices, weather information and sports scores are always available whenever you want them.

Women working outside the home. Homemakers were once a major segment of newspaper readership. With outside jobs, women still shoulder household chores, too. Free time is scarce. Newspaper reading is one of the things they drop.

Young adults who grew up with television and never developed the newspaper-reading habit. Take a look at the obituaries and understand that the death of anyone over 65 today means the loss of another newspaper reader — who is not being replaced.

Sunday Papers Now Sliding, Too

While it hasn't kept pace with the growth in households, Sunday newspaper circulation in 2000 (59.9 million) was 22 per cent higher than it was in 1970 (49.2 million), according to *Editor and Publisher*.

But even on Sunday, the circulation figures peaked in 1993 (62.6 million) and have been sliding since.

One theory for the difference in Sunday and weekday circulation trends is more time to read on Sunday. Readers don't have to go to work. Sunday papers have more advertising, and there's time to shop for bargains in both the classified and display ads.

Audit Bureau of Circulations

How do you know how many people buy a newspaper?

The Audit Bureau of Circulations (ABC) in Schaumburg, Illinois, is the international source for certifying how many newspapers and magazines are sold.

The ABC serves the same purpose as broadcast and cable rating services. It tells advertisers how many people they'll reach if they buy space in newspapers or magazines.

ABC has now expanded into auditing and certifying the traffic on Internet websites. You'll find some of their Internet data at www.accessabc.com.

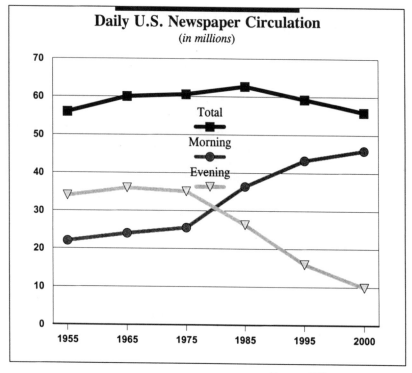

Daily U.S. Newspaper Circulation
(*in millions*)

Total

Morning

Evening

Source: Editor and Publisher

Sickly Afternoon Papers

Television news is blamed for the frail financial health of afternoon newspapers. The last deadline, if the newspaper is to reach your home before dark, is about 1 p.m. Why pay for news that is four hours old, many subscribers reason, when you can catch the 5 or 6 p.m. newscast and be up-to-the-minute?

Most of the videotaped stories on the evening newscast were shot about the same time the newspaper was closing out its pages. But the viewer gets the impression that television stories are much fresher.

Particularly if some of them are done "live." The anchors are always live. Broadcasters have always traded on their immediacy by frequently sprinkling phrases like "at this hour" and "even as we speak" into their scripts.

In the last 20 years, many afternoon papers switched to morning publication to stay alive (see numbers on next page).

Competing Papers

American cities with separately owned, competing newspapers are now extremely rare. In 1956, there were 94. In 1990, the count was down to 43.

By 2000, only a dozen cities in the entire United States had completely separate, competing newspapers. In another 13 cities, morning and evening newspapers were published through joint operating agreements (JOAs).

Joint Operating Agreements

In a JOA, the larger newspaper (usually a morning paper) contracts to print the other paper on its presses, use its circulation department to sell subscriptions, and then deliver the other paper. In most JOAs, the advertising departments are also merged.

The editorial and news staffs for the two papers remain separate, distinct, and theoretically competitive, even though they share the same building, and sometimes the same newsroom.

Congress permitted JOA's with the 1970 Newspaper Preservation Act. They must be approved by the U.S. Justice Department.

Dailies Dropping

The number of daily newspapers continues to drop.

In 1980, there were 387 morning papers and 1,388 evening newspapers — a total of 1,745.

In 2000, *Editor and Publisher* magazine counted 736 morning papers and 760 evening newspapers — a total of 1,496. The total includes 13 "all-day" newspapers, which publish both morning and evening. All-day newspapers are counted twice in these totals.

Most American newspapers are fairly small. Only 16.1 per cent of dailies have circulations of more than 50,000.

Weeklies Increasing

The number of weekly newspapers, on the other hand, has increased in the last 10 years. Some are distributed free — conduits for advertising with little real news. The weekly figures count any newspaper that is not distributed daily.

The National Newspaper Association reported in 2000 that 8,138 weeklies had an average circulation of 5,754. Total circulation nationwide was 74.5 million. That is considerably higher than either weekday or Sunday circulation numbers for the dailies.

Ten Largest Papers

ABC figures as of September 30, 2000, show the 10 largest dailies' weekday circulation figures were:

USA Today	1,777,488
The Wall Street Journal	1,762,751
The New York Times	1,097,180
Los Angeles Times	1,033,399
The Washington Post	762,009
Daily News (New York)	704,463
Chicago Tribune	661,699
Newsday (Long Island)	576,345
Houston Chronicle	546,799
The Dallas Morning News	495,597

Sensationalism & Circulation

Critics often say the print media sensationalize "to sell newspapers." But three-quarters of U.S. daily newspapers are bought, sight unseen. Delivered to homes and offices, paid for in advance. Sensationalism must become unusually offensive before most of those subscribers will cancel their subscriptions.

Sensational stories still sell tabloids. The headlines and front page photographs grab commuters about to board a subway or bus. The smaller size makes this genre easier to read in the cramped space of public transportation.

Buyers in supermarket check-out lines are lured by headlines about celebrities' sexual exploits with aliens, the latest diet craze, a movie star's love agony or secret disease.

Big Newspaper Groups

One of the most dramatic changes in newspapers is the growth of newspaper groups. Traditionally, newspapers were small-town, family-owned, with deep community ties.

No longer. Today, large newspaper groups control 82 percent of national daily circulation, 87 percent on Sunday.

In a few groups, local editors have a great deal of autonomy, as long as the newspaper makes a profit. In most, corporate executives micro-manage the local paper.

Some of them are huge conglomerates, with interests in television and radio stations, magazines and Internet ventures.

Twelve companies control a little more than half the nation's total daily newspaper circulation. In 2000, *Editor and Publisher* calculated their papers owned and circulation:

12 Largest Groups	*Papers Owned*	*Daily Circulation*
Gannett Co., Inc.	73	6,040,874
Knight-Ridder, Inc.	31	3,879,838
Tribune Co.	13	3,614,641
Advance Publications	22	2,786,684
The New York Times Co.	21	2,367,396
Dow Jones & Co., Inc.	20	2,312,952
MediaNews Group, Inc.	46	1,729,583
E. W. Scripps Co.	19	1,382,635
McClatchy Newspapers	11	1,364,903
Hearst Newspapers	12	1,295,600
Cox Enterprises, Inc.	16	1,134,545
Belo	9	943,884

NOTE: Until late 2000, Thomson Newspapers — a Canadian company — would have been on this list. Thomson owned 49 daily U.S. newspapers with a combined circulation of 1.6 million. Thomson sold all its American papers to go into electronic publishing. Twenty-one of those newspapers were bought by Gannett. The former Thomson papers are not included in the figures above.

Advertising Revenue

What you pay for a daily newspaper doesn't even cover the cost of the blank paper. All the profit is in advertising. About 40 per cent of the average paper's gross revenue comes from classified ads. Other media created to advertise real estate, cars and boats have been very damaging to newspapers.

The Internet's format is vastly superior for classifieds. (See **INSIDE THE MEDIA/The Internet**) Newspapers are now banding together to offer their classifieds on the Web to try to stop the hemorrhaging losses. They may be too late.

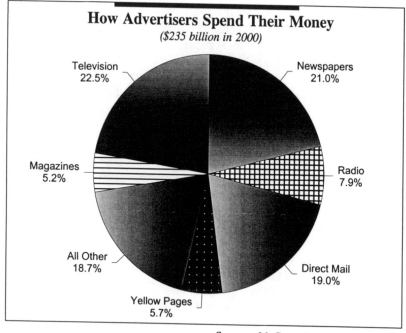

How Advertisers Spend Their Money
($235 billion in 2000)

Television 22.5%

Newspapers 21.0%

Magazines 5.2%

Radio 7.9%

All Other 18.7%

Direct Mail 19.0%

Yellow Pages 5.7%

Source: McCann-Erickson WorldGroup

Newspapers on the Web

To counter the lag time and compete with broadcast news, 10 newspapers in 1989-90 began offering an early, abbreviated version of their next edition by facsimile. But the Internet killed the faxed newspaper, making it expensive and redundant.

Belatedly, newspapers are now scrambling to learn the Internet game and make their stories instantly available on the Web. By April, 2000, the NNA reported, 80 per cent of American daily newspapers were online. Almost all their websites were free.

The Wall Street Journal was an exception. It began charging for access to its online edition in August, 1998. In late 2000, *WSJ* on the web cost $59 per year. Print subscribers got it for $29. The Web version had some special content and services.

I believe that within about 10 years, virtually all daily newspapers will have to be delivered this way. Because advertising dollars are going elsewhere, the traditional newspaper — printed and hand-delivered — will no longer be economically feasible.

The real challenge is to make Internet delivery profitable.

INSIDE THE MEDIA

Privacy

Get Out of Here ...
And Leave Me Alone

Many suits against the media now claim invasion of privacy, not libel. Jurors have strong feelings in this area. So do judges. Privacy cases focus on personal, emotional beliefs in conflict with each other.

Appellate courts take widely different views of similar cases, depending on the judges' personal experience and attitudes about the news media. Jurors are swayed more by an attorney's appeal to their outrage than by the law and legal precedent.

Today's technology gives the media powerful new tools for intrusion into private lives. Cameras are smaller and easier to hide. Conversations are easily recorded surreptitiously. Computers and the Internet provide the ability to rummage through the closets of your life in ways that have never before been possible.

An Evolving Legal Concept

Personal privacy is a relatively new legal concept in this country. It is still evolving.

The Bill of Rights protects citizens against unreasonable search and seizure. But that is a protection from government intrusion — not media corporations, or individual journalists.

We inherited criminal trespass from British Common Law. But that protects your real estate from intrusion. The idea of a right to privacy in your personal life was not even conceived until the 1890s, when newspapers became more sensational with stories of gossip and sexual scandal. They even published pictures.

Law Lags Behind Technology

The law has generally lagged well behind the technology. In the 1950s, the old statutes forbidding wiretaps became ineffective. Better ways had been invented. It was no longer necessary to physically tap into telephone lines. Electronic "bugs" and inductance devices were widely used to pick up conversations and were technically not an illegal "tap."

A comprehensive federal statute to protect the privacy of conversation was not adopted until 1968. There still is no statutory privacy protection from the telephoto lenses of the news media.

Physical Trespass

Trespass is physical intrusion onto your property. It can be a criminal act. Shooting a picture, and publishing or broadcasting it, can be two different kinds of intrusion. If the picture taken by a trespasser is never shown to anybody else, then a simple trespass took place.

Shooting Without Entering

But a picture can be shot and shown to others without entering your property and trespassing. A news story and photographs can bring thousands — perhaps millions — of people into the most intimate parts of your life.

A privacy lawsuit provides a way to punish the media who make your private life a peep show. Courts have said paparazzi stalking you in public places can also invade your privacy.

Where Cameras Can Go

Let's go back now to trespass — physical intrusion — and work forward to the latest electronic eavesdropping.

A photographer has the same freedom of movement as anyone else. If you can walk down the sidewalk, so can a television or print photographer.

We have public places in this society where anyone can legally go, unless a state of emergency is declared. Places like streets, parks, subways, beaches, public buildings.

Privacy decisions in court often hinge on what is reasonable and customary. Customs, and what seems reasonable, change.

No Privacy in Public

Generally speaking, you have little or no right of privacy from the media if you are in a public place. So long as everybody in that public place can see you, the media can photograph you, write about what you did there, and publish the pictures. You have no legal recourse.

If you don't want to be seen, don't go out in public.

Off-Limit Public Places

There are some public places which by custom are not truly open to the public.

A public school classroom, for instance, is a public building, paid for with tax dollars. The teacher is a public employee.

But custom says you can't just barge in and interrupt the class. Even if your child is a student there, you're expected to check in at the principal's office and get permission.

Reporters and photographers are expected to do the same thing, and would probably lose a lawsuit if they suddenly entered, cameras rolling, disturbing the teacher and the students.

It All Depends

Notice in this chapter — even more than in the Libel chapter — how often I use fudge words like probably — apparently — in most cases — in all likelihood.

Because every case is different, and the law so new. The outcome will depend on how judges and juries react to the facts and conflicting values.

Special Media Access

We sometimes give the news media special access so they can represent the public and report what happens. At a major trial, for instance, seats are reserved for the media and many spectators are shut out. There's just not enough room for everybody.

Reporters and photographers are customarily allowed beyond police lines at disasters so they can see, record and photograph the victims and the rescue effort.

Later in this chapter I'll cover cases where journalists accompanied government authorities with special power into people's homes. Can reporters and photographers go with them? For years, the courts said yes. The U.S. Supreme Court now says no.

Cameras in Congress

There are some public places where citizens are welcome but cameras and microphones are barred. Television cameras were not allowed to cover proceedings in the U.S. House of Representatives until the 1970s.

The U.S. Senate allowed television camera coverage of its committee hearings as early as the 1950s (McCarthy & Kefauver committees) but did not allow daily, continuous coverage of proceedings in the Senate chamber until 1986.

Cameras in Courtrooms

Almost all American trials are open to spectators. Because the Constitution guarantees a right to trial by a jury of your peers, case law has almost always said the public has a right to be represented by the media to make sure the justice system is working properly.

But news cameras are not welcome in many courts. Almost all federal trial courts forbid cameras.

News cameras were barred from the trial of Oklahoma City Federal Building bomber Timothy McVeigh. But the trial was televised, through a closed-circuit system, to a room where survivors of the bombing and families of the victims could watch.

That was made possible by a special law Congress passed after survivors and family members pleaded for access. Security was extremely tight, to make sure the news media did not acquire any of the pictures.

The O. J. Simpson Trial

U.S. District Court Judge William Hoeveler of Miami, who chaired the American Bar Association's Resource Team for High Profile Trials told a media-law conference in early 1998:

> *You will not see cameras in the federal courts for quite some time because of the O. J. Simpson criminal trial. It set cameras in the federal courts back at least 10 years.*

In that case, the saturation coverage showed the mistakes and frailties of the judge, police officers, witnesses and attorneys.

Inside the judicial system, there was a protective reaction —
*Maybe we shouldn't let the public watch. The pressure of national
coverage affects people. It can sometimes be embarrassing.*

The Simpson case also made the media look bad, in their mob
scene chases of witnesses; the feeding frenzy for any scrap of
information, the payoffs for exclusive interviews. The backlash
from the Simpson case had a chilling effect nationwide.

Moves to Ban Cameras

When a law or court order allows cameras in courtrooms,
judges have broad discretion to ban cameras if they think the
cameras will interfere with a fair trial. After the Simpson trial,
more judges moved in that direction.

The New York Legislature failed to extend a law that had
allowed cameras in state courts for 10 years when the law expired
in June, 1997. About the same time, U.S. Supreme Court Justice
Antonin Scalia, who once favored courtroom cameras, said he had
changed his mind.

Federal Court Status

Fellow Supreme Court Justice David Souter said publicly,
"The day you see a camera coming into our courtroom, it's going
to roll over my dead body."

Reportedly, there is an agreement among Supreme Court
justices that no cameras will be allowed there unless the nine
justices unanimously approve. It may be a while.

The U.S. Judicial Conference supervised a three-year experiment with cameras in two Circuit Court of Appeals and civil trials
in five District Courts in the early 1990s.

When it was over, the committee overseeing the experiment
recommended that federal courts allow cameras in. A majority of
the judges in the 13 federal appellate courts signed a letter endorsing cameras in their proceedings. Despite the study and the vote,
the Judicial Conference decided in 1995 that cameras should not be
allowed.

U.S. Supreme Court Chief Justice William Rehnquist — chairman of the Conference — sent the proposal back for more study.
Under pressure from the Chief Justice, the Judicial Conference in
1996 left the decision up to individual Circuit Courts of Appeals.

Opponents of cameras in court have always argued that they intimidate witnesses and jurors, and prevent a fair trial. In appellate courts, there are no witnesses or jurors.

Courtroom Construction

In the 1970s, my television station in Miami (WPLG-TV) was the plaintiff in a suit that eventually made news cameras standard in Florida courts. For many years, oral arguments before the Florida Supreme Court have been videotaped and archived.

During that process, I became convinced that all objections to cameras' disruptive influence can be overcome with the construction of soundproof booths in courtrooms. Photographers can work there, shooting through a glass panel, and nobody in the courtroom can even tell whether the cameras are there.

Cameras in State Courts

According to the Radio-Television News Directors Assn., only two states — Mississippi and South Dakota — banned cameras in all courts at the end of 2000.

Six states allow cameras in appellate but not trial courts (Delaware, Idaho, Illinois, Louisiana, Maine and New York). Pennsylvania allows them in trial but not appellate courts.

In most of those states that allow cameras to cover trials, the judge has the right to remove photographers if, in the judge's opinion, they would interfere with a fair trial.

Some states require the consent of both the judge and the litigants in either civil or criminal cases. The majority allow cameras if the judge approves, even if the litigants don't.

Semi-Public Places

Back to personal privacy. The next areas in which the media can intrude on personal privacy are semi-public places. Privately owned, but open to the public. Stores, restaurants, bars, offices. Anybody can walk in. There is an understood, open invitation.

In a truly public place, a reporter or photographer cannot invade your privacy unless they physically harass and intimidate you. When they walk into a semi-public place, the rules shift.

Most cases now seem to indicate still photographers or TV camera crews can come in shooting, but must leave if the owner of the semi-public place tells them to. If they don't leave, they become trespassers. This increases the likelihood a court will decide they also invaded personal privacy. This would apply to almost any place of business. Case in point:

Le Mistral, Inc. v. CBS

61 A.D. 2d 491, 402 N.Y.S. 2d 815, 3 Med L. Rptr. 1913 (1978)

The owner of Le Mistral restaurant in New York City won a privacy suit against CBS, claiming that a television crew barged in, refused to leave, created a scene, and frightened the restaurant's customers. Witnesses disagreed on how long the camera crew tarried, but the jury felt they overstayed their welcome.

The CBS crew had entered the restaurant with a health inspector, hoping to videotape unsanitary conditions in the kitchen.

The restaurant manager couldn't stop the health inspector, but argued that the inspector's right of entry did not include the right for a television crew to tag along. The jury agreed.

If You Go, the Camera Can

Again — the camera crew has the same right of entry as the general public. The photographer has the legal right to walk into the reception area of a doctor's office, but can't barge past the receptionist into the examining rooms, where patients have their clothes off.

In semi-public places, the outcome of a privacy suit often hinges on the behavior of the two litigants. Juries tend to rule against people who are loud or obnoxious, and act like bullies.

If a television crew enters your place of business and you ask them to leave, be nice.

The nicer you are — and the pushier they are — the better your chances of winning a privacy suit.

The Most Private Place

The most private place is the home. Here, criminal law says you commit a felony — not just trespass — if you enter without an invitation, even if the door is unlocked. Because of that long tradition that holds privacy of the home so sacred, many successful privacy suits against the news media involve intrusion there.

Do reporters and photographers have the right to come to your front door and try to talk to you?

The U.S. Supreme Court decided long ago (1943 — *Martin v. Struthers*) that unless there is a "Do Not Enter" sign at your front gate, no trespass is committed if someone enters your property and knocks on your front door. The court followed custom in America.

Once they're asked to leave, they become trespassers if they refuse. A rented home — or a hotel room — carries with it the same sort of privacy rights as a home you own.

Dietemann v. Time, Inc.

449 F.2d 245 [9th Cir.] (1971)

In California, a *Life* Magazine reporter went into the home of a naturopathic doctor and feigned symptoms of cancer. The doctor wired her to a gadget with flashing lights, and told her she was feeling bad because she ate rancid butter on a certain date.

While she was receiving the diagnosis, her "husband," a *Life* photographer, was shooting pictures with a hidden camera. He was also wearing a "bug" that transmitted the entire procedure to a prosecutor parked up the street in a van.

When the prosecutor arrested the doctor, *Life* was there to photograph the bust. The pictures taken inside the house were featured in an article on quack doctors.

The naturopath sued for invasion of privacy. He won the case at trial. In upholding the verdict, the appellate court made it clear that it simply did not like the idea of reporters coming into people's homes with hidden cameras and microphones, acting as agents for law enforcement.

Cantrell v. Forest City Publishing Co.

419 U.S. 245, 95 S.Ct. 465, 42 L.Ed.2d 419 (1974)

In Ohio, a newspaper reporter and photographer returned to an area that had been devastated by a flood. Their story focused on one family, where the father had been killed when a bridge collapsed. The children, at home alone, let the newsmen into the house. The kids told how the flood had changed their lives.

The reporter never saw the mother. But in his story, the reporter cheated. He included a sentence about how tired she looked. "She wears the same mask of non-expression she wore at the funeral." He gave the clear impression that she was present during the interview.

In deciding that the family's privacy was invaded by the story, the court made a special note of the reporter's deception. Another case where the specific behavior of those involved had a powerful influence on the outcome.

Fla. Publishing Co. v. Fletcher

**340 So.2d 914, 2 Med. L. Rptr. 1088 [Fla. S. Ct.] (1976),
cert. denied 431 U.S. 930 (1977)**

In Jacksonville, Florida, a fire killed a 17-year-old girl, at home alone. When firefighters removed the body, her silhouette remained in the charred floor of her bedroom. A fire marshal, who had run out of film, asked a newspaper photographer to take a picture of the room and the unburned spot where the girl died. It was a dramatic shot. The newspaper published it with a caption, "Silhouette of Death."

The mother sued for invasion of privacy, saying the fire marshal had no right to bring the photographer into her home; that the newspaper had no right to invade her life by publishing a picture that caused her so much pain.

At the trial, a jury found the newspaper guilty of privacy invasion. On appeal, the verdict was overturned by the Florida Supreme Court.

The higher court said it was the custom for journalists to accompany fire and police officials at disaster scenes, and the photographer served a semi-official function when he shot the picture at the fire marshal's request.

Police Raids and the Media

Over the years, courts disagreed for many different reasons about cops bringing reporters and photographers along on raids. In my years as a reporter, I went into many private homes and businesses with cops who had a search warrant to enter.

I was not there — but a crew from my station was — the night in the late 1970s when the Hialeah Police Department invited my station along on a huge raid. They were going to break up a major, illegal gambling operation.

Our reporter and photographer sat in on the briefing, then went to a private home with the cops. The reading team was ready for World War III with their riot guns and flak jackets. At a pre-arranged signal, they burst into the living room of the house.

Our photographer was right behind them.

Penny-Ante Poker

Inside were a group of senior citizens playing penny-ante poker. No arrests. No story.

The owner of the home sued my station for invasion of privacy. Our attorney — media specialist Sandy D'Alemberte — persuaded a judge to dismiss the suit. He argued it was standard procedure for the media to accompany the police when they served search warrants. It was.

But later, D'Alemberte warned our news staff that sometime in the future, courts would decide that reporters and photographers have no right to enter a home with the police.

The U.S. Supreme Court ruled on this specific issue for the first time in 1999.

Operation Gunsmoke

In early 1992, the U.S. Justice Department launched "Operation Gunsmoke." U.S. marshals and local police were to concentrate on fugitives with outstanding arrest warrants for drug arrests and violent felonies.

A special public relations brochure was printed, telling marshals how to include reporters and photographers on arrests they planned.

Dominic Wilson was one of the targets of Operation Gunsmoke. Wilson was a fugitive who had violated his probation on charges of robbery, theft and attempt to rob. The wanted bulletin listed him as armed and dangerous.

The Raiding Party

A reporter and photographer from *The Washington Post* were invited to accompany a squad of officers when they raided a home in Rockville, Maryland. They believed Wilson was there.

It turned out to be the home of his parents. At dawn, marshals, county police officers, and the newspaper team entered the house.

Wilson's parents were still in bed. When he heard a noise, the father ran into the living room wearing only his briefs, to find a group of men in plain clothes, some of them with guns drawn.

The father yelled at the group, asked what they were doing, cursed them, and was quickly thrown to the floor. His wife ran in, wearing her nightgown. She was kept in place while officers searched the house. They didn't find Dominic Wilson.

All through the search, the newspaper photographer was taking pictures. The pictures were never published.

The Wilsons sued the officers and the *Post*, claiming their Fourth Amendment rights against unreasonable search and seizure were violated when the officers brought the news media into their house. The search warrant clearly gave the officers the right to enter, they said, but did not give that right to the media.

The Trial and Appeal

The U.S. District Court ruled the law enforcement officers were protected from the Wilsons' suit because they were following standard practice at the time. The decision was appealed. The federal appellate court reheard the case twice.

A majority of the appellate judges finally agreed with the trial court, but were badly split on the decision and the reasons for it. So were other federal appellate courts in similar cases. The Supreme Court decided to hear the case and make a decision that would apply nationwide.

Wilson v. Layne

U.S. Supreme Court, May, 1999
(Full text available at www.findlaw.com)

The Supreme Court ruled unanimously that the Wilsons' Fourth Amendment rights had been violated when the media were brought into the house by the police.

All but Justice Stephens agreed that the police should not pay damages, however, because they were following widely accepted standards at the time.

Writing for the court, Chief Justice William Rehnquist said:

Although media ride-alongs of one sort or another had apparently become a common police practice, in 1992 there were no judicial opinions holding that this practice became unlawful when it entered a home. We hold that it is a violation of the Fourth Amendment for police to bring members of the media or other third parties into a home during the execution of a warrant when the presence of the third parties in the home was not in aid of the execution of the warrant. ... the possibility of good public relations for the police is simply not enough ... to justify the ride-along intrusion into a private home.

Rulings from the Gut

This case, like many others, shows how judges and juries see similar facts in very different ways. After reading as many court decisions as I have, I conclude that they frequently decide from their gut, then look for legal reasoning to support that decision.

Racially segregated schools had the blessing of the U.S. Supreme Court for generations. In time, attitudes change. Court decisions often reflect the common sense in that community, at that particular time.

With new concepts like privacy, and the explosion of new technology that makes invasion of privacy easier and more abusive, the law must race to keep up.

Wiretaps and Telephone Privacy

Most states passed laws against wiretapping in the 1920s and '30s. But they were often more concerned with the bootlegging of telephone service than with personal privacy.

Two and four-party telephone service was common in most American homes through the 1940s. Most people just assumed someone might be listening to their conversations. Privacy is not a big concern if you don't expect it.

A wiretap is a physical connection to a communications line — tapping into the wire that carries information. You can tap into a telephone line or television cable and create an extension of that conversation or TV signal. If the tap is done skillfully, the people who use or own the line cannot tell the wire has been tapped.

This is how bootleggers get cable TV without paying for it.

One of the most vulnerable spots for industrial espionage is a telephone line carrying computerized data or e-mail from one office to another. A wiretap can put you inside the company.

There are no provisions in state or federal law for private citizens to wiretap. **Wiretapping by individuals is always illegal.** The early laws let police agencies wiretap with little control or supervision as part of a criminal investigation.

Electronic Bugs

Federal law enforcement agencies were required to get approval from the U.S. Attorney General before they could wiretap. In the early 1950s, the first small "bugs" were created. Law enforcement began using them on a massive scale, without approval from the Attorney General. There was no requirement that they be reported, and very little law governing their use.

A "bug" is a small combination microphone-radio transmitter. It is easy to hide, and much more intrusive than a wiretap. In a car or a room, it intercepts conversation and transmits it to a radio receiver.

A "bug" can be designed to pick up not only conversation in a room, but also both ends of a telephone conversation from that room. Some of them use house current, or the voltage in the telephone line, and never need new batteries.

Most "bugs" have a limited range. The receiver must be located within several blocks to pick up their signal.

The invention of miniaturized electronics opened up new worlds of possibilities for privacy invasion. Their widespread use by law enforcement, as well as private investigators engaged in industrial espionage, became a major issue in the early 1960s. Congress passed in 1968 — as part of its Omnibus Crime Bill — national standards for electronic eavesdropping.

Federal Standards

Simply stated, federal law says if you participate in a conversation, you may record it. But if you plant a microphone, tape recorder, or bug to *intercept* a conversation you cannot hear, then you have committed a serious federal crime.

It is the *interception* — the listening in — that constitutes a crime in most laws against eavesdropping — not the recording.

Under this law, police agencies must get court approval to intercept conversations if they — or their informants — are not participants. The court approval is an electronic search warrant.

Electronic Search Warrants

If a police officer goes before a judge with sworn information that you have contraband hidden in your home, the judge issues a search warrant. It gives the police the right to go into your home or office and search for evidence of a crime.

In the same way, if a police officer has sworn information that you are about to have a conversation that would become evidence of a crime, the judge can give the officer a warrant to search for that conversational evidence electronically. The officer must certify that conventional investigative techniques will not work; that the eavesdropping is a technique of last resort.

State Eavesdropping Laws

Federal law gives states power to pass more stringent eaves-dropping regulations, if they choose. A few states have laws that make it a crime to secretly record conversation, *even if you partici-pate* in that conversation.

In those states, it is a felony to record your telephone calls — to record any conversation whatsoever — unless everyone whose voice is intercepted knows the microphone or "bug" is picking up what is being said.

In states that have not adopted more stringent laws and use the federal standard, you may record your telephone calls without telling the other person, if you use a suction cup or other induc-tance pickup that does not physically tap into the telephone wires. You can wear a small recorder to tape conversation.

In those states, reporters can secretly record what you say and use it later in their stories.

In the more stringent states, reporters cannot secretly record your voice. If a recorder is in use, they must tell you.

Skirting the Law

Illinois forbids secret recording, but *60 Minutes* came up with a clever way to get around the law.

They rented a storefront in Chicago and put a sign in the window announcing a doctor's office would open there soon. Representatives from a dozen laboratories dropped in to solicit business for blood and urine tests.

There was a hidden microphone, wired so the producer pretending to be a doctor could turn it on and off. When the laboratory owners talked, the mike was off. The labs were offering kickbacks. Send us your business, and we'll give you a cut.

Read My Lips

A hidden camera photographed the kickback negotiations. The audience heard the "doctor" say something like, "Now, let me get this straight — if I send you all my Medicare blood tests, you'll kick back 25 percent?"

The sound went dead, and you saw the lab man nod his head. You couldn't hear the answer, but it was easy to read his lips as he said, "That's right."

Expectation of Privacy

Many of the court cases in this area hinge on whether the person whose conversation was intercepted had a reasonable expectation of privacy. If passers-by can hear, the cases seem to say, the media can record.

Juries and judges often decide against the news media if the reporter broke the law to obtain the secret recording, or gained access under false pretenses to bring in the hidden camera or microphone. In their gut, they don't like that.

Computer Hackers

Computer hackers can get past electronic security barriers and access sensitive data like medical, insurance and bank records to invade your privacy.

Some rare cases have surfaced where the news media apparently used this kind of entry to spy on their competition or targets of investigative stories. (See **STRATEGY/Ethics**)

Hacking does not involve wiretapping. Hackers use a public line, but crack a security code or find unprotected ports to gain entry. Sometimes an insider gives them a "key" — the password.

It *is* a form of eavesdropping, where once inside, the hacker can do a lot of damage. The law is trying to catch up with this kind of violation. Law enforcement in most communities does not have the sophisticated tools to investigate and prove this kind of crime.

Visual Eavesdropping

So far, there are no laws similar to those for audio and telephone privacy that establish visual privacy from the news media. If a telephoto camera lens can see you inside your home or business, it has not invaded your privacy.

The theory seems to be: if you don't close the blinds, you can't blame your neighbors for watching you undress. Some court decisions have restricted law enforcement from using telephoto lenses, but those rulings are concerned with governmental invasion, not intrusion by private citizens.

If a secret camera were hidden inside your home or business to photograph things the reporter couldn't see with the doors and blinds closed, most judges and juries would probably feel your privacy had been invaded. You had an expectation of privacy.

Personal Privacy

Intrusion into the secret details of your personal life is another matter. It may involve some kind of physical trespass to obtain those details, but not necessarily.

The concept was first proposed in December, 1890, in a *Harvard Law Review* article written by two young lawyers who had roomed together in Cambridge — Samuel Warren and Louis Brandeis.

Brandeis would later become one of the legendary justices of the U.S. Supreme Court. Warren's family was prominent in Boston society. They threw lavish parties. Press gossips constantly pestered the family and tried to spy on their parties.

The Right To Be Left Alone

Warren and Brandeis published their novel idea in a *Harvard Law Review* essay. "Instantaneous photographs and newspaper enterprise," they wrote, "Have invaded the sacred precincts of private and domestic life."

Remember now, this was more than 100 years ago.

It is time, they said, to create a new area of law in America that would guarantee the right of personal privacy. Their definition is still used today:

Personal privacy is *the right to be left alone*.

Galella v. Onassis
(487 F 2d 986, 1 Media L. Rep. 2425 (1973)

Even in public places, courts have ruled that paparazzi openly hounding their targets can invade personal privacy. The most famous case involved Jacqueline Kennedy Onassis.

Ron Galella was a free-lance photographer who stalked Onassis, her family and friends. He would bump into them or block their way. She sued in federal court and obtained an injunction preventing Galella from taking photos closer than 150 feet.

The judge said Galella had violated her *right to be left alone*. An appeals court affirmed most of the decision, but decreased the separation to 25 feet. Galella violated the court order several times and was ordered to pay Onassis $10,000.

Human Decency

Suppose a young child has been hit by a truck. The mother is sitting in the street, holding the body, sobbing hysterically. The truck driver, sitting at the curb, is going into shock. He may be having a heart attack. His face is gray. He's having trouble breathing. A police officer is trying to help him.

A news photographer arrives and begins shooting close-ups of the mother and child and the truck driver. Does the photographer invade their privacy? At this point in our history, no.

Police, the Media and Privacy

This kind of incident often leads to major confrontations between the police and the news media. Officers, with feelings of human compassion, step in to stop the photographer.

Sometimes, they seize the camera and arrest the photographer for interfering with an officer by ignoring an order to stop shooting. But the officer has no legal right to stop the photographer simply to protect the privacy of the accident or crime victim. It is a public place. No criminal trespass is occurring.

On the other hand, law enforcement often helps the media invade the privacy of people they have arrested. Because prisoners in a jail cell have some rights to privacy, police officers often arrange a "perp walk." They walk the perpetrator — in handcuffs — in a public place just so the media can photograph him.

Murdered Teenagers

The morning after a teenage couple parked in a car were murdered in Miami, a homicide detective was briefing reporters. The couple's car could be seen in the distance, behind the yellow police tape.

With the TV cameras rolling, a man came up behind the crowd of reporters. "What kind of car is that?" he said, interrupting. He became louder and more insistent. The cameras turned to videotape him as the detective told him the make and model of the car.

"Oh, my God, that's my son's car," the man said as he collapsed. Television stations ran the videotape as part of the murder story. Legally, the man had no right of privacy, but the media became the target of intense community criticism for being so insensitive.

Trauma and Grief

The public seems to be increasingly angry about the media's invading the privacy of people who are in deep trauma or grief. They feel these people have *the right to be left alone*. Photographers chasing relatives of crash victims through airports after major airline accidents are almost universally condemned.

A reporter infiltrated the group of family members in New York after the TWA Flight 800 crash in July, 1996. She was not unmasked for three days. When she was discovered, what she had done was so sharply criticized she never wrote anything. Her newspaper apologized.

The insensitivity of photographers who continued to shoot Princess Diana as she lay dying in the tangled wreckage after the Paris crash brought worldwide cries of outrage.

Libel & Privacy Differences

Let's look at the differences between libel and privacy.

Suppose you are about to be promoted to the presidency of a department store. A reporter discovers that 40 years ago, when you were 15, you were caught shoplifting in that same store.

If the story is published or broadcast, there is no question it will damage your reputation. The embarrassment could even stop your promotion. But you can't win a libel suit, because it's true.

Public Good vs. Privacy

You might be able to win a privacy suit. In deciding whether damages should be paid, the judicial scale tries to balance the public good that is accomplished by publishing or broadcasting information, against the damage that is done to the individual whose privacy is invaded. Example:

Briscoe v. Readers Digest Assn.

4 Cal. 3d 529, 93 Cal. Rptr. 866, 483 P. 2d 34 (1971)

The *Reader's Digest*, in a long-running series on organized crime, included a brief reference to a man who had been convicted of a crime as a young adult. The story did not focus on him. His case was simply used to illustrate a point. His wife and children, his employer, his friends knew nothing of his criminal past before the article was published.

He sued for invasion of privacy, and won. He argued he had paid his debt to society, become a productive citizen, and lived an exemplary life after he left prison.

Any public good that was served by publicizing that part of his early life, he maintained, was far outweighed by the damage it did to his personal privacy.

The court agreed.

Final Exam Questions

A question from my final exam, when I was an adjunct professor at the University of Miami:

A woman calls you with a story tip. Every Saturday night, she says, the people next door throw a very wild party. They leave all the doors and windows open.

From my back bedroom, you can look into their house. By 10 p.m., they're drunk and rowdy. By midnight, they're naked and obscene. Some of them are holding a white powder to their nose and snorting it.

I've called the police with no results, your caller says. How would you like to come sit in the dark, in my house, and take pictures of what goes on next door?

Question A: If you accept the invitation and shoot into the house next door, have you invaded the privacy of the people at the party? Question B: If you publish or broadcast those pictures, have you invaded their privacy?

Final Exam Answers

Answer A: Shooting the pictures will not invade their privacy. You were not trespassing when you shot the pictures. If someone chooses to undress in front of an open window, and you watch, you can't be accused of being a peeping Tom.

Answer B: The best test answer I ever had from a student was one which said, "If it's just a bunch of naked people, you may invade their privacy. A jury might decide their privacy outweighed any public benefit from publishing the pictures. You have no real proof the white powder is cocaine.

"But if one of the people in your pictures is the police chief — or the governor — that's something else." The outcome of a privacy suit in this example will probably hinge on the jury's weighing personal privacy vs. public good.

Senator Eagleton's Past

U.S. Senator Thomas Eagleton of Missouri in 1972 became the Democratic vice-presidential candidate, running with George McGovern. A newspaper reporter discovered that Eagleton, years earlier, had been a patient in a mental institution.

The story caused Eagleton's withdrawal from the race. But there was never even a suggestion that he sue for invasion of privacy. Why? Because he was a public official. Like libel, privacy law offers little protection to public officials.

Gary Hart and Donna Rice

U.S. Senator Gary Hart of Colorado was the front-runner for the Democratic nomination in 1988. There were recurring rumors that Hart had an active sex life outside his marriage.

The rumors became so strong, Hart challenged the media to follow him and prove whether the rumors were true or false.

Acting on a tip, *The Miami Herald* followed model and actress Donna Rice when she flew from Miami to Washington, D. C.

While *The Herald* didn't have photographs of Hart and Rice together, their story suggested the two had spent the night in Hart's Washington townhouse.

Hart attacked the newspaper for scurrilous, slanted reporting; said he had done nothing immoral, and planned to continue as a presidential candidate.

But when the *National Enquirer's* front page later showed Rice on Hart's lap during a weekend boat trip to Bimini, Hart's campaign collapsed and he withdrew from the race.

The stories sparked a national debate on whether politicians have the *right to be left alone* in their private lives. That debate continues. Is nothing in the life of a government official private?

FDR's Handicap

There was a time when certain parts of public officials' lives *were* private. As a result of polio that had made him a paraplegic, President Franklin D. Roosevelt could not stand without leg braces, holding onto something. He spent his days in a wheelchair.

When he left the White House, he had to be carried in the arms of a servant, then placed in the presidential limousine. At his destination, the servant would hold him up while someone else locked the steel braces on his legs. Once on his feet, with his braces locked, he could walk stiffly, slowly, with the aid of two canes. But the process was never photographed.

Throughout his presidency, news photographers avoided pictures that showed how handicapped he was. In an era where the media felt an obligation to censor itself for the public good, they protected his personal privacy.

Campaign Films

Look at old film of Roosevelt campaigning from the back of a railroad car. One of his sons usually traveled with him, standing beside him, discreetly holding his arm, to keep him from falling.

There are 35,000 pictures of Roosevelt in his Presidential Library, but only two show him in a wheelchair. Neither was published while he was alive, according to the Freedom Forum in Arlington, Virginia.

LBJ's Gall Bladder

President Lyndon Johnson insisted on showing the media his scar after his gall bladder operation, and after that, major political figures were expected to show us their stitches. During Ronald

Reagan's term in office, network newscasts gave the nation nightly diagrams of his colon and prostate during separate operations.

Where's Lyndon?

Before John F. Kennedy was assassinated in 1963, Washington reporters began to wonder if they should report on Vice-President Lyndon Johnson's private life. Bored, alienated from Kennedy, Johnson drank a lot. He had an eye for the ladies, and frequently disappeared in the afternoons.

Suppose something happened to the President, the reporters asked themselves. If there was a national emergency, would anybody know where to find Johnson? And if they did, would he be able to make critical decisions?

Johnson became President, got back into working trim, and the stories were never written. The reporters were relieved. Most reporters and public officials were men, and men had a gentlemen's agreement not to talk about certain things.

The Stripper's Swim

The watershed event for stories on politicians' sex lives occurred in 1974, when U.S. Rep. Wilbur Mills, 65 and married, got into a spat with his stripper girl friend, Fanne Foxe. Mills was chairman of the House Ways and Means Committee. He and Foxe, riding in a car one night, got into a fight. She jumped out of the car, into the Tidal Basin, and onto the front page of nearly every newspaper in the country.

From that point on, it seemed that nothing in a politician's private life was sacred. There was an avalanche of stories about the sex lives of former presidents. Mills retired in 1976.

Clinton and Lewinsky

When the Monica Lewinsky story broke in early 1998, many people were puzzled by the public's reaction. Polls showed most people believed the President had been unfaithful to his wife. But Clinton's popularity was not affected, and many of those surveyed seemed more unhappy with the media than with Clinton.

Perhaps they were just weary of sleazy stories. The Lewinsky scandal followed Paula Jones' and Gennifer Flowers' accusations, and a long run of stories where it was hard to distinguish between "respectable" media coverage and the tabloids. Stories like:

- White House political consultant Dick Morris' long-term relationship with a prostitute

- Sportscaster Marv Albert's fetishes, and a criminal charge for rough sex with a former girlfriend

- Sportscaster Frank Gifford's secretly filmed rendezvous with a flight attendant who was not his wife (TV star Kathie Lee)

- New York Mayor Rudolph Guiliani's disintegrating marriage and his friendship with another woman

Public People: Less Privacy

The rule of thumb seems to be: the higher in government, and the more contact with the public, the less privacy you have. Judges, police officers and school teachers probably have less privacy than government auditors or secretaries, on the theory that their character can affect the quality of their public work.

Outside government, the more visible and newsworthy you are, the less privacy you have. Officers of a major labor union or corporation give up some of their privacy. Lawyers who represent famous clients can become public figures, along with journalists, entertainers and professional athletes.

We are still trying to determine how far the media should be allowed to go in invading private lives.

The lines are difficult to draw. Verdicts in one state disagree with those in another. It is new law, growing and being reshaped each time a jury wrestles with the facts in a specific case.

Recap Libel & Privacy

Let's recap —

- If the story is true, you can't win a libel suit

- If the story is false, public officials and a public persons can win a libel suit only if they *prove* the story is false; and was published with malice and/or *reckless disregard for the truth*

- Libel cases have determined that one sure indication of malice is to know a story is false — or to have serious doubts about the facts — and run the story anyway

- True or false, a story can invade your privacy
- You have almost no privacy from a camera in a public place
- If you are in a private place, a news photographer outside, shooting with a telephoto lens, does not invade your privacy
- Broadcasting or publishing what is shot with a telephoto lens *can* invade your privacy if a court decides your privacy outweighs any public good served by the publication or broadcast
- Photographers can come into a privately owned place where the public is invited, but may invade privacy and become trespassers if the owner asks them to leave and they refuse
- Federal law does not prohibit secret recording of telephone conversations by people who participate in those conversations, but some states have more stringent laws that prevent *all* secret interception and/or recording by private citizens
- Spreading facts about your past — and intimate portions of your present — may do more personal damage than public good, and therefore become an invasion of your privacy
- Invasion of privacy verdicts are often returned when a jury feels:

  They shouldn't do that.

  I wouldn't like it if they did that to me.

  That person had a right to be left alone.
- In the near future, court cases could decide that people have a right to privacy, even in public places, during moments of deep grief or other emotional stress

INSIDE THE MEDIA

Ratings

Will They Know I Switched
From Opera to Wrestling?

Television is probably America's most fiercely competitive industry. Very slight changes in the audience can shift profits by millions of dollars.

It is an industry constantly in metamorphosis, looking for some new game or gimmick that will entice a few more people away from the competition. If the audience wants a little more sex, a little more violence, that's what it gets.

Every producer of TV programming is constantly trying to guess next season's fad or fashion, hoping to invent a show or character or situation that will play to the appetite of that fleeting, fickle audience.

Spin-offs

Once a show becomes a success, there is a stampede to copy and clone it, hoping to squeeze every penny of profit out of the idea before it gets stale and the audience moves on to whatever turns them on.

All in the Family begat *Archie Bunker's Place*, until the audience eventually became weary of the characters and dwindled away. *Happy Days* bred *Laverne and Shirley*. *The Cosby Show* became *A Different World*. *Cheers* led to *Frasier*. Sometimes the spin-offs work. Sometimes they don't.

At the very top, television news is controlled by the same people who program entertainment. They're always looking for the magic formula that will seduce people away from the competition.

They're constantly doing research. If the studies show the audience wants more flash and trash, stories become flashier. Trashier.

From city to city, television news is as varied as radio station formats. There are newscasts anchored by gray-haired veterans as bland and dated as elevator music.

Hard Rock News

In other markets, young, hyper anchors shout stories with the intensity of hard-rock radio. It doesn't matter so much what the words say, so long as you keep the rhythm and beat. Keep it breathless and intense.

"The City Manager's Secret Agony! Tape at Eleven!"

"A Psychic Says UFOs Will Disrupt The Governor's Inauguration! I'll Talk With Her Live, at Five!"

How do they know we'd rather learn about a new diet than the defense budget? How do they know who — and how many — are watching?

Ratings.

Ratings & Demos Set the Price

As a general rule, the cost of commercial time on television is based on how many people will see the advertising. But *who* is in the audience also has a powerful influence on price. TV advertisers will pay more to reach fewer people, if that smaller audience has the right "demos" — demographics.

An audience with a lot of 18 to 49-year-olds is more desirable to advertisers because they spend more. Advertisers use ratings to target a specific audience.

Gillette, advertising a new razor, wants to know how many men of shaving age are watching. Revlon wants a show with a lot of women. Lexus and Lincoln will place their commercials in shows that appeal to a mature, affluent, status-conscious audience.

What the Market Will Bear

There are no hard and fast rules. The price is based on what the market will bear. It has to be competitive with other forms of advertising. The price keeps going up.

In early 1983, the last installment of *M*A*S*H* set a new record — $450,000 for each half-minute of commercial time.

Seinfeld's Farewell

The next all-time high was the final *Seinfeld* episode in May, 1998, where commercials cost $2 million per 30-second spot.

Unless there is an unusual show like the *M*A*S*H** and *Seinfeld* finales, telecasts of Super Bowl games usuallly contain the most expensive commercial time on the tube because they have the largest audience of the year.

Super Bowl Commercials

Thirty-second spots during the January, 2000, Super Bowl went as high as $2 million, and averaged $1.85 million, according to *Broadcasting and Cable* Magazine. As this book goes to press, CBS is asking $2.4 million for 30-second spots in the 2001 game.

Some portions of the game are more expensive than others. Spots toward the end of the game are usually cheaper, because the audience is expected to gradually tune out.

The national economy affects sales. At the last minute in 1992, CBS had to offer advertisers special deals on other commercial time to sell all its Super Bowl spots.

Buyers don't always get what they pay for. The runaway score at the 1990 Super Bowl (San Francisco 49ers 55, Denver Broncos 10) drew the smallest Super Bowl audience since 1969.

Make-Goods

Broadcasting and Cable reported that CBS sold national advertising for the 1990 game with no guarantees on the size of the audience. Some local stations, however, had promised a minimum audience in their market for local spots during the game.

Those local affiliates had to make other advertising time available to those advertisers at reduced prices because of the game's low ratings. (See **INSIDE THE MEDIA/Networks** for how networks and affiliates split advertising time and profits)

The industry calls those "make-good" commercials. The station or network makes good its promise to deliver a certain number of people per dollar spent on a commercial.

Nationwide, advertisers spent about $53 billion in 2000 for commercial time on TV. Newspaper advertising totaled close to

$50 billion; radio advertising about $18.5 billion. (See **INSIDE THE MEDIA/Newspapers** for chart showing how advertising is split between all media)

Ratings Are Estimates

The entire economic foundation of television and radio in this country is built on audience estimates. Broadcast rating services use several techniques to calculate how many people are listening or watching at any given time.

They sell their results to broadcasters and advertising agencies. Advertising prices are based on those numbers.

Polling Is Mysterious

The process has always been mysterious to outsiders. Polling techniques are very complicated, and few people who don't have Ph.D.s in statistics understand how a small sample, properly drawn, can accurately tell you what millions of people are doing or thinking.

The entire system is constantly under attack. Periodically, powerful network executives say they're unhappy with the system and would support a new company if it could make ratings more accurate. They only complain if their numbers go down.

Nielsen and Arbitron

Two firms — Nielsen Media Research and Arbitron — have historically been the major ratings services. In 1993, Arbitron abandoned national television ratings, leaving Nielsen with a monopoly.

Arbitron continues to be the dominant ratings service for radio. It also specializes in telephone surveys and those that track buying patterns of audiences exposed to specific commercials.

Internet Ratings

In late 1995, Nielsen launched a new service to measure how many people are logged onto the Internet; their demographics, and which sites they visit. The information is valuable to broadcast networks — who are trying to figure out where their audience is going — and to future Internet advertisers, who want to know how to target their message. (See **INSIDE THE MEDIA/Networks** and **The Internet**)

Internet users are extremely attractive to advertisers. They're young, affluent, highly educated. Internet advertising hit $4.6 billion in 1999 — a growth rate of 1,700 per cent in three years.

In 2000, two major research firms — Nielsen and Media Metrix, Inc. — said the number of American homes connected to the Internet passed the 50 per cent mark. Another firm — Forrester Research, Inc. — predicted 70 percent would be online by 2004.

Rating Techniques

Rating services use four basic techniques:

- Telephone surveys
- Viewer/listener diaries
- Electronic meters that show when a TV set is turned on
- People Meters that show WHO is watching what, and when

Choosing a Sample

For all four methods, the rating services develop small, random samples that are designed to accurately reflect the local or national audience. Age, gender, ethnicity, education, income, neighborhood, family status, are all factors.

Nielsen constantly tracks about 5,000 TV households through People Meters for its national sample. Another 20,000 metered homes produce reports for local TV markets. During "sweeps" four times a year, about 100,000 additional families keep diaries logging what they watch. There are fewer diaries at other times.

Nielsen tracks the programming of 1,700 TV stations and 11,000 cable systems. Part of its service tells advertisers when their commercials are transmitted, and the audience that saw or heard them.

Household Diaries

The diary households are supposed to make an entry every 15 minutes when the set is turned on, showing which station is on, and who's watching. Once a family agrees to keep a diary, their viewing habits may be monitored for long periods of time.

Their identity is a secret, to avoid any outside influence on their choice of shows. But diary-keeping is a real chore, and there has always been a concern that some families aren't very precise.

Viewing Meters

In 1959, Nielsen began using viewing meters in New York City to supplement its telephone surveys and viewer diaries. The company selects metered households in much the same way it chooses a family to keep a diary.

The family gives its permission for the rating service to connect a meter to its TV set. Any time the set is turned on, the meter automatically keeps a record of the time and which station it is tuned to.

By April, 2001, Nielsen will have meters in 50 market areas that contain about 66 per cent of all TV viewers in the U.S.

In each market area, meters in homes are connected by telephone lines to computers. At 3 a.m. each morning, each meter sends its data for the last 24 hours to Nielsen. Instant, overnight ratings are then tabulated for those who subscribe to the service.

"Voting" A Show

In some ways, meters are much more accurate than telephone and diary reports. People in viewing samples have a tendency to cheat. If they have a favorite series, they "vote" for it, reporting that they watched it, even if they didn't.

Viewers also tend to tell the rating service they watched shows they think they *should* watch. They may say they saw a *National Geographic Special* or a symphony concert when they were really watching wrestling.

Newspaper Readers Also Fib

The same thing happens when people are surveyed about their newspaper reading habits. People want to appear educated and well-read.

In the 1998 Pew Research Center survey, for instance, 10 per cent of those polled said they read *The New York Times* regularly. But *The Times* only sells enough copies to reach one per cent of the homes in America. In that same survey, 28 per cent said they read

USA Today regularly. The publisher only prints enough copies of *USA Today* to reach 1.6 per cent of the population.

Meters eliminate the inaccuracies of diaries in families that have literacy or language problems; or families that get sloppy, and fill out their diaries at the end of the week, relying on memory to report what they watched.

But meters have their own inaccuracies. They report viewers if a set is turned on, even when nobody is watching. Nielsen's formula is a secret, but if the channel is not changed within a certain time, that family is dropped from the day's sample.

Meters Increase Viewing

When a family gives permission for a meter to be installed, they watch a lot more television for a while. There's a subtle psychological effect. Their inclusion in the sample makes them feel like their choice of shows is suddenly more important. That tendency to increase viewing time slacks off after several months.

The families aren't told this, but the rating service usually doesn't start tabulating their viewing until that early period of heavy TV watching has passed.

Independent stations seemed to be the big winners when meters were first added to diaries and telephone surveys. One study showed daytime ratings for independents doubled in homes where meters were installed. The analysts could only guess why.

Meter Mysteries

One explanation — people at home alone during the day didn't want their spouses or parents to know how much time they spend watching daytime television. In those homes without meters, viewers were not reporting accurately in their diaries.

Meters seemed to make little difference in audience numbers during prime time, from 8 to 11 p.m. But after 11 o'clock, one early metered rating period showed independent stations 42 percent higher than before. Hard to explain.

People Meters

For advertisers, WHO is watching is just as important as HOW MANY are watching. You don't advertise beer in a children's show, or toys on *20/20*. So Nielsen began using People Meters in

1986 to find out WHO is watching in carefully selected sample groups.

The People Meter is very much like a remote-control TV device. A miniature computer about the size of a paperback book is attached to the TV.

The meter has lights that blink red and green. There is a light for each family member, and additional lights for guests. When the set is turned on, the red lights start blinking. The people watching push a button on the remote device to log in.

The light for that person changes from red to green. If someone new comes into the room to watch TV, or if someone leaves, they're supposed to use the remote control to tell the meter.

Time to Push the Button

After a certain time, or if the station is changed, the red lights start flashing again. Each person watching must log in to be counted. Using a remote control to quickly surf other stations doesn't require a new tally if the set is returned to the original station within a certain number of seconds. Stay away from that channel too long, and the meter asks again who's watching.

If the set stays on without a change of stations, and nobody responds when the red lights blink, Nielsen drops that family from the viewer count that day.

People Meters are subject to cheating, too. One member of the household can log in absent family members. But you can't go back and "vote" a show that was on two hours earlier.

There are other measurement problems that Nielsen is trying to solve. Like picture-in-picture sets that allow you to see two stations on the same screen at the same time. Or videotaped shows, viewed later, where the viewer zaps commercials. And the new devices that are constantly recording shows on a computer hard drive that can pause or replay sections of shows and skip commercials.

Translating the Numbers

Radio and TV programs are measured in two ways:

- **Rating** — The *percentage of homes watching or listening* to a specific show. This figure is technically the percentage of *homes who have radio or TV* that watched. In most communities, more than 99 per cent of the homes have at least one radio and TV set. So the rating number is really the percentage of total households. Ratings are tabulated for local market areas as well as nationwide. Before the actual 2000 U.S. Census count, the Census Bureau estimated 104.5 million households in the country. Nielsen's estimate was 100.8 million TV households.

- **Share** — The *percentage of households with their sets on* who were tuned to a particular program. It is that station's *share of the audience* which is watching or listening at any given time.

HUT Levels

The TV industry has another shorthand term in its jargon — HUT. Households Using Television. A HUT-level of 10 means your show was being watched by 10 percent of the households using television in that particular time slot.

If a town has 100 households and five are watching television — but all are watching the same show — then that show will have a 5 Rating/100 Share. Only five per cent of the homes are watching television. But 100 per cent of the people watching TV at the time are all watching the same show.

A program with a 12 Rating/26 Share was seen by 12 percent of the households who own TV sets and by 26 percent of the households who were using TV during its time slot.

Prime and Drive Time

Rating numbers go up during evening prime time hours (8-11 p.m.) when more people watch television. Share numbers in any market total 100, no matter how many people are watching.

Radio audiences are generally highest during "drive time" — rush-hour traffic periods — when large numbers of people listen as they commute between home and work.

In addition to the rating and share figures, the services can report detailed demographic information on the people watching, by age, sex, ethnicity, education, whether employed, and by income level.

They report whether the households have cable, and/or pay-per-view and/or direct broadcast satellite television.

If a subscriber wants to know more about the audience, it can arrange for the rating service to expand the information on households in the sample.

All this can be useful to advertisers who want to target a certain audience, but it's expensive. Some of this detailed data is routinely included in markets with People Meters.

Market Size

The Nielsen numbers establish audiences in 210 television markets and rank them by size. Reporters and anchors are always looking for opportunities in higher-ranked markets because the size of the potential audience means stations there can charge more for their advertising, and the salaries of TV news people are higher.

The 2000 market rankings, with number of households in the top 15 markets, and their percent of the national audience were:

		Households	% of U.S.
1.	New York	6,874,990	6.820
2.	Los Angeles	5,234,690	5.193
3.	Chicago	3,204,710	3.179
4.	Philadelphia	2,670,710	2.650
5.	San Francisco-Oakland-San Jose	2,423,120	2.404
6.	Boston	2,210,580	2.193
7.	Dallas-Ft. Worth	2,018,120	2.002
8.	Washington, DC (Hagerstown)	1,999,870	1.984
9.	Detroit	1,855,500	1.841
10.	Atlanta	1,774,720	1.761
11.	Houston	1,712,060	1.698
12.	Seattle-Tacoma	1,591,100	1.578
13.	Tampa-St. Petersburg (Sarasota)	1,485,980	1.474
14.	Minneapolis-St. Paul	1,481,050	1.469
15.	Cleveland	1,479,020	1.467

High-Priced Anchors

Slight shifts in audiences can mean millions of dollars. If a network show increases its ratings just one point, that means the audience for the program and its commercial messages increased by about 2.6 million people. That's why on-air "talent" — anchors, sportscasters and meteorologists — are paid so much.

A popular anchor or sportscaster who moves to a competing station can sometimes bring the fans to the new station and cause dramatic shifts in ratings. Most rating changes are much more gradual. Humans are creatures of habit. Changing their viewing or listening patterns takes time.

Popular anchors have job benefits like a chauffeured limousine; an extravagant expense account and clothes allowance; a reporting assignment outside the country at least once a year, where the entire family can tag along.

"Hi, Jane"

Network anchors are even more pampered.

Television is an unusual medium. Its anchors have more celebrity status than anyone except the President of the United States. Walk a movie star and Jane Pauley down the same sidewalk, and many more people will recognize Pauley. More than just recognize her. They'll speak, wave, call her Jane.

They think they know her personally. If you questioned them, they'd have a complete personality in mind, based entirely on their perceptions of her from visits in their living room over the years.

The ability to create that kind of relationship with viewers is an extremely valuable commodity. It's hard to document, but network salaries topping $7 million per year have been reported for on-air talent like Dan Rather, Diane Sawyer and Pauley.

Simpson Verdict Sets Record

When the jury announced its "not guilty" verdict in the O. J. Simpson murder trial October 3, 1995, it set a new record for the most Americans watching a single event, Nielsen reported. Because it happened at 1 p.m. on a Tuesday, millions of viewers were watching at the office and were not counted in the estimate.

The combined audience for the verdict was a 42.9 rating/91 share. That means 42.9 per cent of the nation's households and 91 per cent of the viewers in those households were tuned to the verdict.

That was a combined rating/share for identical video carried by ABC, NBC, CBS, Fox, CNBC, CNN, Court TV, E!, ESPN, Headline News and Warner Brothers.

Until the Simpson verdict, Nielsen said the previous records were the first moon landing and the events following the assassination of President John F. Kennedy. Each had a combined 90 share.

The "Sweeps"

The major rating periods are called "sweeps." They take place four times a year — in November, February, May and July. You'll notice local newscasts promoting themselves a lot more during the sweeps, trying to improve their numbers and advertising prices.

More Nielsen diaries are in use during sweeps. At many stations, special reports and series are broadcast only during the sweeps, to maximize the audience for advertising purposes.

With more meters and People Meters operating year-round, the hyping of shows during sweeps could eventually be eliminated.

Shooting Craps

Because the ratings are so critical and so fluid, television news is in a constant state of flux. If the ratings get stuck or go down, you change the format or the pacing or the people.

It's like shooting craps. If the new anchor, weather forecaster or news director doesn't bring the ratings up, fire them, one at a time, and try another roll of the dice. Keep changing people until you hit a winning combination.

Consulting firms charge small fortunes to study newscasts and newscasters, looking for the magic formula that will increase ratings. They lock test viewers in a room, show them videotape, and then debrief them on what they saw, what they like, what they remember. The test group is called a focus group.

The Magic Elixir

And, like magic, some new gimmick works. For a while.

The process never stops. To be effective in America today, information must be packaged in 10-second thoughts, with subliminal hints, visual imagery and human chemistry.

Television has changed the American brain and the way it receives, remembers, and reacts to information. There are purists who balk at the idea; who say TV is ephemeral and shallow; that its performers are pretentious and plastic; that its motives are crass and demeaning. Why should I learn to be like them?

To some extent, all those criticisms are valid. But when TV is good, it is *very, very good*. No other technique has yet been invented to reach so many people so quickly with so much power.

Book Order Form

If you'd like more copies of this book, use the order form below, or our website: **http://www.winning-newsmedia.com/bookordr.htm**. We offer discounts for carton-lot orders. (See next page)

The book is **$23.95 per copy, including shipping** by U.S. Postal Service **BOOK RATE**. Mailed from Tampa, Florida, books will reach the West Coast in about a week; the Midwest and Eastern U.S. in two to five days.

Add $1.00 per copy for U.S. Postal Service, **PRIORITY MAIL**. The Postal Service strives to deliver PRIORITY packages nationwide in two days, but does not guarantee that delivery time.

SEND YOUR ORDER TO:

Video Consultants, Inc.
5220 S. Russell St. # 40
Tampa, FL 33611
Voice: 813.832.4137 - FAX: 813.832.9039

e-mail: cjones@winning-newsmedia.com

I need _____ copies of *Winning with the News Media* @ $23.95 each.

_____ copies X $ 23.95 .... $ _____

Plus $1.00 per copy for PRIORITY SHIPPING .... +_____

Plus Florida orders add sales tax -- $1.56 per copy......... +_____

TOTAL ENCLOSED............ $ _____

Name _____

Street or PO Box _____

City _____ State _____ Zip _____

CARTON-LOT DISCOUNTS ON NEXT PAGE

Carton-lot Discounts

We offer discounts for carton-lot orders, which will be shipped out of the printer's warehouse in Ohio. **A carton contains 28 books.** For each carton ordered at the same time, the price drops $2.00 per copy, to a maximum of four cartons ($8.00 per copy off the $23.95 Cover Price).

	TOTAL
One carton (28 books) is $21.95 per book, including UPS GROUND shipping	$ 614.60
Two cartons (56 books) is $19.95 per book, including UPS GROUND shipping	$ 1,117.20
Three cartons (84 books) is $17.95 per book, including UPS GROUND shipping	$ 1,507.80
Four cartons (112 books) is $15.95 per book, including UPS GROUND shipping	$ 1,786.40

**More than four cartons is $15.95 per book,
Including UPS GROUND shipping**

**For UPS SECOND-DAY AIR,
ADD $ 1.00 per book
For any carton-lot order**

**Our website cannot calculate
carton-lot discounts. Those orders
must be placed by phone, FAX or e-mail
(previous page)**